SEVEN
DAUGHTERS
OF THE
THEATER

SEVEN DAUGHTERS OF THE THEATER

- *Jenny Lind* -
- *Sarah Bernhardt* -
- *Ellen Terry* -
- *Julia Marlowe* -
- *Isadora Duncan* -
- *Mary Garden* -
- *Marilyn Monroe* -

By
- *Edward Wagenknecht* -

A DA CAPO PAPERBACK

Library of Congress Cataloging in Publication Data

Wagenknecht, Edward, 1900–
  Seven daughters of the theater.

  (A Da Capo paperback)
  Reprint. Originally published: Norman : University of
Oklahoma Press, 1964.
  Bibliography: p.
  Includes index.
  1. Actresses—Biography. 2. Singers—Biography.
3. Dancers—Biography. I. Title.
[PN2205.W3 1981]   791'.092'2   [B]   81-5549
ISBN 0-306-80153-1 (pbk.)   AACR2

This Da Capo Press paperback edition of
Seven Daughters of the Theater
is an unabridged republication of the
first edition published in Norman, Oklahoma, in 1964
It is reprinted by arrangement with the author.

Published by Da Capo Press, Inc.
A Subsidiary of Plenum Publishing Corporation
233 Spring Street, New York, N.Y. 10013

FOREWORD

THREE ACTRESSES of the legitimate stage, two opera singers, a dancer, and a film star—these are my seven daughters of the theater. The oldest—Jenny Lind—died thirteen years before I was born; the youngest—Marilyn Monroe—was born twenty-six years after me.

My portrait of Jenny Lind has been condensed and rewritten from my early book, *Jenny Lind,* long out of print, published by Houghton Mifflin Company in 1931. The Garden, the Duncan, and the Marlowe were also, in their original forms, written long ago, though only the Marlowe has been previously published in any form: in *Modern Drama,* Vol. I (1959), 244–55. It is included here by courtesy of the editor, A. C. Edwards.

The Marilyn Monroe is less of a portrait than the others and more of an essay—or elegy—for the wound which Marilyn's death left in the world's psyche and in mine is still too fresh to permit me to treat her with the detachment which psychography requires. Though this book contains much material which I wrote long before I had ever heard of her, she was still the "onlie begetter" of the volume as it stands, for it began with my feeling that I must write something about her, and because what I had to say was not long enough to be published by itself, I conceived the idea of constructing the book around her, to build, as it were, a house for her to inhabit. I have not included a formal dedication because it would have been superfluous: *Seven Daughters of the Theater* has been Marilyn's book from the beginning, and I was content to have it so.

EDWARD WAGENKNECHT

CONTENTS

PICTURES

Sources of Illustrations: Picture 1 is from Henry Scott Holland and W. S. Rockstro, *Jenny Lind: The Artist*; Picture 3 is from Mrs. Raymond Maude, *Jenny Lind*; Pictures 4, 6, 7, 8, 10, 11, 12, 13, 14, 15, 16, 17, 18, 19, and 20 are courtesy of the Harvard Theatre Collection; Picture 5 is from *The Theatre* (December, 1916); Picture 9 is from Ellen Terry, *The Story of My Life*; Picture 21 is from Arnold Genthe, *Isadora Duncan: Twenty-Four Studies*; Picture 22 is from the author's collection; Picture 23 is from *The Theatre* (January, 1909); Picture 24 is from *The Theatre* (December, 1912); Picture 25 is from *The Theatre* (May, 1910); Pictures 27, 28, 29, and 30 are courtesy of Twentieth Century-Fox.

· I ·

JENNY LIND

The Nightingale
as Avatar and Evangel

I want to be near trees; and water; and a cathedral.

JENNY LIND, 1849

She passed *through* life. That is what she made one feel: she was on her way somewhere else: it was a movement across a scene—her life. On she passed: often in perplexity and surprise at what she found here.

HENRY SCOTT HOLLAND

The youth of her day have borne her in their hearts across a generation, and their hearts still rise at the mention of her name, as the Garde du Roi sprang up cheering to their feet when the Queen appeared.

GEORGE WILLIAM CURTIS

A feeling of uplifted life spread over the metropolis. She melted the souls of thousands, and purged the craft of money getting. We came away from her as from a higher realm.

EDGAR LEE MASTERS, *Children of the Market Place*

I *Jenny Lind*[1]

MORE THAN A CENTURY AGO, our ancestors went mad over a simple Swedish woman, not generally considered a beauty and austerely disdainful toward most of the fetching idiosyncrasies of the prima donna, whom a great museum impressario and self-styled professor of the art of humbug had brought to the United States for an extensive concert tour.

It was the first such tour ever undertaken by a European celebrity, and it still remains the most spectacular and successful of them all. Like printing, the art of ballyhooing a singer was born at a very high point of development, and the name of its Johannes Gutenberg was P. T. Barnum.

In the large cities the box office was not good enough for her tickets: they must be sold at public auction. The record "high" was reached in Boston, where the first ticket was purchased for $625 by a minor vocalist named Ossian F. Dodge. When the news was conveyed to Jenny Lind herself, she called Dodge a fool. But she was wrong, for she did not understand the intimate New World connection between art and commerce. The next time Dodge gave a concert he advertised it by means of a vivid poster which showed Barnum introducing him to Jenny and reaped his reward.

Henry Wadsworth Longfellow, being a mere poet and college professor, could not hope to compete in such a running: he spent $8.50 and sat in the gallery. But of course even $8.50 is a good deal of money, a fact nowhere more clearly or profitably realized than by the ingenious proprietor of a livery stable located near the Boston concert hall, who provided a number of chairs at $.50 each, which were taken up by optimists who hoped that if the wind were favorable, some of the divine melody might reach them there.

[1] *Jenny Lind* was first published in book form by Houghton Mifflin Company in 1931. It was copyrighted in that form in 1931 and 1959 by Edward Wagenknecht.

This was by no means the most ridiculous incident of the tour. There were times when the enthusiasm of the populace approached the riot stage. But perhaps the sweetest tribute was reserved for Providence, where the thrifty chambermaid of the hotel where Jenny Lind was staying lined her pockets by the simple expedient of selling hair from her own blonde head to undesigning purchasers who were persuaded that she had taken them from the great singer's brush.

When Jenny Lind arrived in New York on Sunday, September 1, 1850, thirty thousand people turned out to meet the boat. In the excitement several persons were injured, and one man was swept off the dock into the water. The crowd trailed along to the Irving House, and by night Broadway was completely blocked. Escorted by the Fire Department, the New York Musical Fund Society gave a concert in her honor which did not terminate until well past midnight.

"Milliners, mantua-makers, and shopkeepers" besieged her, naming articles for her, presenting them to her, begging favors in return. Barnum mentions Jenny Lind gloves, bonnets, riding hats, shawls, mantillas, robes, chairs, sofas, pianos. Songs and poems were dedicated to her, and dances were named after her. Her name and her picture appeared on water carafes. Hotels served their choicest dishes *à la Jenny Lind*. There was a Jenny Lind teakettle, "which, being filled with water and placed on the fire, commences to *sing* in a few minutes." In Lynn, Massachusetts, Jenny Lind sausages were placed on sale. There was a Jenny Lind pancake too, and in faraway Alaska the time was coming when, in Gold Rush days, a baker would nail out a shingle announcing Jenny Lind cakes. Though she loathed tobacco, there was a Jenny Lind cigar, and in Boston there was a Jenny Lind Hotel which was little more than a common barroom. In Rensselaer County, New York, she was nominated for the assembly. She received a vote for lieutenant-governor in Massachusetts, and in New York City several persons voted for her for mayor. At the same time, all sorts of fantastic stories were circulated about her. From her individual method of dressing her hair, massing its coils on each side of her head, arose the legend, widely believed, that she had no ears.

The morning after her arrival, and before she had sung a note on this side of the water, the New York *Tribune* had four columns on the front page describing her reception and a poem with fifty-two footnotes explaining the Scandinavian allusions in it. The papers published a facsimile of the ticket to her concerts and listed the names of the purchasers. In a special column they reported from day to day the "Movements of the Swedish Nightingale." The New York *Herald* found her appearance "as significant an event as the appearance of Dante, Tasso, Raphael, Shakespeare, Goethe, Thorwaldsen, or Michael Angelo" and hailed it as a sign "that the wand of civilization has fallen from the hands of the southern nations and passed to the hardy northern races." "She has changed all men's ideas of music as much as Bacon's inductive system revolutionized philosophy."

The American visit was of course simply a brief interlude in a long musical career. In Europe Jenny Lind's admirers generally used somewhat less rowdy methods of manifesting their enthusiasm, but the enthusiasm was there just the same. And no more than with us was it confined to the upper classes; it filtered down through the strata of society until her name had become a household word to thousands who had never heard her voice. The great composers, the artists, the poets of Europe had accepted Jenny Lind as their peer. Queen Victoria —Victorianism incarnate—had officially placed the sanction of the age upon her. And even Disraeli, whom we do not usually think of as a sentimentalist, had said of her career as artist and philanthropist that it almost reached "the high ideal of human nature."

When she set out on her tour of the English provinces, the Bishop of Norwich—Arthur Penrhyn Stanley's father—invited this opera singer to make the episcopal palace her headquarters during her stay in the city, and though there were fanatics on both sides of the Atlantic who objected, the incident is still significant of the attitude that was taken up towards her. In Boston the famous Father Taylor of the Seaman's Bethel, who opposed dancing, theatergoing, and cardplaying but loved music, was in the midst of a passionate tribute to her talents and many virtues when a long, lank individual rose from the seat he had been occupying in the crowded church on the pulpit stairs and inquired whether a person who died while attending one of Jenny's concerts would go to heaven. The preacher glared at him disgustedly as he replied, "A Christian will go to heaven wherever he dies; and a fool will be a fool wherever he is—even if he is on the steps of the pulpit."

II

To a woman of Jenny Lind's combined idealism and *pudeur* the fact that she was born out of wedlock, in Stockholm, on October 6, 1820, necessarily must have occasioned much grief of mind. The circumstances, even now, are difficult to understand. Her mother, Anne-Marie Fellborg, a passionate puritan and an impossible woman (from whom Jenny inherited all her "difficult" qualities), had divorced her husband, Captain Erik Johan Rådberg, for infidelity. She seems therefore to have been legally free to marry Niclas Jonas Lind, whom, for reasons best known to herself, she considered her husband "in the sight of God," but she did not choose to do so until Jenny was fifteen. Lind was a good-natured man, with an attachment to the bottle and little real character, and after Jenny became famous, both he and his wife seem to have been primarily interested in getting as much money out of her as possible, thus occasioning her many difficulties including conscientious qualms over her inability to feel for them what she thought a daughter ought to feel toward her parents. As a baby, she had been separated from her mother at the earliest possible moment and placed in the care of one Carl Ferndal, organist of the parish church at Ed-Sollentua, fifteen miles from Stockholm. Positively and constructively, her mother meant little or nothing in her life, but Jenny was devoted to her grandmother, who deeply influenced her religious outlook.

In 1820, when Jenny was only nine years old, her voice was discovered by Mlle Lundberg, a dancer at the Royal Opera House, whose maid had chanced to hear the child singing to her cat. The dancer at once enlisted the interest of Herr Croelius, court secretary and singing master of the Royal Theater, through whom Jenny was introduced to Count Puke and entered as a pupil in the theater-school, to be trained as a singer and actress.

Her first appearance on the stage occurred in 1830 in a melodrama by Kotzebue, *The Polish Mine.* Technically her operatic debut took place in 1836, when she appeared as Georgette in Lindblad's *Fondö-rene,* but this was of small importance and attracted little attention, and her real debut did not come until March 7, 1838, when she appeared as Agatha in *Der Freischütz.*

She remained in Stockholm until 1841, when, becoming dissatisfied with her progress, she reluctantly journeyed to Paris, to seek instruction from Manuel Garcia. Garcia (1805–1906), brother of Malibran and Viardot and inventor of the laryngoscope, was possibly the greatest singing teacher who ever lived. In any case, he taught Jenny Lind what singing is in the technical sense, and from then on her progress was rapid. Enlisting the good will of Meyerbeer, she appeared in Berlin, as Norma, on December 15, 1844, with triumphant success. On April 22, 1846, she made her Viennese debut in the same character, and a little more than a month later she created a tremendous sensation when she appeared as featured soloist at the Lower Rhine Music Festival at Aix-la-Chapelle, singing both in Haydn's *Creation* and in Handel's *Alexander's Feast.* She appeared for the first time in London, on May 4, 1847, at Her Majesty's Theater, as Alice in *Roberto il Diavolo,* and her farewell to opera was sung at the same theater and in the same character, almost exactly two years later—May 10, 1849.

Meanwhile she had begun to identify herself with oratorio, with which her name was so long to be associated in England, and which was to win her a unique place in the heart of the nation. On December 15, 1848, she had sung in London in Mendelssohn's *Elijah;* now, on August 19, 1850, she established her supremacy in the new field when she sang in that most beloved of all oratorios, Handel's *Messiah.*

It was immediately after the *Messiah* that she crossed the ocean, her first American concert being sung at Castle Garden, New York City, on September 1, 1850. She remained in America until May 24, 1852, when she made her last appearance in New York. During her stay in the United States, she married, at Boston, on February 5, 1852, the young German pianist, Otto Goldschmidt.

After returning from America, Jenny Lind and her husband lived for a time in Dresden, but Jenny had fallen in love with England, and in 1856 she returned to its shores, thenceforth to call it home. In her later years she was more interested in teaching than in singing. From 1876 to 1883 a good share of her energy went into leading and training the sopranos of the Bach Choir, of which her husband was founder and director, and from 1883 to 1886 she taught singing at the Royal College of Music. Her last public concert was at Malvern Hills, where she lived, on July 23, 1880. She died there, after a long and distressing illness, on November 2, 1887.

III

In considering Jenny Lind as an artist, we must not assume that her popularity was due to her art alone. "Other famous singers," writes George William Curtis, "charmed that happy time. But Jenny Lind, rivalling their art, went beyond them all in touching the heart with her personality." And Barnum himself remarked, looking back upon the famous tour from 1890: "It is a mistake to say the fame of Jenny Lind rests solely upon her ability to sing. She was a woman who would have been adored if she had had the voice of a crow." One of her Swedish biographers, Tobias Norlind, has developed ably and in some detail the thesis that she served her time as an avatar of a romantic ideal, expressing the tendency toward simplification, the union of art and religion so profoundly characteristic of the whole Romantic Movement, and that in no other period could her gifts have awakened quite the response that they did just then.

"As a singer," wrote Washington Irving, "she appears to me of the very first order; as a specimen of womankind, a little more. She is enough of herself to counterbalance all the evil that the world is threatened with by the great convention of women." Longfellow declared: "She is very feminine and lovely. Her power is in her presence, which is magnetic, and takes her audience captive before she opens her lips. She sings like the morning star; clear, liquid, heavenly sounds." The great Victorian actor Macready called her "the most charming singer and actress I have ever in my life seen. Her energy, vivacity, archness, humour, passion, and pathos are equally true." Best of all, perhaps, is the tribute of Mendelssohn: "She is as great an artist as ever lived; and the greatest I have known."

Of course there were famous persons who did not care for her—among them Carlyle, Thackeray, Whitman, and Wagner—but except for Wagner, these are all so obviously crotchety that they do not help us much. It may be more rewarding to turn to those who, while appreciating Jenny Lind's gifts and gladly acknowledging that she enriched their artistic experience, yet insist that she had marked limitations. One of these was the famous British critic Henry F. Chorley: "In short, Mdlle. Lind's opera repertory was limited,—one which must have exposed her on every side to comparisons should she have remained on the stage till enthusiasm cooled, as it must inevitably have done." Even in *La Figlia del Reggimento* Chorley considered her inferior to Sontag, and he calls her Susanna in *Le Nozze di Figaro* "stiff, heavy, and conscientious," but he fully appreciated her Julia in *La Vestale*—which she herself considered her finest piece of work—"a real, pathetic, admirable piece of acting—by much her best tragic character." Sir Julius Benedict too named five roles—Alice in *Roberto il Diavolo,* Amina in *La Sonnambula,* Marie in *La Figlia del Reggimento,* Lucia in *Lucia di Lammermoor,* and Elvira in *L'Elisir d' Amore*—as the only ones in which "she held an undisputed sway over her audiences." And even the entirely sympathetic Longfellow found it advisable to discriminate: "Jenny Lind has a Northern soul and sings Northern music better than Southern."

Like others who think it necessary to express their own personalities in the roles they portray, Jenny Lind sometimes failed with a character with which she was not in perfect sympathy. This seems to have been the case with *Les Huguenots* in 1846. Sometimes, as with Norma, she recharactered a role so as to bring it more in harmony with her own tastes and point of view. Macready found her Norma "very womanly, loving, passionate, and grand," but doubted "whether it will be a *popular* performance—it wants more vulgar effect to be so." Most observers agreed that this characterization was "womanly" and "loving," but the English were inclined to think it lacked passion and grandeur, and the American Parker Willis, who adored Jenny Lind, found even the "Casta Diva," which she sang so often in her concerts, deficient in this regard. "On Jenny's lips," he wrote, "the devout purity and imploring worship and contrition, proper to the stanzas in which the Deity is addressed, are continued throughout; and the Roman, who has both desecrated and been faithless to her, is besought to return and sin again, with accents of sublimely unconscious innocence."

She had a range of two octaves and three-quarters, from B below the staff to G in the fourth line above it. Her high F-sharps were of unusual beauty, and it was with the idea of displaying them advantageously that Mendelssohn composed his "Hear ye, Israel." The upper A appeared prominently in a syncopated passage in a "Casta Diva" cadence, as well as in one of her Swedish songs. She always improvised her cadenzas, which most hearers found beautiful and in excellent taste. Richard Hoffman thought her voice "not so brilliant as it was deliciously rounded, and of an exquisite musical timbre." Henri Appy compared its timbre to that of a clarinet, "penetrating and tearful and sweet." "She possessed two qualities of voice," he writes—"one sombre, the other of a clear, sunny ring, brilliant and sparkling. She carried her middle voice in one quality up to high B flat without a break, and sang there in the same rich tone as in her middle octaves."

At the basis of her technique [writes Joan Bulman], was her perfect breathing-control. People believed that she must have an exceptional lung capacity, but in fact it was comparatively small. She could sustain her voice so long that it was rumoured she had an ability to sing on the indrawn as well as the outgoing breath. What she could do was to replenish her lungs so skilfully that not a sign could be seen or heard. Once at Aachen she was reported to have held on to a note for sixty seconds. She could hold on until the audience believed she must be at the very end of her resources;

but then, instead of breaking off, it would gradually swell out in an unbelievable crescendo of sound. Her breathing control was the secret of her wonderful pianissimo, that incomparable achievement that filled everyone with amazement and that Chopin loved so. It was a true pianissimo, scarcely more than a breath of sound, yet as full and rich as her mezzo voice and it penetrated to every corner of the largest theatre or concert hall. People spoke of it as creeping up to you and touching you. Audiences held their breath as they strained to catch the moment at which the note faded away into silence.... Her top notes, brilliant beyond words, could be softened down to a pianissimo as perfect as that of the veiled notes of the middle register. Her shake, which was executed with fantastic speed and accuracy and unapproachable brilliance, could be toned down to a whisper that was like nothing in nature but the warbling of a bird.

Some of Jenny Lind's listeners have attempted to describe not her voice alone but their own emotional reactions to it. "At the first tones of her voice," wrote John Addington Symonds, "I quivered all over. It was not her wonderful execution, her pathos, varying expression, subtle flexibility, that surprised me, but the pure timbre which so vibrated and thrilled my very soul that tears came into my eyes." And Henry Cabot Lodge always remembered her as he heard her in his youth, on a European holiday: "She was a plain woman, very simply dressed, and looked elderly to my youthful eyes. She sang, among other things, one or two English songs, which I particularly remember, and her voice seemed to me the most wonderful I had ever listened to. It had a quality of beauty which dwells with me still and which I have never heard surpassed."

IV

It is clear that nature was kind to Jenny Lind in giving her a good ear and natural musicianship. When she was only three years old she reproduced on the piano a fanfare she had heard from military bugles in the street. Nor did she ever forget the passage; many years later she wrote it down for her daughter. And in her maturity the Schumanns were literally dumfounded when she sang two of Robert's great songs,

"Marienwürmchen" and *"Frühlingsglaube,"* at sight, and sang them magnificently.

She continued to sing until long after she had passed her prime, apparently without giving anybody a suggestion that she knew her voice to be in any sense impaired. As late as 1861, however, so fine a musician as Moscheles calls her organ "as fine as ever." Of course she was never the kind of singer whose appeal rests on technical dexterity or on the sensuous beauty of her tones alone. "I suppose her high notes are a little gone," wrote Lady Frederick Cavendish in 1863, "but the matchless expression and *heart-feeling* can never go out of her voice, and there is a ringing purity of tone unlike anything else." And when Lady Westmorland heard gossip to the effect that Jenny had lost her voice, she said, "Never mind; if she has still got her soul, she is better worth hearing than all the other singers of the world."

Nature did not give her everything however, nor did nature do all her work for her. The technical chapter in the authorized biography and the letter written in 1868 to Professor Bystrom[2] make it abundantly clear that she analyzed her voice down to its minutest detail, knew its strength and its weakness, and built it up consciously to what it ultimately became. She began singing in Sweden without adequate training and continued to sing thus until she almost wore out her voice. When she arrived in Paris, Garcia refused even to consider her as a pupil until her vocal organs had had six weeks of absolute rest, yet in later years he was to tell his biographer that "he had never heard her sing even a hair's-breadth out of tune, so perfect was her natural ear." Nor did she ever repeat an error. "Jenny Lind would have cut her throat sooner than have given me reason to say, 'We corrected that mis-

[2] *Musical Quarterly*, Vol. III (1917), 548–51.

The author wishes to explain an apparent inconsistency in footnoting. In dealing with periodicals which are bibliographically respectable, i.e., which number their pages continuously throughout the volume, I follow the conventional style of reference: volume number, year of publication, pages. But in dealing with popular magazines which begin with page 1 in each issue it is not possible to do this; in these instances, therefore, I have gone to the extreme of simplification by giving, both in the bibliography and in my notes, merely the date of the issue in which the article in question appeared.

take last time.' " "For twenty-five years," she wrote Bystrom, "have I steadily worked on the chromatic scale and only five or six years ago did it come perfectly—when I no longer needed it." When she was in her prime, a certain veiled quality at times in her middle register seems to have been the only important technical deficiency in her singing.

Certainly there can be no question concerning her devotion to her task or her willingness to work. "If I had nothing but music in the world," she said, "it would be enough." No detail was too insignificant to demand and to receive hours of practice if necessary. She once practiced on the word *zersplittre* on a high B-flat in the opening recitative of *Norma* for several hours, and to the end of her career she always rehearsed during the day the opera she was to sing at night. When she began her work with Garcia, she was already a famous singer in her own country, but they went back to fundamentals, quite as remorselessly as if she had never sung a note:

> I have to begin again from the beginning; to sing scales, up and down, slowly, and with great care; then, to practice the shake—awfully slowly; and to try to get rid of the hoarseness, if possible. Moreover, he is very particular about the breathing. I trust I have made a happy choice. Anyhow, he is the best master; and expensive enough—twenty francs for an hour. But, what does that signify, if only he can teach me to sing?

Benedict says she invariably did her best: at Natchez and at Memphis, where they had small audiences, largely colored, she was every bit as conscientious as she had been in Boston and New York. When he mentioned this circumstance to her, she replied, "I value my art much too highly to degrade it even occasionally by any wilful disregard of what I consider due to it." Chorley speaks of this same conscientiousness, though without being sure that it always improved her performances:

> Of all the singers whom I have ever heard Mdlle. Lind was perhaps the most assiduous. Her resolution to offer the very best of her best to the public seemed part and parcel of her nature and of her conscience. Not a note was neglected by her, not a phrase slurred over. Unlike many of the

Italians, who spare themselves in uninteresting passages of any given opera to shine out in some favorite piece of display, she went through her entire part with a zeal which it was impossible not to admire, and which could not be too generally adopted as a principle by every one, great and small, who presents himself to an audience. But perhaps owing to this remarkable strenuousness, many of her effects on the stage appeared over-calculated. Everything was brought out into an equally high relief.

Considering the brevity of Jenny Lind's operatic career, her repertoire of thirty operas seems very large. Besides the works already mentioned, perhaps the titles now most familiar are *Il Flauto Magico, Don Giovanni, I Puritani, Der Freischütz, Euryanthe,* and *Semiramide.* Verdi designed the role of Amalia in *I Masnadieri* for her, but the opera was not liked. In opera she was not of course in control of her own repertoire, and her own taste cannot always be safely inferred from it. The one occasion in her career when her common sense seems completely to have deserted her was when, having determined to leave opera, she consented to give, at Her Majesty's in London, a series of "Grand Classical Performances" of opera in concert form. The opening bill was *Il Flauto Magico,* and with it Jenny met her first and only true popular failure. In fairness to her, it should be noted that at the time she was strongly under the influence of one Captain Claudius Harris, of whom there will be more to say hereafter, and also that so good a musician as Arthur Coleridge rated the performance as a high musical achievement. She herself recognized her error immediately and agreed to offer a series of farewell performances on the operatic stage.

We can tell more concerning her own tastes from her concert programs. In early life at least, her natural tastes in music were not austere. When she was a child, military music always delighted her, and her biographers tell us that even in later years the sight of a regiment of soldiers never failed to thrill her. Sir Charles Hallé's opinion is suggestive at this point: "Whether her judgment in music kept pace with her marvellous genius as a singer I have not been able to decide, for I have seen her cry when hearing a beautiful masterpiece well sung by a good chorus, and seen her cry also when some very commonplace ditty was given by the same chorus." And Appy speaks of her "child-like simplicity of character" as being best expressed in her ballad singing.

In this country at least, she generally appeared as part of a concert company, and judged by modern standards her programs often look pretty thin. Look at the opening concert in New York, for example. There was the "Casta Diva" to begin with, and that was splendid enough. But what followed? A duet with Belletti from *Il Turco in Italia,* a Swedish song, and a miserable "Welcome to America," the music of which had been hastily improvised by Benedict. And that was all. The "Welcome to America" was Barnum's fault. She sang it under protest; the lyric (by Bayard Taylor) had been chosen as the result of a public contest; she could not have refused without upsetting Barnum's applecart. But at her last concert in New York, when she was no longer under Barnum's management, she did something quite as bad on her own responsibility when she sang "Farewell to America" to a lyric by Christopher Pearse Cranch. Once she even suffered Barnum to persuade her to offer "Hail, Columbia," and we are told that her "interpretation" was not good. She was happier with the songs of Stephen Foster, which she discovered over here, and the later wide-spread concert use of "Home, Sweet Home," which had been largely forgotten, dates from her rediscovery of it.

Taken in the large, the range of her musical interests stands up more impressively. She began with music of the Meyerbeer type, but as time went on she won distinction as an interpreter of "the Divine Mozart," as she called him, of Mendelssohn, Handel, Haydn, Schubert, Schumann, and finally Bach. In 1876, when, under her husband's direction, Bach's *Mass in B-Minor* was first sung in England in its complete form, she trained and led the sopranos in the choir. Being a very positive person, she always had her blind spots and prejudices however. One was Brahms, and another was Wagner, whose music she considered injurious to the voice. Indeed the "new music" of her later years did not please her in any way. "Where are there now any song-composers," she asked in 1881, "since Bellini, Rossini, Donizetti, Lindblad, and Josephson are gone? At that time there was song-music—now there is music which is *supposed* to be song; it is purely harmonic difficulties which disregard the simple and the beautiful." "Mlle. Lind's sympathies," writes her daughter Mrs. Maude, "were entirely with the Italian school of singing as against the German."

v

An operatic artist, however, must be more than a singer. Jenny Lind was carefully trained in elocution and dancing as well as singing, and she was always extremely impatient of singers who moved awkwardly, who did not articulate clearly, or whose appearance while singing was not pleasant. Her diction was universally praised, and she is said to have articulated with quite unusual clarity, even when she was singing in a comparatively unfamiliar language. Humble as she was about her singing, she considered herself practically infallible as an actress and asked no advice from anybody. Berlioz and Chorley agree that as Lucia she was the only singer who prepared the mind of the audience for the climactic scenes of Lucia's madness.

But she was not a good showman. She disliked the artificial aids to effect which the actress habitually employs; sometimes refused, as Duse did, to use even rouge on the stage. In her concerts she often wore a simple white dress, and her general aspect suggested simplicity and purity, not the complicated, highly emotionalized set of reactions habitually associated with the prima donna. "I see Jenny Lind gliding down the stage with consummate grace," writes George P. Upton—"she never seemed to walk." "She would trip on and off," says Richard Hoffman, "as if in an ecstasy of delight at the opportunity of singing, bowing and smiling to her audience, and giving every one present a flattering sense of contributing in a measure toward the success of the evening."

Jenny Lind's passionate puritanism naturally involved a certain artistic honesty. In *La Sonnambula* she never permitted a substitute to cross the bridge for her in the sleepwalking scene, as was then the custom, but insisted upon doing it herself, though the strain unnerved her and sometimes interfered with her singing in the scene which followed. "I should have been ashamed to stand before the audience pretending that I had crossed the bridge, if I had not really done it." She tried to identify herself with her character—or thought she did— from which followed her unwillingness to enact base characters. "I scarcely ever think of the effect I am producing, and if the thought does sometimes come across me, it spoils my acting. It seems to me, when I act, that I feel fully all the emotions of the character I represent. I fancy myself—in fact, believe myself—to be in her situation; and never think of the audience." More concretely, when she was asked about a certain effect in *Roberto il Diavolo,* she exclaimed passionately, "How could I tell how I sang it? I stood at the man's right hand, and the Fiend at his left, and all I could think of was, how to save him."

Jenny Lind never followed tradition blindly, nor shrank from introducing a new interpretation of even a well-known role when it seemed to her that such departures were in the interest of art and of truth. Both her Norma and her Euryanthe marked a clear break with tradition. When preparing to appear in *La Vestale* at Berlin, she insisted on many changes in the libretto. And it is said that she was the first to sing the "Casta Diva" in the key of F, with which it has since been generally identified, rather than the key of G, in which it was composed.

As to the artistic value of her departures, it was natural that there should be differences of opinion. In England, Chorley wrote of her that she "seemed resolved to dominate beyond any artist whom I have ever seen." Benedict lends color to this view when he tells us that at the close of *La Sonnambula* she "destroyed the effect by doubling the part of the tenor in order to introduce a few high notes." And Sims Reeves's account of one feature in her management of *Lucia di Lammermoor* is so specific that one can hardly doubt his very substantial accuracy:

At the end of the magnificent *finale* to the second act . . . Lucia appeals to the indignant Edgardo, who throws her back into her brother's arms; upon which the curtain falls. Jenny Lind, however, as if to concentrate all attention on herself, rushed to the front of the stage, indicated by her gestures and general demeanour that she was losing her reason, and remained, as if demented, before the footlights, while the curtain fell behind her.

The judgment of the Continental critics, however, does not sustain these views. Indeed the difference seems so striking that one wonders whether, in her most striking departures, Jenny may not have been following Continental as opposed to English tradition rather than indulging in any self-glorification on her own account. In any case, the Continentals felt that she always envisaged the opera as an entity, never played for points, adjusted herself to a coherent interpretation of the entire work, and reserved her own striking dramatic effects for climactic situations where the emphasis naturally fell upon the character she was portraying.

It is hard to remember that this singer whose gifts had been recognized more widely and greeted with more passionate adoration than those of any other diva of her time voluntarily left the operatic stage behind her at the age of twenty-nine. At the very height of her European success she determined to leave the theater as soon as possible, and once the determination has been formed she recurs to it again and again until her desire has been accomplished.

It is true, of course, that though Jenny Lind retired early, her career in the theater—as distinguished from her operatic career, strictly speaking—covered nineteen years. It may well be that had she entered upon theatrical life at a less early age, she might not have wearied of it as soon as she had entered her prime. Moreover, her temperament being what it was, she could hardly have been expected to look forward to a steady diet of *La Sonnambula, Lucia,* and *La Figlia.* Sooner or later she must have taken the step she took, passing on to Bach and the great oratorios. For all that, she did not despise the theater. In her early days, her love for it was strong enough to overcome even her family's pious, middle-class Swedish prejudice against it. Many years later she sturdily opposed the dislike which her extreme evangelical friends felt toward it. Herself she remained a passionate theater-goer as long as she lived.

It is clear that she suffered terribly from stage fright. Before her Berlin debut she was in a mood of hopeless despondency. She looked forward with dread to her engagement in Vienna, and when she arrived, and saw the auditorium there, she was so sure her voice could not fill it that she wished to cancel the engagement. She was always so afraid of losing what she held that she could not open her hands for more. "And yet—only think!—what if I lose my whole reputation!" "It is not a question of money, but simply of my existence as an artist, which would be compromised by my appearance in London, and perhaps annihilated by my debut at Drury Lane."

Indeed it was in connection with the long and complicated negotiations preceding her London debut that Jenny Lind appeared most brilliantly as a performer of the hesitation blues. Her admirers have all taken it for granted that she was quite justified in breaking the contract with Alfred Bunn which called for her debut at Drury Lane, but Bunn's cool, objective account of the controversy, in his pamphlet, *The Case of Bunn versus Lind,* makes it clear that there was another side to the matter. When she declared that she could not master the English language in time for her proposed debut, he offered to permit her to sing in either German or Italian instead. When she wished to pay him £2,000 to be released from her contract, he agreed, provided she would sing three times at Drury Lane before singing elsewhere in England. Finally he professed himself ready to give up even these performances if she would furnish "written assurance, that you were not deterred from appearing on the Drury Lane stage by any other motive than the one assigned in your letter of the 17th of October, 1845, wherein, on asking me to cancel our agreement, you offered me an ample indemnification should you ever appear at her Majesty's Theatre. I make this final proposal to you to restore our former good understanding, to avoid further litigation, and to dispense with any

more public discussion." This communication Jenny Lind did not see fit to answer, whereupon Bunn took legal action and won his case. Moreover, she came very near going through the same comedy when Benjamin Lumley engaged her for Her Majesty's. Even after she had come to London for the express purpose of appearing at Her Majesty's she could not bring herself to do so. Hopes for her appearance had been well-nigh given up and discussion had been dropped when, at last, upon hearing that the opera business was at a standstill and Lumley losing money every day, she decided suddenly to take the plunge. And then she chose *Roberto il Diavolo* for her debut because it would give her a chance to make her first entrance on a crowded stage and have time to collect her faculties before she should be called upon to sing.

Yet Jenny Lind was not devoid of personal ambition. Her more fanatical admirers have always denied this, but the evidence is against them. She was indeed a severe critic of her own work, and her extreme conscientiousness would not permit her to accept gracefully any suffrages that she did not feel she had fairly earned. It was this consideration which led her to Garcia. "I am gifted by Nature; and to that I am indebted for a certain amount of success; but Art I did not know, even by name. I felt this bitterly; and it made me receive the applause of the public with sorrow rather than with joy: for I felt that I did not deserve it." And Hans Christian Andersen tells how, when she was received with enthusiasm at Copenhagen, her response was to retire to a corner and weep. "Yes, yes, I will exert myself, I will endeavor; I will be better qualified than I am when I again come to Copenhagen."

She did exert herself, for art and for God, no doubt, but she also felt the sting of competition, and she would not have been human if she had not also exerted herself for Jenny Lind. To be sure, she never participated in conflicts with other singers. In Berlin, in 1844, when she learned that Leopoldine Tuczec considered herself entitled to the role which Meyerbeer had designed for Jenny in *Das Feldlager in Schlesien* she immediately insisted upon relinquishing it to her. The real sting came closer to her when she was called upon to measure her gifts

against those of Henrietta Nissen, who was to her what Breslau was to Marie Bashkirtseff.

Nissen, like Jenny Lind, was a pupil of Garcia's, and she had some gifts which Jenny lacked. Jenny thought they were distinctly of the superficial variety, and it hurt her that Garcia did not see the difference between them quite so clearly as she thought he ought to see it. Indeed for a time Nissen seemed to be making better progress than Lind.

> I am not depressed on Mademoiselle Nissen's acount. Ah no! Besides, how foolish it would be not to stand aside for a merit greater than my own—and this I do. Thank God! I feel no jealousy, and—shall I tell you?—it is true that I can never get her voice; but I am quite satisfied with my own. And, furthermore, I shall be able, in time, to learn all that she knows; but she can never learn what I know. Do you understand? She is a nice girl; and with all my heart I wish her every happiness. Her stay here is of great advantage to me, for she spurs me on.

When it came to returning to Stockholm, there were other factors and personalities to consider, and we find Jenny writing the officials of the Royal Theater with this consideration in mind:

> I shall certainly return, in a year and a half—quite certainly—but not if I meet with coldness, or am regarded as altogether unnecessary. I am almost afraid of that. Elma Ström has everything in her favour, which I have against me. She has a much softer and better voice to work with than I ever had, during the whole time of my working period. She ought, therefore, to sing very well. The actress, probably, will come later. I do not wish to stand in her way, or in the way of any one. Rather than that, I would settle down here to give singing-lessons; for Garcia's method is the best of our time, and every one, here, is striving to follow it.

Her exalted estimate of her own character and powers did not tend to diminish as she grew older, and it finds perhaps its best expression in the precious letter she wrote in 1865 to the editor of the Swedish *Biografiskt Lexicon*. "For me," she said, "mankind, in general, has done very little. I never was in want of anything, and asked help of no one." And again:

> As to the greater part of what I can do in my art, I have myself acquired it by incredible work, and in spite of astonishing difficulties; it is from Garcia alone that I learned some few important things. To such a degree had God written within what I had to study. My ideal was (and is) so high, that no mortal could be found who, in the least degree, could satisfy my demands; therefore I sing after no one's "methode"—only that of the birds (as far as I am able); for their Teacher was the only one who responded to my requirements for truth, clearness, and expression.

Of course Jenny Lind's faith in herself was not calm and unwavering; neither did her performance always—or perhaps often—reach her own ideal. Personally I am much less troubled by her self-confidence than I am by her professions of humility, which often have an unconvincing, pietistic flavor about them. One feels that "the lady doth protest too much," speaking not from inner urging but because the good pastors have taught her that humility is a Christian virtue. In 1845 she declined to appear in Paris before "the finest audience in the world." "For," she says, "the more I think of it, the more I am persuaded that I am not suited for Paris, nor Paris for me." And I, for one, do not believe that she felt the advantages all to be in favor of Paris. Take, again, her thought about the autobiography she never wrote. "My life—especially as an artist—has furnished material for a biography in such abundance, that I almost look upon it as a duty to produce something of the kind, before leaving a world where I had been called upon to take so active a part." Is that why people write autobiographies? When Jenny gave up her "duty" in this connection, she justified herself by reference to the indignation she felt at the treatment which had been accorded Carlyle's *Reminiscences*: "If they could so treat him, who was so great, what respect would they pay me? No! let the waves of oblivion pass over my poor little life!"

Hesitant as Jenny Lind was to embark upon an untried enterprise, a challenge to her pride rarely passed unheeded. A. A. Bournonville has told of his amusing experience in persuading her to sing in Copenhagen in 1842. She doubted her ability to cope with a foreign stage; she feared the competition of Fru Heiberg, and so on. She became so excited that she finally accused him of having set a trap for her. "This both frightened and wounded me; and I promised to cancel all. But now the 'woman' came to the front; for as I began to doubt, she waxed firm."

Sometimes her advisers deliberately played upon such stubbornness. In 1844, after she had studied in Paris, the Royal Theater at Stockholm offered her an engagement for eight years at a salary of $5,000 a year, to be continued later as a pension for life. Though her friends strongly urged her not to tie herself to a single theater, she was more than a little inclined to accept this paltry offer. While the question was still hot, one of her friends happened to mention the matter to a certain consul general who set himself up as an authority on music, and who at once replied that she was wise, since her powers would not be equal to a Continental success. "Well knowing the effect which this absurd misrepresentation ... could not fail to produce upon Jenny's mind, her friend lost no time in making her acquainted with it; and then and there he had the satisfaction of seeing her tear up the fatal contract and thus put an end to the discussion for ever."

VI

How, now, did this strong individuality manifest itself in non-aesthetic connections? Jenny Lind was not a beautiful woman, and she knew it well. She will not even allow herself the endearing graces of childhood: she was "a small, ugly, broadnosed, shy, 'gauche,' altogether undergrown girl." The broad nose remained with her in later years, and she had too the extremely high checkbones and the wide, frank, open features so often characteristic of the Swedes. Once a German asked her about Swedish beauty. "All the Swedes are beautiful," she replied. "It is seldom that one sees anyone like me." And when the Bournonvilles brought up the much-mooted matter of her refusal to sing in Paris, she said, "I am too ugly. With my potato nose, it is impossible for me to have any success in Paris."

She was of medium height—five feet, five inches—though it is said she appeared taller. In her Berlin days, an observer who saw her first sitting at the piano before a private concert was able to discern only "a thin, pale, plain-featured girl." Frederick Locker-Lampson pronounced her "a fair-haired and blue-eyed Puritan—an excellent woman, with serious enthusiasms and a plain but impressive personality." But when Lillie de Hegermann-Lindencrone first saw her in 1866, she found her "neither handsome nor distinguished-looking; in fact, quite the contrary: plain features, a pert nose, sallow skin, and very yellow hair."

John Addington Symonds is more specific. He met her in 1862, when she was forty-two and he twenty years younger. "She was quite in black, and looked to me an old worn lady with a large head and a small person. She wore no crinoline, and her dress with its loose waist reminded me of grandma's." He goes on to a careful description of her physiognomy:

> First, the face is terribly thin and worn. The eyes are small, and very glaucous grey. They soon screw up when she looks attentive. The nose is immense and broad at the base. The mouth broad, and lips thin, with the skin about it pink and irritable. Her hair is profuse and yellow. Her throat is immense, with a large larynx. The whole face is mobile and expressive.

The deficiencies that nature had left in her were never covered up through skillful dressing, for clothes did not interest her. One night she started out for a ball with the Bournonvilles, and her appearance was distinctly shabby. At the last moment Mrs. Bournonville begged her at least to put on a few bracelets. She complied without protest, then turned to her friend. "How is it now?" she asked indifferently. When she did sometimes burst forth in gorgeous attire, her taste does not seem always to have been good. On one occasion she is spoken of as wearing four large gold rings on the middle and one on the third finger. And once a visitor who called upon her at eleven o'clock in the morning found her "dressed in a white brocade trimmed with a piece of red silk around the bottom, with a red, blousy waist covered with gold beads sewed fantastically over it . . . and gold shoes!"

Jenny Lind's admirers have never claimed beauty for her: what they do claim is that her features were extraordinarily transparent, expressive, and alive. "When she smiled," says Madame de Hegermann Lindencrone, "which was not often, her face became almost handsome." Longfellow said, "There is something very fascinating about her; a kind of soft wildness of manner, and sudden pauses in her speaking, and floating shadows over her face." When she sang she became another woman. Mrs. Price Newman describes this with special reference to her interpretation of "I Know That My Redeemer Liveth":

> The pale face became a little more pale, the rather wide mouth became peaceful, the eyes glowed with calm intensity as they raised themselves to the Heaven whence [*sic*] her soul had ascended. She was translated to the beyond and chanted with the angels her credo of faith.

But less impressible observers may serve us better here. When Lord Broughton heard her as Amina, he was "charmed beyond measure, not only with her singing but her acting, and forgot her plainness." Symonds speaks of another occasion when she was not on the stage: "As she sat there singing, she became beautiful, and her profile seemed really classical." Most important of all is her own observation in this connection: "I become a different thing when I sing—different body, different soul."

Her health was no better than she needed. Toward the close of her operatic period, her nerves were in a bad state: she suffered continually from severe neuralgic headaches, and for days after a performance of *Norma* she would be good for nothing. "Yes, I gave too much of myself in my art," she wrote in later years; "all of my life's strength was on the point of being extinguished." Naturally the strain of the American tour, with the unfamiliarity and the physical discomforts involved, did not improve her condition. In 1853 she wrote a friend that the ordeal of singing in America to "Barnumish" houses—"you will understand all I mean with that only word"—had exhausted her.

When she was older she was harassed with rheumatism, and at the end she was stricken with cancer, but did not die of it. The immediate cause of her death was a cerebral hemorrhage.

VII

Jenny Lind was an intelligent woman but in no sense an intellectual. Her early education had been "quite simple and unscientific," and she was in no position to put herself through any very rigid intellectual discipline during later years. We are told that, while she was not a conversationalist, her talk was full of vivid flashes and swift glimpses, none of which she ever stopped to develop logically or consistently. Parker Willis found that "her occasional anticipations of the speaker's meaning, though they had a momentary look of abruptness, were invariably the mile-stones at which he was bound to attain."

In science and in abstract thought she shows no interest whatever, and since she found all she needed to know about God and destiny in the creed of her church, there was no need for her to engage in metaphysical or philosophical speculation of any kind. Politics as such did not interest her either. She was disturbed and depressed by the revolutions of 1848, and she was rabidly pro-German in the Franco-Prussian War, but that is all.

Her interest in literature was much greater, but this too was haphazard and unsystematic. She disliked Goethe because she thought his influence had made the Germans irreligious. She read Hans Andersen's stories as they were published and wept over them and praised them extravagantly. She was greatly moved too when the elder Symonds read Tennyson to her, and she refused to sing after he had finished. "The vibrations will clash," she said. *Uncle Tom's Cabin,* as might have been expected, made a strong humanitarian appeal to her. She disliked biography because it reveals the faults of great men. "What good can we get from seeing how Bacon fell? Ah, that did give me pain. I would sooner have known evil of some near friend."

I am quite unable to understand her dislike of Sir Walter Scott, whose novels, she declared, did her soul no good.

She had decided convictions on the relationship between poetry and music. Milton, Dryden, and Heine might all be set to music, but in her view Shakespeare, Shelley, and Tennyson were far too complex. The composer needed one harmony, one feeling, not a series of broken lights. "Tennyson takes all the solid sharp words and puts them together. Music cannot come between. He does not flow."

The art galleries of Dresden and Florence appealed to her emotions deeply, but she was always quite the layman in her observation of pictures. J. A. Symonds writes in 1862:

> Papa was asking her about pictures. She admired at Dresden the great Madonna, Titian's Tribute Money, and Carlo Dolci's Christ Breaking Bread, more than any. "The Madonna," she said, "is not painted—it is thought—it is there—you see it—you cannot call it painted." But of ordinary art-criticism she had none. Simple feeling was all that gave her a preference for one picture over the other.

As a lover of nature, however, she need yield to none. "I believe the good God did his best when he raised the mountains," she writes; and when she traveled through Switzerland, she was tremendously impressed by both their beauty and the majestic commentary which they made on the petty pride of man. When she crossed the Atlantic, the ever-changing moods of the ocean was a subject of endless fascination to her. But it was not only the spectacular or theatrical aspects of nature that appealed to her. She spent the first years of her life in the country, and the impressions thus early implanted did not wear off. She loved birds and water and flowers—wild flowers, not cultivated ones. She felt most at home among peasants, and she loathed the city with its dirt, crowds, and excitement. Once, with some friends, she watched a nightingale. Observing his observers, the bird suddenly stopped singing. "There!" she exclaimed, "he has seen us! Now that is just like me. I should have done the same, if I had caught anyone intruding on my solitude. And, indeed, those who compared me to the nightingale were not far wrong, for I have a great deal of the nightingale in me."

Naturally, since she had first learned to love nature in Sweden, the Swedish aspects of nature held a special charm for her. And this is what her Swedish patriotism was: a love of home, a loyalty to the associations of formative years. As late as 1868 she felt that "Scandinavian voices have a charm which no other voices in the whole world have," and she attributes this to the natural beauty of their country. But, with fine honesty, she immediately adds that instruction is miserable in Sweden and that the strange, contrasted slowness and excitability of the national temperament create a great handicap. After first going abroad, she suffered much from homesickness, but when she returned from her study in Paris, she was much disturbed by the unrest she found in her native land, then just beginning to hear the echoes of the general European revolutionary movement. France she loathed always, but there was no patriotic animus involved: the French point of view and her own simply would not go together. Indeed I think the only thing she ever found out about France was that Paris is a wicked city. In the deepest sense she was always loyal to Sweden—"One's heart is in one's own country, and mine, certainly, is Swedish to the very backbone of my body and soul"—but the charms of England grew upon her more and more during her later years, and it was in England that she finally made her home.

VIII

Neither Jenny Lind's faults nor her virtues were such as to fit her supremely for social success. When she was on a concert tour, she once astonished her companions by carefully stopping up her ears with wool before retiring for the night, to shut out—she said—the noises of the world. There are times when the action seems symbolic of her whole social attitude. "In later years," writes her daughter, "there was a sense of aloofness and almost haughtiness with those who were not her friends, this attitude giving offence to intruders on her private life whose visits she resented, and Mr. Goldschmidt had to use all his inherent powers of tact and diplomacy to put things right again." But it was not only in later years that this tendency was manifested. Even Hans Christian Andersen, who afterwards became such a close friend, was received "distantly, almost coldly," when he first called upon her. "I had," he writes, "the impression of a very ordinary character which soon passed away from my mind."

When Jenny Lind was first received into "society," as it is called, its novelty and glamour rather charmed her, but this did not last long. She had the Old World deference for rank and position, and when she was staying with the Bishop of Norwich she never addressed either her host or his wife until she had first been addressed; neither did she take a seat until invited to do so. But she had the independence of the artist also, and when, upon her arrival in London, Queen Victoria invited her to come and sing at the palace, she simply excused herself on the ground that she must save her strength against her debut at the opera house the following evening.

Sometimes her frankness went so far as to be amusing, as when she told a fashionable hostess to her face that she pitied her because she had too much money. When the mayor of Boston greeted her with praise of her "character," she interrupted him sharply: "What do you know of my private character? What *can* you know of my private character? Sir, I am no better than other people, no better." And once, when she suspected Horace Greeley of tricking her at a séance they attended together, she suddenly called across the table to him, "in the tone and manner of an indifferently bold archduchess," commanding him to take his hands from under the table, and poor Greeley, who was quite incapable of such trickery, was so nonplussed that he did not know what to make of her.

Like the rest of us, she sometimes allowed her social attitude to be governed by her moods. Once the officials of a convent to which she had made a donation came to her in state: a procession of children, banners, robes, and ten or twelve priests. "I will not see them," she said; "they have nothing to thank me for. If I have done good, it is no more than my duty, and it is my pleasure. I do not deserve their thanks, and I will not see them." But when a poor old Italian dancer whom she had helped wished to call on her and bring his performing dog with him, she was so touched that she wept. "Poor man, poor man," she said to Barnum, "do let him come; it is all the good creature can do for me. I like that, I like that; so let the poor creature come and bring his dog. It will make him so happy."

Her complete indifference to the pleasures of the table did not contribute to Jenny Lind's social success either. She liked Swedish *Knäckerbröd;* "herrings and potatoes—a clean wooden-chair, and a wooden-spoon to eat milk-soup with"—that was her idea of a good meal, and nothing bored her more than being compelled to sit at table after she had finished eating. Symonds describes her table manners: " . . . holds her knife *à l'Allemande,* cuts up her meat, and eats it with a fork, rests her knife on a piece of bread." Clara Schumann records that "she drinks neither wine, nor tea, nor coffee—in every respect she is an ethereal being!"

In her case, social success was of course complicated by the fact that she was a celebrity. She always resented being made an object of curiosity at social gatherings, and she was righteously indignant when she discovered that she had been asked as a guest when she was really desired to sing for the other guests. On the other hand, she rejoiced to sing freely for those who had not laid a trap for her. Indeed, when she was in good spirits she would sing anywhere, as once at a hotel in Garmisch, and on such occasions the assistance and co-operation of the persons about her would be "commanded" in the style of a queen giving orders to her obedient subjects.

One evening, Lady St. Helier and her husband, having made a mistake in the date of their invitation, burst in upon Jenny Lind at dinnertime. Said she, magisterially, "We waited dinner last night for you till nine o'clock, and you did not come. Tonight Madame Schumann is dining with me, and has made it a condition that we shall be absolutely alone. Therefore I cannot ask you to stay to our dinner." The even-tempered Goldschmidt could not with alacrity embrace such heroic methods. Surely they would be able in some way to provide for their guests! But his strong-minded wife, restating her objections, overruled him, and the nonplussed visitors withdrew with as good grace as possible to seek their dinner in a restaurant.

On another occasion, Miss Gaynor Simpson, who was very intimate with Jenny Lind and a frequent guest in her house, asked her to write in an autograph album. The singer rose abruptly. "Well," she said, "I did not think you had been a commonplace person." And she stalked out of the room into the garden. In a little while she came back, a rose in her hand as a peace offering, and continued the previous conversation. Finally, as the girl rose to leave, she asked suddenly, "Now, where is your birthday book?" and taking it, quietly wrote her name in it.

If this was her manner with friends, it can easily be imagined how she would treat intruders. In Charleston, Barnum told her of a wealthy young lady who was so eager to meet her that she had disguised herself as a servant in the hope of gaining access to her. But Jenny flatly rejected all suggestions that she receive the girl. "It is not admiration— it is only curiosity, and I will not encourage such folly." In later years she used to sit in her garden with a large red umbrella beside her, and if any bold spirit presumptuously peeped in at the gate, she would shoot the umbrella open and hide herself behind it. Once some Americans succeeded in forcing their way into her drawing room. Jenny entered, stiff as a poker, and asked them to state their business. Somewhat abashed, they replied that they had merely wished to see her and make her acquaintance. "Well," said Jenny, "here is my front!" and she made a profound bow. Then, turning about: "There is my back. Now, you can go back home and say that you have seen me." With which she stalked out of the room. But after they had gone, she was overwhelmed with remorse for her rudeness.

Yet she had humor. Her first Christmas in America she presented Barnum with a statue of Bacchus, in honor of his temperance principles. When Hans Christian Andersen's perpetual wooing became more than ordinarily distasteful, she reminded him of his extreme unlikeness to Apollo by silently handing him a mirror. She used to take childlike pleasure in showing her treasures to her friends. "And they all came out of here," she would say, laughing and pointing to her throat. After she had attended services in the cathedral at Peterborough, the dean injudiciously asked her how she had enjoyed the choir. "Oh, Mr. Dean," she replied, "your *cathedral* is indeed most beautiful!" And once when somebody asked her what sort of man George Grote was, she replied, "Oh! Mr. Grote, he was like a nice old bust in the corner; you could go and dust him!"

Nor did her humor stop short at herself. Andersen, visiting her in England, found on her sitting-room table a caricature of herself, "a great nightingale with a girlish face; Lumley was shown putting sovereigns on the tail to get her to sing." When the singer Lablache declared fervently that her every note was a pearl, she seized his hat, sang into it, and then returned it to him with the observation that she had made him a very wealthy man. But what I like best of all in this connection is her reply to the earnest souls who asked her what heavenly thoughts had filled her mind when, as Alice in *Roberto,* she was clinging to the cross. "I believe," she said, "I believe I was thinking of my old bonnet."

There was something childlike about her, as there often is in very serious people. She loved animals, enjoyed playing with them and making friends with them, and they were often in her conversation and her thoughts. Despite her extreme puritanism, she was devoted to dancing, enjoyed it tremendously herself and in later years gave dancing parties for her children. Once she and Bournonville settled an argument by dancing a polka. She even played cards with Sims Reeves when they were on a concert tour together. In England she learned to love horseback-riding, though it is said that she used a chair to mount the horse, and when she was in Havana she played ball on the lawn of her house, insisted on Barnum's playing with her, and teased him about his fatness and laziness when he tired too easily. As a hostess she was assiduous and careful, delighting to give personal attention to the wants of her guests. When she went to the Oberammergau Passion Play with Arthur Coleridge and her husband and children, she secretly brought a large cold roast goose with her, and gleefully served it to them in her room. She retained her gift for mimicry to the end; once she played a maid in some children's theatricals. "You see I have not lost my old art!" she would exclaim. And we have one delightful picture of her at a children's party, "thumping out the 'Swedish Dance' at the piano . . . ; smiling with joy at the emphatic rhythm of stamping feet; and then springing up to dance herself with all the brisk, bright playfulness of a child."

Only she could never be thus for long. And beside the story of the children's party we need to place Barnum's account of the New Year's Eve which he and Jenny shared. Up until a quarter to twelve she was full of high spirits. Then suddenly she stopped the festivities. "Pray, let us have quiet; do you see, in fifteen minutes more, this year will be gone forever!" And she sat down in silence and rested her head on her hand.

IX

The warmth of her nature shows best in her relations with her friends. She felt great need of her friends and clung to those she trusted almost desperately. Sometimes her expressions of dependence even sound a little servile to modern ears. But there can be no question as to her sincerity. She held back because she would not give herself where she could not give herself completely. In 1849 she told Mrs. Stanley that she had no wish to make any more friends: she had enough. How seriously she took the obligations of friendship may be inferred from her saying that it would not be wise to make friends in America, "for I love my friends so dearly that I shall be too unhappy to leave them." She did not shrink from devoted and intimate offices of friendship; she nursed Arthur Coleridge tenderly when he had ophthalmia; she also nursed the violinist Guerini. When Mendelssohn died, she was shaken to the depths—"everything seemed to me to be dead"—and for two years she could not bring herself to sing his songs. Later, when Ruskin mentioned Mendelssohn to her, she inquired had he known him. "No." "Better for you you did not." "How so?" "The loss—too great."

In choosing her friends she seems to have been guided by an intuition which she trusted implicitly and followed wherever it led. She was fond of discussing the sympathy of sensitive natures and the magnetic influence they have upon each other. As is often the case with shy or reserved people, when she found a really congenial spirit, there was little formality, and intimacy developed quickly. She found one such in the actor Macready, who, so far as the world in general was concerned, was as austere as she was. "You will wonder that I speak so open to you," she writes him in 1860, in her broken English, "although we have seen so little of each other, but I feel that we must well understand each other's way of feeling, and, born with the artistical flame in our hearts, we have wandered through much the same pains and trials, and this makes me to feel no stranger to you, dear Mr. Macready!" But she did not confine herself to such persons: one of her most intimate friends was Arthur Penrhyn Stanley, later the famous dean of Westminster, who is indeed said to have once proposed marriage to her, and he was a man who could not tell one note from another and listened to music with positive pain.

Where Jenny Lind gave her friendship she demanded something in return. Even in her kindness she was inclined to be somewhat dictatorial. Sims Reeves said of her: "Her temper was equal, her feelings always under control. I never knew any one so strict in the observance of self-prescribed rules." But he also found that the best way to get on with her was to do as she wished. When they were on tour together she invited him to dine with her. He declined on the ground that he wished to spare himself any possible fatigue preceding the concert. Jenny rang for the waiter: "Place Mr. Reeves's dinner on my table," she said. It must, one fancies, have been a gay meal.

Sometimes, being human, she failed in friendship, as she did finally with Clara Schumann, when they quarreled over Brahms's music, and though there was no actual estrangement, they were never really intimate again. And from Arthur Coleridge she withdrew her favor, without a quarrel, after more than twenty years of friendship, apparently for no better reason than that he had dared to suggest the name of a man she disliked as her husband's successor in an important musical post. Where a moral question was involved, it is hardly necessary to add, she gave no quarter whatever. Once a friend who had indulged in innuendo in her presence was abruptly shown the door.

Through her charities, however, Jenny Lind in effect made friends with all mankind. Nothing about her was more characteristic of her than her conviction that the money she earned did not belong to herself alone but must be invested where it would do most good for God and for mankind.

It might be supposed that a woman who so thoroughly appreciated the value of money would have a good business sense, but this does not seem to have been the case. To be sure, Barnum's account of the adjustments made in the American contract as having proceeded wholly from his own generosity is contradicted by Maunsell B. Field, the lawyer in the case, who insists that not once but many times Jenny insisted upon alterations, always to her advantage, and that Barnum always yielded with very good grace. But this does not mean that she knew anything about the science of money, or that if she had been left to her own devices, she would have acquired very much of it. She had already shown her innocence in this regard in connection with the Bunn negotiations in England, and her principal contributions to her American manager consisted of a series of complaints that he was charging too much for tickets. After she had left Barnum she remarked to him one day that it was very annoying to give concerts on her own, since everybody cheated her.

Nevertheless she wanted a lot of money—to give away, and probably no other singer ever gave so much away as she did. Her very contract with Barnum provided that, after she had sung twice for him in any city, she should be free to sing again for charity if she chose. In Sweden she never sang a note for her own profit after she became famous. Of the $10,000 she received for her first concert at Castle Garden she never saw a penny. It was divided among the charitable institutions of the city, the apportionment being determined by Barnum and the mayor of New York. As a matter of fact, none of the money Jenny Lind earned in America was for herself. She kept it in a separate fund, and only twice in her life did she dip into it. At her death, it was devoted to benevolent purposes.

But statistics cannot tell the whole story. In many cases she herself selected the object of her benevolence and personally bestowed the gift. There is the pretty story of her secretary coming in one day to tell her that he had stood next to a poor girl in the lobby who had paid three dollars for a ticket with the remark, "There goes a week's wages, but I must hear Jenny Lind." Forthwith he was hurried out to search the audience for that girl and give her twenty dollars with Jenny Lind's compliments. There was the student in a German university who wrote her how desperately anxious he was to hear her, begged her to send him a ticket, and promised to pay for it as soon as he received his next allowance. Jenny immediately sent two complimentary tickets, and, remembering their location, thoughtfully rewarded the boy's devotion with a smile from the stage. Finally, there was the poor countrywoman. Wandering along a lonely road one day, Jenny Lind stopped at a little cottage and asked for a drink of water. The woman was friendly, and the singer sat down to rest for a while and chat. The story she heard was one of poverty and misfortune. Jenny Lind's name came into the conversation, and the woman asked her guest if she had ever heard her. "Yes," she replied, "I, too, am a singer, and if you like, I will sing you one of Jenny's songs." When she had finished, she added, "Now you, too, may say that you have heard Jenny sing," and pressing a five-pound note into her companion's hand, she left the cottage immediately without waiting to be thanked.

x

The subject of friendship suggests the greater subject of love and marriage. Jenny Lind was a very domestic woman, and she wanted the normal surroundings of a woman's life—husband, children, home. Fame could not take the place of these things. In early days, lamenting to a friend over the breakup of a love affair, she remarks that though she has many interests, many duties, "the finest, the most sacred of all —I mean, a mother's love, is forbidden—nay! denied to me!" On her American tour she once greeted a young mother with the passionate exclamation, "Ah! how I envy you! you have something to live for!" There are several stories of Jenny Lind's kindliness to children in the early days, and once when a child burst into tears over her singing, she was greatly moved and called it her finest triumph.

Not much has been recorded concerning Jenny Lind's relations with her own three children, though her daughter wrote a book about her. They came somewhat late in her life, the first in 1853, when she was thirty-three, and the youngest in 1861, when she was forty-one. When her first pregnancy occured, she solemnly and uncomplainingly prepared for death, not supposing that she could bear a first child at such an advanced age. To her astonishment, the delivery was so easy that she declared she would hardly have known that anything had happened. Once she quarreled with a governess and sent her away. But after the girl had taken a new place, she decided that she could not get on without her, the successor having "no soul, no heart, no head"; so she swallowed her pride and sent for her again. She did not wholly approve of the liberating influence of England upon her children. "They think they know everything far better than mother," she once complained—*"yes, even music!"*

As to love itself, one observer declares of Jenny Lind that "in her own character, she was not a woman to fall in love with; she was too reserved." Several, first and last, seem to have managed it however. Adolph Lindblad fell in love with her, though he was a married man, and if her principles had not been as strict as they were, considerable turmoil might have resulted. It is possible that she and Mendelssohn might have loved and married if he had been free. Hans Christian Andersen proposed to her again and again but always received the same answer. Of Giovanni Belletti, who took the American tour with her, Maunsell B. Field says that he would "lie in bed all day, weeping and howling over his unrequited affection." But her first serious love affair was with Julius Günther, an operatic tenor in Stockholm, to whom she was informally engaged as early as 1844. During her career on the Continent she seems to have drifted away from him. But in 1848 the engagement was definitely renewed and rings were exchanged. It seems, however, that Jenny did not love Günther as deeply as she felt she ought to love the man she married. In 1847 she confessed that she had "very high thoughts of finding a being, to whom I could utterly and entirely surrender myself." She did not find him in Günther, and though the details of their parting are not clear, her reluctance to marry an opera singer at the very moment when she herself was trying to break away from the theater seems to have had something to do with it.

The next suitor was an Englishman, Claudius Harris, a young captain in the Indian Army. And, oddly enough, as she had broken with Günther because he would have kept her in the theater, so she broke with Harris because he insisted on turning her against it. In her own words, he wanted her "to think the theater a temple of Satan, and all the actors priests of the Devil." She was "not only to abandon her profession, but to be ashamed of it," and "to go down to Bath, among people who care for nothing but clergymen and sermons, as a sort of convert or penitent."

There was an added difficulty in the fact that though Captain Harris regarded the theater as "a temple of Satan," he had not the slightest objection to coming into possession of money that had been earned there. While the question of marriage was under consideration, both he and his mother—a formidable lady who looms up somewhat ogreishly in the background of the story—sternly informed Jenny Lind that it would be "unscriptural" if she were to attempt to control her own fortune after her marriage. Jenny Lind liked to give, but she also liked to be a free agent, and she saw no particular reason, either in the Scriptures or out of them, why Captain Claudius Harris should control a fortune not one penny of which he had ever earned.

Finally, after many misgivings, she decided that in spite of everything she would go through with it. Captain Harris threatened her with eternal damnation if she broke her engagement, and she seems to have felt that he was an authority on the subject. But alas! the anticlimax: "when in the joy of reconciliation she was singing to him, she turned round and saw that he had gone to sleep." Now Jenny Lind could marry a man who would not have her without her fortune; she could even marry a man who threatened her with eternal damnation. But to ask her to marry a man who could not keep awake while she was singing—no! that was too much to expect. The whole thing is as lovely a comedy of errors as you are likely to find in a long summer's day, and of all those who have dragged themselves into history on the skirts of the great, none ever succeeded more gloriously in making a fool of himself than did Captain Claudius Harris.

And then, finally, there was Otto Goldschmidt. She met him first in Germany, where he was studying music at the time of her first great Continental triumphs. When Benedict withdrew in America, she sent for him. He came at once, and though he was eight years younger than she was, they soon fell in love. He was one of the few who could satisfy her as an accompanist, a matter about which she was extremely particular. "Herr Goldschmidt is our accompanist, and whether he accompanies me or I accompany myself, it is absolutely the same thing." Unquestionably Goldschmidt knew his business, but audiences found him lacking in glamour. All Jenny Lind's native stubbornness came out in response to the challenge. Instead of going backstage to rest during his piano solos, she stationed herself on the platform and listened to him attentively, and once when an audience had been rude to him, she delivered a cutting rebuke by meeting him as he was leaving the stage and warmly shaking his hand. Goldschmidt was of Hebrew extraction, but in 1851 he was converted to the Christian faith, Jenny Lind standing sponsor for him at his baptism. On February 5, 1852, they were married in Boston, and Edward Everett witnessed the ceremony. Thereafter her concert billing read: "Madame Otto Goldschmidt (late Mlle. Jenny Lind)." It is clear that in many things the husband was subordinated to the wife. But, in theory at least, Jenny Lind was firmly of the conviction that the man is the head of the house. In private life she called herself "Madame Lind-Goldschmidt" and was, says her daughter, "mortally offended if addressed otherwise." When her English neighbors referred to Goldschmidt as "the Prince Consort of Song," she was very angry, and found her own way of expressing her displeasure at the intimation "that her husband should be put second, instead of first, in their home."

The Prince Consort comparison has been made again and again. For some mysterious reason the world has always regarded it as somewhat disgraceful for a man to marry a woman who is more famous than he is himself, and Goldschmidt has been abused for much the same reasons as Prince Albert himself, and quite as unjustly, for he was as good a man as ever lived. To be sure, the gossips got busy before the honeymoon was over, but there is nothing wonderful about that. The talk began to reach Jenny while they were still living at Northampton, Massachusetts. "Why," she exclaimed, "I have known him since a boy, and I love him, and am so proud of him, too, for he is a fine composer as well as player." Much later, at a time when the rumors were particularly vicious, she took legal action to silence them and collected damages. There can be no doubt that she loved him; indeed she sometimes pushed her devotion to his interests beyond the bounds of decorum. Clara Schumann relates with suitable indignation that when, in 1853, Jenny was asked to appear at the Düsseldorf Festival, "she replied at once that she would sing gratis if they would let her husband conduct the Festival," which offer was accepted. But he was easily as valuable to her as she was to him, and she cannot have been an easy person to live with, as she well knew. "Mr. Goldschmidt begs me to send you his best compliments," she wrote Joseph Burke in 1853; "he continues to make justice to my opinion of a true, uninterested friend of mine, he is very kind and faithful to me, bears with great patience and mildness my many infirmities, and my impulsive nature gets smoothed by his equal and dignified temper. God bless and lead him on in the right way, as I have every reason to love and respect him."

XI

But there was one absorbing interest, one abiding, all-embracing passion that stirred Jenny Lind more deeply and thrilled her more profoundly than all the varied wonders of music and art. That passion, that goal for life, was God. "I have always put God first," she told her biographer, and she quoted with approval Janotha's saying, "What is this 'world' of which people speak? I play for Jesus Christ." When Jenny was four years old, her religious impulses were awakened by her maternal grandmother. Not until much later did she realize that her religion was vitally and intimately connected with the musical aspirations which so early engrossed her: it is said to have been the composer Lindblad who taught her, as she was later to teach Andersen, that the artistic life is itself a consecration of the artist and all his powers to God. Thenceforth the core of her being was sound and whole.

Some observers felt a cold austerity in Jenny Lind's religion. She was not narrowly sectarian. Though she grew up a Swedish Lutheran, she later felt sympathetic toward all evangelical bodies, and in England she was quite at home with the Low Church Anglicans. Yet Joseph Joachim complains of her "thoughtless, superficial piety—she often invokes God when talking of the most ungodly things, such as money and fame." And when Maude Valérie White met her as "an old lady in rather a severe poke bonnet," she listened impatiently to Jenny's pietistic harangue. "While she was speaking to me I felt as if I were being birched! I longed to say something frivolous, something positively outrageous."

Judged by modern standards, Jenny Lind may have been too much concerned with the formal externalities of religion, or even with the "moral," in the narrower, fussier sense. She was not entirely consistent in such matters, and sometimes the charm of a particular personality would completely conquer her; so she accepted Chopin into her circle of friends, called him a "good" man, and made excuses for his connection with George Sand. Yet when Clara Schumann was robbed, she wrote her a letter of condolence in which she said, "There must certainly be a hell in store for the wicked, wicked men." Then, catching herself, she adds, "At least they must be far from God—and that is hell enough." Her prejudice against the French has already been spoken of. When Ruskin met her, in 1849, she told him that this people "seemed to be a nation shut out from the common portion of God's blessing upon men, and deservedly so." Ruskin tried his best to put in a good word for them, saying "that the peasantry were not altogether spoiled, that they only wanted an honest government and true religion. 'You have said All in that last word,' she replied." The dislike of Catholicism comes out again, much more amusingly, in Liza Lehmann's story of what happened one day when she and her mother were having tea with Jenny. A little Italian boy brought in the muffins, "and when he had left the room, she turned to us and in a tense voice said, 'You see that boy? I am trying to conquer myself—to *bear* with him—but—*he is a Roman Catholic!*'" And she could be something of a spiritual snob even where no creedal prejudice was involved. When her boat passed Blackwell's Island en route to Boston from New York, the prisoners were gathered on the shore to wave greetings to her as she passed. She was pleased at first, but when she learned that these men were convicts, she hurried to the other side of the boat. Early in life she "cut" a singer of whose way of life she did not approve; later she rejoiced that she had not had to appear at the Bavarian court, where she would have been obliged to encounter Lola Montez.

This, however, is not the whole story, and it would be absurd and unjust to leave it there. To Jenny Lind it seemed, as she grew older, that she was gaining in grace and in strength, that in return for her devotion the good God was giving more and more of himself to her. "Ah! much, very much," she wrote in 1850, "must one live through, before one learns to fasten on the Life, the Higher Life." Of the Bible she wrote, "I drink therein rest, self-knowledge, hope, faith, love, carefulness, and the fear of God; so that I look at life and the world in quite another fashion to what I did before." In religion she had found finally an excitement, a stimulus that made everything the theater had given her seem hollow and artificial. Late in life she wrote that all stage tears were sham tears, and quoted the words written on the margin of her Bible: "my newly-found Lord, who first taught me to shed the genuine tears."

Not that perfect answers were always given even here. In her youth she had been much troubled by spiritual doubts. These passed away in later life, but now and then they would return to plague her. Not long before her death, Henry Scott Holland found her one day pondering the old questions:

"Why is evil so strong? Why does wickedness increase? Why is there pain, and misery, and earthquake, and famine, and war? Why does the good which one sets oneself to do, fail? Why do the best efforts win no fruit?" The old desperate enquiries! They stirred her to the very depths. The faith which she firmly grasped for her own salvation, did not seem to spread out as an illuminative interpretation of the world around her.

Sometimes the light would seem to break through from another world. When she looked on the dead face of her friend Mrs. Nassau Senior, she caught an impressive glimpse of it:

It was not her *own* look that was in her face. It was the look of another, that had passed into hers. It was the shadow of Christ that had come upon her. She had seen Christ. And I put down my candle, and I said, "Let me see this thing. Let me stop here always. Let me sit and look. Where are my children? Let them come and see. Here is a woman who has seen Christ."

For herself she was sure that she too would one day look upon His face. "I feel very strongly the beginning of the end, and think it a blessing to look forward to eternal rest. What is the whole miserable earthly life worth in comparison to one single glance of the sinless, holy Saviour?"

The great problem in Jenny Lind, however, is the curious interworking of her religion and her career. It was her own view that with-out religion she could have had no career. "She told Catherine," writes Mrs. Stanley, wife of the bishop of Norwich, "that, every morning, when she got up, she felt that her voice was a gift from God, and that, perhaps, that very day might be the last of it." She was *led* to Paris, to Garcia. She was *led* to London. When she crossed the ocean to America, again it was God's hand that pointed the way:

> I have for a long time had a most eager wish to earn, somewhere, a great deal of money, so as to endow a school, for poor, lost children, in my native country. And the invitation to America came as a direct answer, so that I go there in this confidence; and I pray to God in Heaven, out of a full heart, that he will guide me thither as ever before, with his gentle hand; and will graciously forgive me my sins, and my infirmities. But since I have no less an aim before me than to help in widening God's Kingdom, the littlenesses of life vanish in face of this.

It was from this vantage point that she justified the "heavenly—yes, heavenly career" that was hers. "If you knew what a sensation of the nearness of a higher power one instinctively feels, when one is per-mitted to contribute to the good of mankind, as I have done, and still do! Believe me, it is a great gift of God's mercy." She prayed too "that what I gave my fellows may continue to live on through eternity, and that the Giver of the gift, and not the creature to whom He lent it, may be praised and acknowledged." It may be that her prayer will be answered. At least her fame has long outlasted that of any other singer of her time, and Frieda Hempel, who spent much time and energy during her later years giving Jenny Lind Concerts, once told Leonidas Westervelt that she felt Jenny Lind was not dead.

Of course there have always been those who have urged that Jenny Lind's religion put an end to her career; if it had not been for her reli-gion, she would have continued longer in the theater and won an even prouder place for herself in the history of music. Even so devoted an admirer as Hans Christian Andersen was of this opinion. "She has left the stage," he wrote; "that is a wrong done her spirit; it is to give up her mission, the mission that God chose for her." And M. R. Werner remarks that "she was held back from supreme triumph in this world that she might enjoy comfort in the next, and it is to be hoped that her spiritual promises to herself have been fulfilled."

The answer depends somewhat upon what one's conception of a great career may be. Jenny Lind had limitations of health and of temperament that would probably have taken her into retirement at a fairly early age even if religion had not been there powerfully to reinforce them. For the theater is a highly eclectic art. It embraces within itself the ministries of all the others; through its powerful visual capacity and its tremendous gift of inducing sympathetic realizations, it can enlarge the individual's vision of life as no other art can. But this supreme mistress of the artist soul is not always chaste. There are too many rhinestones on her gown, and her cheeks are heavily rouged. She is Cleopatra, not Desdemona:

> *Age cannot wither her, nor custom stale*
> *Her infinite variety.*

As we have already seen, Jenny Lind rejected the extreme puritanical attitude toward the theater, though there were times when she approached it. According to Charlotte Bournonville, Jenny told Charlotte's father in 1854 that she now considered it sinful to appear in a theater. How can that be? asked Bournonville, in effect. When you sang in the theater, you made it into a church. You brought a spiritual message to those who could not be reached in any other way. Now that you confine yourself to churches, people go to divine service not to worship God but to hear your voice. Which is better, to bring the church into the theater or to bring the theater into the church? Goldschmidt agreed entirely with Bournonville's reasoning, but Jenny became angry and dismissed the matter by saying that since the Archbishop of Canterbury had said that it was a sin to sing in a theater, the matter was no longer open for discussion. This was not her settled view however. She invested much interest and energy long years after her retirement in training singers, and she was not the woman to gather recruits for the House of Belial. What she did feel, quite consistently, was that she herself could not achieve what her spirit craved in the distracting surroundings of backstage life. For that she needed something different altogether: "trees; and water; and a cathedral." So she gave it all up, and it must have cost her something to do it.

One asks oneself whether the baser, coarser side of the theater ever tempted her. The answer must be yes and no. Exalted as she seems to us, her contemporaries found in her an abundance of arch, coquettish arts and graces. "There were always the few who questioned her rendering of her tragic roles," writes Joan Bulman; "her comedy was supreme." I do not mean of course that she could ever have been attracted by debauchery or promiscuity. But there are aspects of theatrical life more alluring than debauchery and promiscuity. There are glitter and tinsel and vanity, the temptation to take the show for the reality, to enter so readily into the joys and sorrows of others that one has no insight or energy left to build an honest set of emotional reactions for oneself. And these things I believe Jenny Lind may have felt. Her authorized biographers, who knew her well, assure us that she had the artistic temperament with all its temptations and difficulties, and that it cost her a hard struggle to bring it within bounds. That she could not achieve it, to her own satisfaction at least, so long as she remained in the theater, is perhaps not wholly without significance; there are others who have done so. On January 8, 1845, she wrote a letter filled with rejoicing over her triumph in *Das Feldlager in Schlesien*: "Sontag herself had not so brilliant a triumph." "I almost think I achieved a greater triumph than in *Norma*." She goes on to tell of a happy evening spent with Goethe's Bettina. "We did not return till after twelve!" And she adds: "Nowadays the world is influencing me very considerably." It has its comic side—this dreadful dissipation of visiting Goethe's Bettina and staying out until after twelve! Nevertheless she seems to have felt that there were possibilities in that direction. And far more significant is the priceless story of the friend who found her, on the English coast, with an open Bible in her lap, looking out into the sunset. "Oh, Madame Goldschmidt, how was it that you ever came to abandon the stage at the very height of your success?" And she replied quietly, "When, every day, it made me think less of *this*" (laying her finger on the Bible), "and nothing at all of *that*" (pointing to the sunset), "what else could I do?"

So it seems to me that Jenny Lind's religion contributed far more to her art than it took away. It is quite possible that without it she would have sung more roles and sung longer, but she would never have made the peculiar impression which is associated with her name.

Above everything else, she gave her audiences the impression that they were seeing and listening to an exceptionally pure and high-minded woman, and it was for this as much as for anything that she was loved. Nor were her audiences deceived. She stood before the world as a priestess of beauty, but she sensed the underlying harmony of beauty and goodness. Once she spoke to J. A. Symonds of "the sorrow of sin which destroys beauty. We who have an ideal see that, and cannot bear the discord."

Sympathetic critics sensed these things from the very beginning of her career. "One sentiment . . ." wrote a German critic in 1846, "pervades all her Art-pictures—the spirit of holiness." Meyerbeer speaks of "those indelible graces which modesty and candour and innocence give only to their favored ones." And Hans Christian Andersen testifies, "Through Jenny Lind I first became sensible of the holiness there is in art; through her I learned that one must forget one's self in the service of the Supreme."

Of her Susanna it was remarked that she emphasized the womanliness, the loyalty, the purity of the character, beneath all the surface frivolities with which other singers had been content. Of her Amina one critic wrote: "She reads the character differently from all her predecessors—appearing not as a village coquette . . . but as a fond, loving girl, faithful to her lover, and rejecting for his sake the attention of the stranger count." Of her Donna Anna a German reviewer remarked, "In one word, Jenny Lind clothes the part in her own modest purity—no other conception would be intelligible to her." And the fundamental difference between her conception of Norma and Grisi's may be indicated in the words of Parker Willis: "Jenny Lind is the betrayed and heart-crushed woman; Grisi, the jealous mistress, panting for vengeance for her wrongs." C. G. Rosenberg's description may help us to see how the contrast worked itself out:

> In the *duo* with *Adalgisa,* or rather in the scene which immediately precedes that *duo,* the grandeur of Grisi is concentred in the moment, when, as if inspired by the spirit of vengeance, she springs forward with the poniard lifted against the lives of her two children. With Jenny Lind it is the pathos of the outcry as she staggers back, unable to consummate her fell design. In Grisi's love for *Pollione,* the senses of the audience are appalled by the intense passion and vehement bitterness of her reproaches. With Jenny it is in the mingled sadness and sorrow of her humble spirit that the observer realizes her passion for the Roman warrior.

Finally we must remind ourselves that great as Jenny Lind was in opera, she had a much longer career in concert and oratorio. In oratorio especially, she found congenial material. In 1849 she writes: "I have begun to sing what has long been the wish of my heart—Oratorio. There I can sing the music I love; and the words make me feel a better being." Here she used no cadenzas, no ornamentation of any kind. Lyman Abbott speaks of her interpretation of "I Know That My Redeemer Liveth": "it was impossible to doubt the Resurrection while she was singing. . . . She seemed a celestial witness; to doubt her testimony was to doubt her veracity." Nor was this a singular reaction. Once, as she finished the number, Daniel Webster, surely no particular connoisseur in piety, rose from his seat in the center of the balcony and made her a profound bow. Richard Hoffman says that, as she sang it, "Her rapt expression of face and never-ending volume of voice made her appear like some inspired seraph delivering a divine message." Appy testifies, "She sang with such a fervor of religious passion that it caught one up, as it seemed, into the sacred presence." And George William Curtis declares that "the lofty fervor of the tone, the rapt exaltation of the woman, with the splendor of the vocalization, made the hearing an event, and left a memory as of a sublime religious function." Perhaps, indeed, this was her supreme expression of herself in art. When she died, the words "I Know That My Redeemer Liveth" were engraved upon her memorial in Westminster Abbey.

And so my mind goes back to the woman on the seashore. "When, every day, it made me think less of *this,* and nothing at all of *that,* what else could I do?" The Bible and the sunset! And the world well lost!

There is always a peculiar interest attaching to those who conquer the world and then throw it away. Vice and greed have been the most popular motives inducing such a relinquishment. Jenny Lind threw it away for God.

· II ·

"The Greatest Actress in the World"
SARAH
BERNHARDT

The existence of Sarah Bernhardt remains the supreme marvel of the nineteenth century.

EDMOND ROSTAND

She understands the art of motion and attitude as no one else does, and her extraordinary personal grace never fails her.

HENRY JAMES, 1878

She is in truth an element, ageless, fearless, dauntless.

GERALDINE FARRAR, 1916

The secret of that astounding utterance baffles the imagination. The words boomed and crashed with a superhuman resonance which shook the spirit of the hearer like a leaf in the wind. The *voix d'or* has often been raved over; but in Sarah Bernhardt's voice there was more than gold: there was thunder and lightning; there was Heaven and Hell.

LYTTON STRACHEY

She will always be one of the permanent and beautiful guesses of mankind, one of the lasting dreams of poets, one of the most magical speculations of artists, like the charm of Cleopatra, the beauty of Mary Stuart, the voice of the masters of *bel canto,* the colours of Greek paintings and the melodies of Greek music.

MAURICE BARING

1 *Sarah Bernhardt*

WHEN I WAS TWELVE years old, my mother took me to the *sanctum sanctorum* of the spoken drama in Chicago, Powers' Theater, to see Sarah Bernhardt in Louis Mercanton's film production of Emile Moreau's play, *Queen Elizabeth*. Though I was not to see her on the stage for another five years, I was duly impressed by the great lady, especially during the scenes depicting Elizabeth's agony over the fall of Essex, and I tried to exercise my budding critical capacities by remarking on how wonderfully nervous she had seemed. "She is the greatest actress in the world," my mother replied. "It would be a pity if she couldn't act nervous!"

"The greatest actress in the world"! It was not the expression of a personal judgment but the enunciation of an axiom. The theater is less important today than it was then, but even in the more limited area of the world which it now inhabits, who is there concerning whom such a statement could go unchallenged? If any theatrical personality since Jenny Lind has achieved a fame or established a legend to equal hers, surely it must be "the Divine Sarah."

In many ways indeed Sarah surpassed Jenny Lind. Her career lasted much longer; many more people saw her; her activities were much more widely distributed. She was called the most famous Frenchwoman since Joan of Arc, and when World War I began she was asked to leave Paris because it was understood that she was one of the persons the Germans planned to hold as hostages should they succeed in taking the city. "I should be the one to bow," said the Czar of all the Russias when she curtsied before him after having played in St. Petersburg. At a wayside station in Scandinavia she had to be wakened in the night because some hundred peasants were standing on the tracks waiting for her train to pass through and would not move until they had seen her. "Will you give the enclosed to the Supreme and Infinitely Glorious One," wrote the great painter Burne-Jones to Graham Robertson, "kneeling as you give it? She is not to dream of troubling to answer.

Who am I, great powers, that she should take a moment's trouble!" When she played *Athalie* in Paris in 1920 every theater in the city closed that the actors might have an opportunity to see her, and when, at the very end, in a physical condition which would have sent any other woman to the hospital or to her grave, she appeared in London in Louis Verneuil's *Daniel,* a critic wrote: "One does not analyze genius; one prostrates oneself." She took *Daniel* to Spain, and the men in the railroad station spontaneously removed their coats and spread them on the floor to make a carpet for those who carried her chair to walk on, and when at last she lay on her deathbed, the people of Paris knelt and prayed in the street outside her house as at the death of kings. In London, royalty attended the memorial service in the Abbey; in Paris the funeral was a municipal affair and the ceremonies lasted for days, with thousands upon thousands of people passing her bier, and with sumptuous floral offerings from the great of all countries piled up to the ceiling and (what Sarah would have valued more) stacks of violets and single roses and little bunches of spring flowers brought in by humble people who had nothing more to give her. Five years later Rebecca West, seeing Maria Falconetti in *La Dame aux Camélias,* found herself weeping bitterly, not for Falconetti but for Sarah, "whom I saw in this part twenty-five years ago when I was a child of ten, whose every movement and inflection I can remember as this woman speaks the lines."

Yet two legends could hardly have been more unlike than those of Sarah Bernhardt and Jenny Lind. "The Swedish Nightingale" was almost as much Christian and puritan as artist and singer; she had the cool northland behind her. Sarah, too, was a Christian, a Catholic, though of one-quarter Hebrew extraction, but she was a *Parisienne,* and as such, in her time, she would have carried a different aura than Lind's even if she had lived as a devotee, whereas she lived instead, as she once remarked in one of her extremely rare bursts of self-confidence, as "one of the *grandes amoureuses* of my time," so that when she came to America, she not only could not, at the outset, be received in "society" but bishops fulminated against her, and there were grave, soul-searching debates as to whether so dangerous a creature might even be viewed across the footlights without contamination. Worse still, the aura of wickedness was commingled with that of the freakish and fantastic, for everybody knew that this woman traveled with and sometimes slept in a rosewood coffin, kept dangerous beasts as pets, slapped the faces of those who displeased her, violated contracts and paid enormous fines whenever her exuberant temperament got out of bounds, and indeed was reputed to have done a great many other things which nobody ever really did outside a madhouse. The various aspects of the legend were not consistent with each other, and very little of it seemed reconcilable with what those who encountered Bernhardt in the theater saw her do on the stage, but the publicity value of the combination for "the greatest actress in the world" was priceless, as she must have been well aware, though she professed, during her later years at least, to be greatly distressed by it all.[1]

Yet it must not be supposed that it was roses, roses all the way for Sarah Bernhardt or that she either won or held her great position without bitter struggle. Early and late she had many disastrous box-office failures, and her numerous foreign tours, "farewell" and otherwise, were motivated by the necessity of regaining abroad the money she had lost in Paris. Influential critics opposed her too. In the early days, Matthew Arnold could not forgive her for not being Rachel; Bernard Shaw, who never gave her a decent word, admitted after her death that he found it impossible to be fair to her because she reminded him of his Aunt Georgina; in later years, many "intellectuals" insisted upon sacrificing her to Duse.[2] Once, in 1891, according to Arthur Symons,

---

[1] "I seem to attract all the mad people in this world," she once said, and again, "I do believe that I am the most vastly and variously lied about woman that ever wore a bonnet," surely a sufficiently mild statement from one who was accused of having had affairs with Napoleon III, the Czar, and the Pope! A good example of the kind of garbage that found its way into print is a scurrilous pamphlet published in New York: *The Amours of Sarah Bernhardt: Secrets of Her Life Revealed.* Two versions of this are in Harvard's Widener Library, in the Bernhardt pamphlet collection numbered FL 398.7.25.

[2] Sarah's own judgment of Duse was that "she is a great comedienne, a very great

she was hissed off the stage in Harancourt's *La Passion de Jésus Christ* because the audience did not think it suitable that a Jewess should appear as the Blessed Virgin![3] It would be interesting to know what they thought *she* was, but however that may be, any young actress of today who is distressed over the stupidities and brutalities of contemporary criticism is entitled to all the comfort she can derive from the knowledge that "the greatest actress in the world" went through it all before her.

II

Sarah Bernhardt was born, in Paris, on the wrong side of the blanket, and a good deal about her early life and family background has, perhaps intentionally, been left obscure. The accepted date is October 23, 1844.[4] Her mother, who is generally called Julie Van Hard, was a Dutch-Jewish cocotte of the Second Empire, and apparently a person of no character whatever. Her father, whose name is given as Edouard Bernhardt, was a French Catholic. Julie never loved Sarah or encouraged her in any way, and when she was a young actress, her mother's presence in a theater was the only thing that could always be counted on to unnerve her completely.

---

comedienne, but not a great *artiste*." That there was an air of exaltation about her which Sarah did not possess is beyond dispute, but Sarah had more variety and vitality, a vastly more dazzling technique, and certainly more poetry. When Duse wished to play in Paris in 1897, Sarah generously placed the Renaissance at her disposal without charge, but Duse (then strongly under the influence of D'Annunzio) had the bad taste to choose a repertoire in which she directly challenged her hostess on her home ground. After the Italian poet had seen Sarah, he is said to have told his mistress that she was mad to dare such a contest. After D'Annunzio had published *Il Fuoco*, in which he made literary capital of his connection with Duse, Sarah openly proclaimed her disgust of a man capable of such an outrage against a woman. See Maximilian Harden, *I Meet My Contemporaries* (Holt, 1925).

[3] "Impressions of Sarah Bernhardt," *London Mercury*, Vol. VIII (1923), 595–99.

[4] This date is accepted by her grandson-by-marriage Louis Verneuil, apparently on the authority of her baptismal certificate; see *The Fabulous Life of Sarah Bernhardt*, page 35, but cf. the document reproduced by Mme Pierre Berton, *The Real Sarah Bernhardt*, facing page 34. According to May Agate, Sarah herself was not sure of her birthdate and sometimes said she thought it was earlier than 1844.

Her pitiful, neglected childhood, when she was passed about from pillar to post, must have done much to develop the unstable elements in her temperament, and she does not seem ever to have been looked after properly until 1853, when she was placed in the Convent of Grand-Champs at Versailles, where, though she can hardly be said to have been a model pupil, she conceived such affection for the wise, understanding Mère Sainte-Sophie, whose mere memory, she afterwards said, made her a better woman than she could ever otherwise have been, that for a time she aspired to become a nun herself.

Instead, she was sent, at the instance of her mother's protector, the Duc de Morny, to the Conservatoire (she had at this time very little interest in the theater) and made a quite undistinguished debut at the Comédie Française, on August 11, 1862, as Iphigénie. She soon quarreled with the directors of the Comédie, left and appeared at the Odéon and elsewhere, was invited back when she had become a celebrity, and broke her contract again when she saw London and New York and world stardom beckoning. It was at the Odéon that she may be said to have become the darling of Paris, her first hit being in 1868, as Anna Danby in *Kean,* a play by Alexandre Dumas *père,* who had played an important role in preparing her for the stage. In 1869 she created a sensation as the page Zanetto in the one-act, two-character play, *Le Passant,* which established the fame of François Coppée.

Meanwhile, on December 22, 1864, she had borne her only child, Maurice Bernhardt, to Prince Henri de Ligne.[5] When the Franco-Prussian War came in 1870, she turned the Odéon into a hospital (young Ferdinand Foch was one of her patients) and manifested the most unselfish devotion and, what is more, the most amazing practical efficiency and common sense under the most difficult possible circumstances.

In 1872 she conquered Paris in Victor Hugo's *Ruy Blas,* followed, five years later, by *Hernani.* In 1874 she took up the great role of her

---

[5] The fullest account of this liaison is given by Louis Verneuil, who makes Sarah behave more or less like Marguerite Gauthier, long before she had ever seen *La Dame aux Camélias.*

life, Phèdre. Her first appearance in London, in June, 1879, made the visit of the Comédie Française in effect a Sarah Bernhardt starring season, and in 1880 she undertook the first of her many tours of the United States.

On the way thither, in what must surely have been one of the strangest encounters in history, she saved the widow of Abraham Lincoln from a bad fall which might well have killed her; she also saved a pregnant Portuguese girl in the steerage from throwing herself into the sea, stood sponsor to the baby when he was born, and denounced all and sundry when she learned that a ship carrying 1,050 persons had life-saving equipment for only 250, and that, in case of an accident, no attention would be paid to anybody in the steerage until all the higher-priced passengers had been taken care of.

In 1883, in London, Sarah Bernhardt married a degenerate Greek aristocrat, Ambroise Aristide Damala; there was a legal separation the next year, but he continued to be a burden to her until his death in 1889. Between 1891 and 1893 she undertook her most extensive world tour. From 1893 to 1898 she controlled and directed the Renaissance Théâtre, where her productions were not notably successful; in 1899 she moved to the Théâtre des Nations, which she renamed Théâtre Sarah Bernhardt.

She first acted in *La Dame aux Camélias* in New York on her first engagement there, having no idea at the time that this was to become her greatest popular success and an unfailing lifesaver whenever she should turn back to it after a new production had failed. In 1882 a whole new phase of her career began with Sardou's *Fédora*, followed in kind by the same author's *Théodora* and *La Tosca*, and, less spectacularly, *Cléopâtre, Gismonda*, and *La Sorcière*. She discovered Rostand with *La Princesse Lointaine* in 1895, and though neither it nor *La Samaritaine* were great financial successes, in 1900 he gave her in *L'Aiglon* one of the great roles of her life.

In 1914 Sarah Bernhardt became a chevalier of the Legion of Honor, and in 1915 she was forced to have her right leg amputated;[6]

[6] Nobody ever seems really to have found out what was wrong with Sarah Bern-

as soon as she had got out of the hospital, she set out to entertain the soldiers on the western front. At the very end of her life, with *Daniel* and *Régine Armand,* Louis Verneuil furnished her full-length plays in which she was able to appear without walking. Until this happened, she was forced to content herself with one-acts or with scenes from her former successes that could be played sitting down or reclining, and it was under this handicap that she made her last long tour of the United States in 1916–18. She had first faced a motion-picture camera in 1900, when Clément Maurice filmed the Duel Scene from *Hamlet* for the Paris Exposition, and she was facing it again, in her own house transformed into a motion-picture studio, because she was too sick to leave it, when uremia finally struck her down in March, 1923, and she died on the twenty-sixth of the month.

III

Sarah Bernhardt was an aesthetic type if any woman ever was, but it would be an exaggeration to say that art completely absorbed her. She loved her family as passionately as she could have loved them if she had had nothing else to do, and nobody who is old enough to remember World War I needs to be reminded how she stood forth in

hardt's leg; there are even variant versions of the injury with which the trouble began. Louis Verneuil places it in Rio, on October 9, 1905, when she jumped from the battlements in the last scene of *La Tosca* and the customary mattresses were not there, but her granddaughter Lysiane dates it much earlier, carrying it back to a fall on shipboard in 1887, while Mme Berton speaks of an injury received in 1890 while Sarah was appearing as Joan of Arc at the Porte St. Martin. The only thing that is really clear is that whatever the trouble was it grew progressively worse, causing increasing difficulty about locomotion, until at last unbearable pain or the spread of poison throughout her system (or both) necessitated amputation. Sarah Bernhardt rarely spoke of her loss, the most pathetic exception being her remark to Houdini that since he could do the impossible, he ought to be able to restore her leg. When Charles Henry Meltzer considerately turned away from her when her servants came to carry her upstairs at her house in Paris, she said, "Oh, you needn't mind me!" But she had wept long before when her little granddaughter, asked what she wished to be when she grew up, confused her medical terminology and replied, "I'm going to be an oculist, so as to be able to see what's the matter with your knee."

her crippled, indomitable condition as the very image of her embattled country. For many years after 1870 she refused to act in Germany, and she once almost created an international incident by amending a German ambassador's toast to France as a toast to all of France.[7]

Yet there was a conflict in her at this point. She was not unaware of the faults of the French—their "determined ignorance . . . concerning all things foreign," for example—and she hated war and dreamed of a day when difficulties between nations should be settled at the council-table and "the monarch who wants war will be dethroned and imprisoned as a malefactor." Edison reminded her of Napoleon, but she thought him greater because he was "creative" where Napoleon was "destructive," and when it was first suggested to her that the conquest of the air would create a valuable new arm in warfare, she was so horrified that she almost banished the man who had spoken of such atrocities from her presence. "Each war, even if won," she cried, "is a fresh defeat for our intelligence." When World War I began, her indomitable courage wavered, and she wept. "To live through two wars is too much."

She was interested in the emancipation of women, but the vote in itself did not seem very important to her. She opposed capital punishment—"we ought never to cause what is irreparable"—and it was she who, believing in Dreyfus from the beginning, persuaded Zola to take up the cudgels in his defense. For this cause she even risked a break from her beloved son, a pronounced anti-Dreyfusard, and took her public stand when it was a real danger to do so, so that the anti-Dreyfus papers proclaimed: "Sarah Bernhardt at Zola's. The great artist is with the Jews against the army!"

But all this, however one may admire or respond to it, is not much more than one might expect from a sensitive, intelligent, courageous woman, and it must be admitted that Sarah Bernhardt's understand-

---

[7] When R. Percy Burton asked her whether it was true that when a German manager telegraphed her for terms, she replied, "Alsace-Lorraine," she said, "No, but I wish it were; it is so clever."

ing of public affairs as such did not go very deep. Despite her reservations concerning him, her anti-militarism did not keep her from admiring Napoleon; in her old age she was even taken in by Mussolini. Like many comparatively uninformed persons, she simplified political problems; if she could rule the world (so Sir George Arthur reports her), "pain and poverty should be banished—pleasure and sunshine should be permanent—beauty should be everywhere." Yet she could nourish and express prejudices quite out of harmony with her general humanity, as against the Chinese, for example. Like everything else about her, her patriotism functioned best in connection with her art, and she proudly and justifiably declared, "I have journeyed across the ocean, bearing with me my aesthetic ideal, and the genius of my nation has triumphed."

Yet her aesthetic interests were not wholly confined to the theater. I do not indeed find that her interest in natural beauty was ever overwhelming. "I adore the sea and the plain, but I care neither for mountains nor for forests. Mountains seem to crush me, and forests to stifle me." But anything that could be done in a studio appealed to her. She painted. She sculptured. She wrote. Did she do these things well? The answer hardly matters. The remarkable thing is that she should have done them at all. She undertook ambitious pieces, she exhibited and won awards, and there were times when she became so absorbed in her studio work that acting itself was pushed into second place. Moreover, she always finished what she had started, though if she did not like it, she might smash it afterwards, even though she had a customer waiting, as with the bust of Rothschild. It is true that there was something facile about all this, sometimes even something childlike: when she built her house, she wondered if she ought not to have become an architect! Yet she hated inspecting public buildings, and her principal architectural conviction seems to have been the idea that all erections "higher than a mill" were bad. "I have nothing to say against the Pyramids, but I would a hundred times rather they had never been built."

Her taste in home decoration was as florid and crowded as her period encouraged, and her house was more like a museum than a home. She was always dressed to the nines, in colorful, swirling silks and velvets, trimmed with fur, and she wanted everybody else dressed the same way, even children: if her friends dressed their children simply or plainly, she would complain that they looked as if they did not belong to anybody.

Her large library brought an excellent price after her death,[8] but it is hard to see how she ever could have found much time to read, and, since she was an excellent listener, one suspects that she derived more from her multitudinous contacts with distinguished men and women than from books. Her principal aesthetic weakness was in music. She herself says that it was only noise to her, and she is often described as tone-deaf, but this does not seem to have been literally true. It seems strange that she cared nothing for the opera, which is, after all, half drama. She composed at least one piece for the piano—"The Dance of the Bears"—and played it on one occasion for Reynaldo Hahn, who often played for her. She sang on the stage on a few occasions, and in the early days she played the piano in *La Femme de Claude*; grown older, she refused to do this, having passed the age when one "dares all without counting the cost."

Of Sarah Bernhardt's religion, Gamaliel Bradford remarks, in his by no means unsympathetic portrait of her,[9] that "what the Almighty thought of her as an adherent, it may be easy to conjecture." Forgive me, "myn owne mayster deere," but is not this, perhaps, a little too New England? What the Almighty thinks of any of us as adherents is a subject that hardly bears our thinking about with comfort, as you yourself were always beautifully aware. Nobody would be so silly as to think of Sarah Bernhardt as a devotee, and she herself admitted, when she grew older, that there was more drama and aesthetic sensi-

[8] See *Bibliothèque de Mme. Sarah Bernhardt* (2 pts., Paris, Librairie Henri Leclerc, 1923).

[9] "Eve in the Spotlight: Sarah Bernhardt," in *Daughters of Eve* (Houghton Mifflin, 1930).

tiveness in her early inclination toward the cloister than genuine religion, but she could hardly have distinguished between the two if religion itself had been quite a closed book to her.

She was a Catholic from the time of her baptism in the convent, and she received the last rites of the church just before she closed her eyes for the last time. In her milieu she had nothing to gain by pretending anything she did not feel along this line; neither was it in her nature to do so. She was intensely superstitious; she herself said that she retained through life all the superstitions of her childhood and superimposed upon them all the superstitions of the countries through which she traveled. But she also had a mystical side to her complex nature, and I see no reason for supposing that, within the limitations of her milieu and her temperament, her religion was not quite as genuine as everything else about her. In her sentimental novel, *The Idol of Paris,* she attributes what we now call extrasensory perception to a heroine obviously modeled upon herself, and once at least, when her father died, she seems herself to have experienced this. She tried table tipping with Sardou, and in 1897 she mounted his play *Spiritisme,* which was an utter failure.

She seems to have been quite as effective in her religious roles—as Joan of Arc, the Woman of Samaria, and Saint Thérèse—as she was as the tiger women that Sardou created for her, and she herself writes that "it was God Himself who inspired the work of M. Rostand."

Christian love filled the theater with the joy of infinite purity [she writes of her production of *La Samaritaine*]. I felt myself transported to the beyond as I recited the beautiful words, and other hearts beat in my heart as I wept those saltless tears devoid of bitterness, those pure tears that lave, remove, and wash away for ever the dross of our souls, of our lives too long for the wrong that we do, too short for the good that we could do.

As a matter of fact, she had a touch of the unworldly and the ideal about her, even in nonreligious roles. "Mme. Sarah Bernhardt," wrote Jules Lemaître, "always seems like a very strange person returning from very far away," and Ellen Terry thought that even in her incomparable love scenes, "it is a *picture* of love that she gives, a strange orchidaceous picture rather than a suggestion of the ordinary human passion as felt by ordinary people." Her Phèdre was not demoniacal like Rachel's but a picture of genuine human affection misdirected and consequently fraught with anguish. And Francisque Sarcey, by no means always an admirer, declared that she had placed *La Dame aux Camélias* itself in a new light. "It isn't a courtesan who dies of consumption. . . . It is a courtesan killed by scorn of her trade and her powerlessness to get out of it. With a single stroke she opened a window on to the ideal."

But what impresses me most about Sarah Bernhardt in this connection is the way she turns to religion to illuminate even what most of us would consider purely secular matters. The norm is *there,* and we can understand what is *here* only by reference to it. Arguing the need for the theater, she says that "just as each soul feels the need of prayer, so each mind needs to evoke dreams, to create legends, and to conjure up the departed." And when she gave a performance that really satisfied her, she could find only three words which expressed her sense of what had occurred: "God was there." She may not always have served God, but a world without Him would have been both inconceivable and intolerable to her.

Her sensitiveness has often been misjudged even by people who ought to have known better. One night Mrs. Patrick Campbell, watching her stain the palms of Cleopatra's hands, asked her why she took so much trouble with something which nobody in the audience would be able to see. "*I* shall see it," she replied. "I am doing it for myself. If I catch sight of my hand it will be the hand of Cleopatra. That will help me." And the same principle is much more seriously involved in Yvette Guilbert's account of how, visiting her at Mount Sinai Hospital, where she had to undergo an operation during her last visit to America, she found her "terribly made up and powdered, her eyes thick with black, her lips scarlet, her red hair crimped and fluffed up—a lion in bed! She terrified me. Heavens! think of not being oneself in the midst of fever and agony, and to be wearing a mask and stage trappings, to deceive—whom?"

This sounds a good deal more intelligent than it is. Sarah Bernhardt, at the end of her tether, having borne more than any ten women should ever be called upon to bear, was certainly not trying to "deceive" anybody. And as for being herself "in the midst of fever and agony," what else in heaven's name did Yvette Guilbert think she was doing? She was confronting life as she had always confronted it; she was preserving the amenities. If she had done anything else, it would have meant that she had surrendered, was giving up the fort. And she had probably never in her life been more heroic.

IV

Yet when all is said and done Sarah Bernhardt was basically an actress. "When she was off the stage, she always seemed to be acting," says Bradford; "she always seemed to be living when she was on it." She was. It was her way of living. God Himself manifested best to her in the theater. Or, as she puts it, "And in this fleeting moment which brought near me all the beauty of life, I felt myself very near to God."

It is impossible even to suggest, in a brief study, the range and richness of the Bernhardt dramatic world. In her excellent biography, Joanna Richardson has tried to describe the Bernhardt type, the woman that she created and embodied on and off the stage:

It owed something to Baudelaire's "Vierge du Mal," something to Swinburne's "Our Lady of Pain," something to the Mona Lisa, and something to Burne-Jones. It was a rich, intensely exotic ideal: the quintessence of the splendid and the feminine, the embodiment of Oriental exoticism, the strange chimeric idol-woman. It was Rostand's "Princess Far Away," it was Sardou's la Tosca and Théodora. It was something sublime, relentless, something epic, something cruel and magical as Circe, and perhaps no actress but Sarah could have given it incarnation. But she, with her wraith-like figure, her aureole of hair, her compelling eloquent eyes: she, with her voice, could realise the dream.

She has been blamed for leaving the Comédie Française, and it is certainly true that if she had stayed there she would have become a more important French classical actress. (She loved Racine but hated Corneille.) On the other hand, she would have missed much—international stardom, for one thing—and she would certainly have left a less vivid and varied imprint upon the life of her time. One reason why her career was so long was that whenever she seemed to have exhausted a particular type of character or play, she was always able to find a new playwright who could give her something fresh and different, so that her whole career seemed to be starting over again. Some of these playwrights it is now fashionable to scorn, Sardou particularly, and it was when Sarah was in her Sardou period that even the admiring Jules Lemaître felt constrained to declare that "she is only completely herself when she is killing or dying. Nowadays she is only the incomparable actress of last acts, of sinister and bloody dénouements."[10] But I always doubt that a critic who dislikes melodrama really cares for the theater, and despite the frequent charge that Sarah Bernhardt coarsened her art by playing broadly enough so that she could make herself comprehensible to foreign audiences, I must say that she never allowed herself to be typed in any period. Of course there were times when God did not come, and she played spiritlessly or mechanically. But run over the list of her innumerable productions and revivals and you will find a quite bewildering variety; read what responsible critics have written about what she did in this or that forgotten item in her vast repertoire—sometimes a disregarded achievement upon the like of which many another actress has based a whole career—or about the gestures and inflections which have been carried in loving memory across a lifetime, and you will marvel, as I have done, at the range of this woman's sensitiveness. Suze Rueff cites her wonderful repetition of *"j'écoute"* as the Woman of Samaria drinks in the words of Jesus, "pouring out her whole soul in those few syllables." "To see Pelléas raise that face to Mélisande and bathe and drown in those black tresses," says James Agate, "to behold the passion of Jeanne

---

[10] For an extreme statement of the anti-Bernhardt point of view, see Signa, "Sarah Bernhardt and Aimée Desclée," *Cornhill,* N.S., Vol. LXVI (1924), 61–73.

d'Arc burn like a flame swaying in the wind, to gaze upon rapt inviolacy, pity and ruth—this was to know the shining facet of a supreme artist."

Sarah Bernhardt believed in the theater and was completely in earnest in her attitude toward it. "The theater propagates new ideas, it arouses slumbering patriotism, it exposes turpitudes and abuses by sarcasm, educates the ignorant without their knowing it, stimulates those of little courage, strengthens faith, gives hope, and enjoins charity." Nor could you ever give an audience less than your best: "Remember you are playing for the one intelligent person who is probably in the gallery. There is always that one person, even in the poorest house, for whom one does one's best."

It is interesting to know that she never conquered stage fright, and Lysiane preserves the picture of her with her hands ice cold before a first night: "My God, my God! If only the theater would burn down!" But she only experienced this before a friendly audience. If she thought her audience hostile, she was calm and collected, with "only one idea, one resolve"—to subjugate the beast.

In formal dramatic theory Sarah Bernhardt's thoroughly feminine mind took little interest. She had no sympathy with "The Tradition," the stilted, prescribed directions with which the Comédie had identified itself; from the beginning she must play her scenes not as "The Tradition" or her masters required but as she herself felt it, which was often in a quieter, though intenser, way. "Do not be afraid to laugh in Tragedy and cry in Comedy," she told her pupils.

For all the glory of her vocalism, which survived miraculously unimpaired until her death (it is amazing to learn that her voice was originally weak and that she built it with deliberation to what it finally became), Sarah Bernhardt believed that action came first in the theater.[11] Technically there was nothing she did not know about the re-

[11] Sarah Bernhardt's films were all silent, but *Queen Elizabeth* at least preserves something of her gift for gesture, and her voice may still be heard on her phonograph records, some of which are magnificent. Both her reading and her acting have been well described in Maurice Baring's *Sarah Bernhardt,* May Agate's *Madame Sarah,* and

lationship between ends and means; she calculated her effects and knew how to produce them exactly as she wanted them. She knew the value of the pause, recognized the necessity of varying pace, and always prepared the audience for striking effects so that they might be thrilled but not shocked. "Sufficient air must be inhaled for four lines or twenty-six words at least"—and she considers the shape of the jaw and of the roof of the mouth and the position of the teeth as affecting this. She adds: "She who writes these lines clenches the teeth a little too much, especially at dress rehearsals or on the first night when she has an attack of stage fright." The simplest chance gesture can ruin everything unless it has been considered and adjusted to the total effect desired. "Never, under any circumstances, allow both your hands to drop to your sides, unless you want deliberately to convey despondency."

But unless the actor's *idea* is right to begin with, all the mechanism in the world will accomplish nothing. "Comprehensive study" must precede the performance; you soak yourself in your character, including extensive reading if you are appearing in a period play, but when it comes to the actual performance, "you must be able to find everything you want on the stage in the excitement created by the general collaboration"; otherwise you will fail in spontaneity. Even after she had acted *La Dame aux Camélias* hundreds of times, she could, when "God was there," play it so that not the audience merely but the actors on the stage beside her would virtually dissolve in tears. She was too creative to stereotype a performance or reproduce it mechanically. Sometimes she altered Marguerite's lines; sometimes she

---

Jules Lemaître's *Literary Impressions* (London, Daniel O'Connor, 1921). Cf. Baring on her use of her eyes: "No actress or actor ever made greater play with the eyes: now wistful and wondering, now like 'magic casements' opening on all that was most far away and most forlorn; now like glinting gems, hard as metal and cold as ice, and now like darts of flame, piercing you with their pointed brilliance; now blazing with fury or flooded with passion; now sad with all the sorrow of all the world; and sometimes, as when in *Le Procès de Jeanne d'Arc* she faced her judges, and spoke of '*la grande clarté,*' the sights and sounds of Paradise were reflected in her eyes and echoed in the fervour of her voice."

would spend her time on tour studying the text of plays in which she had acted, then exclaim: "I have found something new in this scene! We must do it tonight."

Being, as she was, one of the most mercurial creatures ever born, Sarah Bernhardt could be both petty and wonderfully generous toward her fellow actors. She always got along better with the women than she did with the men, and she sometimes showed more tendency to be jealous of mediocrity than of genius. But she was quite clear that the individual actor was "not himself the keyboard, but that he forms part of a general harmony," and she was too good an artist to be guilty of magnifying her role beyond its proper proportions. She met a real test in this connection when she played Roxane to Coquelin's Cyrano to return the favor he had done her in accepting the comparatively small role of Flambeau in *L'Aiglon,* and she passed it triumphantly.

She is nowhere more interesting than in her consideration of the relationship between the actor and his role, between his own emotions and those which he simulates. She is quite clear that "the actor cannot divide his personality between himself and his part; he loses his *ego* during the time he remains on the stage, and thus his consciousness skips from age to age, from one people to another, from one hero to another." But the distinctions here involve almost mystical subtleties, and she knew it well. "Once the curtain is raised, the actor ceases to belong to himself, he belongs to his character, to his author, to his public. He must do the impossible to identify with the first, not to betray the second, and not to disappoint the third." She rejected the view of Talma and Coquelin that the actor himself should feel no emotion (she considered Coquelin to lack sensibility), "as I contend that it is necessary to feel all the sentiments that agitate the soul of the character it is desired to represent." From some of her remarks on the subject one would almost think her a "Method" actress; thus she reacted to Mario's torture in *La Tosca* by reminding herself how she would feel if something were to happen to Maurice. She even claimed to have "touched real death" on the stage; "sometimes it has taken more than an hour for me to come to life." Yet one cannot but feel that she came closer to Coquelin in practice than in theory. May Agate says that in one performance the tears would stream down her cheeks, while in the next she would be dry-eyed, *"but the effect on the audience was the same."* Was "God" really "there" in the first performance, or was Sarah merely having an emotional orgy? She could play practical jokes on her colleagues or scold them, apparently without interfering with the effectiveness of her performance; once she delivered a tirade against Mme Berton in the midst of a death scene.

Sarah Bernhardt had no difficulty with youthful roles when she was an old woman, and a rather astonishing number of her triumphs were in male roles. Of course there is difference of opinion about her Hamlet—and an English reader must admit that a fifty-six-year-old woman who should undertake this role in a French prose translation must have several strikes against her at the outset—but most of the adverse criticisms came from those who were still in bondage to the Coleridgean Hamlet, and I must say that everything I read against her interpretation leaves me feeling more strongly that her critics were wrong and that she was right.[12] *L'Aiglon* and Alfred de Musset's *Lorenzaccio* are nearly always placed among her great achievements; we have already seen that her Zanetto in *Le Passant* played an important part in launching her; she was generally admired in *Pelléas et Mélisande* and in *Les Bouffons* of Miguel Zamacoïs; she is said to have been altogether delightful at sixty-three as Prince Charming in the fantasy by Jean Richepin and Henri Cain, *La Belle au Bois Dormant.*[13]

[12] For various views, pro and con, see Anon., "The Two Spectacles," *Blackwood's,* Vol. CLXVI (1899), 228–30; Elizabeth Robins, "On Seeing Madame Bernhardt's Hamlet," *North American Review,* Vol. CLXXI (1900), 908–19; William Winter, *The Wallet of Time* (Moffat, Yard, 1913), I; Baring, *Sarah Bernhardt;* Max Beerbohm, *Around Theatres* (Knopf, 1930), I.

[13] Cf. W. Graham Robertson, *Time Was* (Hamish Hamilton, 1931): "Was Sarah Bernhardt beautiful? Was she even passably good looking? I have not the slightest idea. Beauty with her was a garment which she could put on and off as she pleased. When she let it fall from her she was a small woman with very delicate features, thin lips, a small beautifully modelled nose, hooded eyes of grey-green shadowed by a fleece

She had a theory about women in men's roles, but here again it does not seem to me completely consistent or very important. What she said was that she preferred "not male parts, but male brains," and that "generally speaking, male parts, are more intellectual than female parts." But she also believed that the dramatic art was essentially a feminine art, better adapted to the character and personality of women than men, that it attracted a better type of woman than man, and that it was the only art "where women may sometimes prove superior to men." She argued further that "a woman can only interpret a male part when it represents a mind in a feeble body," but her own performance of Hamlet did not support this view; rather, this would seem to be the conception of Hamlet against which she revolted. Finally, I must confess that she seems to me to be talking nonsense when she declares that Hamlet, L'Aiglon, and Lorenzaccio, all three, "always gain when they are played by intellectual women, who alone are able to preserve their character of unsexed beings, and their perfume of mystery."

Her feelings about realism and romance in the theater proceeded from deeper levels of her being. She never failed in proper attention to realistic detail: with her own hands she once broke down a pair of boots worn by a super, applying grease paint and fuller's earth so that they should not look new. And there were times when she produced realistic plays—*Magda* and *Sapho* and *Madame X* and others of much less value—when she saw something in them which promised to give her the opportunity to create a spectacular effect. In the course of so long and varied a career, she played almost everything that could be played; once she even deprived herself of her *voix d'or* to appear in a pantomime. But these are not the plays with which she identified most profoundly or by which she is best remembered. "On the stage, to be natural is good, but to be sublime is always better." "Be more mystical."

of red-gold hair, strong slender hands, and a manner full of nervous energy. But when she would appear beautiful, none of these details were to be perceived; her face became a lamp through which glowed pale light, her hair burned like an aureole, she grew tall and stately; it was transfiguration."

"Art is exalted. . . . Do not imagine all emotion is artistic." This is the real Bernhardt. Compare even her naturalistic effects with those created by other actresses in the same roles, and you will find that in every case she refined and exalted her material without compromising its truth. William Winter disliked her and absurdly denied her poetry. But listen to him on *Frou-Frou*: "Her acting in the Death Scene was pathetic in its fidelity to nature, yet never once marred by the literal touch which so often makes death scenes offensive on the stage." And again on *La Dame aux Camélias*: "The subject is coarse: her treatment of it comprehended personal reticence." Such things cause one to believe that she was just when she said of herself, "The only fault which I have never had, which I never shall have, is vulgarity."

v

I have said almost nothing of the freakish, fantastic Sarah of legend or of the *"grande amoureuse"* she admitted herself to have been. It is reported of an Englishwoman watching Sarah Bernhardt in *Cléopâtre* that what impressed her most was the extreme unlikeness between what she was seeing on the stage and "the home life of our own dear Queen." She might perhaps have been similarly affected by Sarah's life off stage, for it would be silly to pretend that her conduct could be squared with the "conventional" principles of "Anglo-Saxon" morality. But it would be even more of a mistake to assume that she had no standards. "My mother's house was always full of men," she says, "and the more I saw of them the less I liked them." She never did like the kind of men that her mother attracted, and if she seems very "French" when she tells Mrs. Patrick Campbell how shocked she is by the English habit of flirting because it is immoral to rouse desires which you do not intend to gratify, she is much less so in her rejection of all the early suitors proposed for her because, though her ideas of marriage were vague, "I understood enough to make me not want to marry without being in love." However wide and varied her sexual experience may have become, she was not coarsened or brutalized by it; neither was she, in any sense, a dissipated woman. She ate and drank sparingly,[14] and she did not smoke. It is true that she lived in a "fast" set early in her career, but this did not last long; as a mother and grandmother her views were as "correct" as those of any French matron, and she believed in marital fidelity and was properly indignant over managers who paid young actresses a wage they could not possibly be expected to live on. She abhorred drug addiction and perversion. She never sold herself for advantages,[15] and she would have nothing to say to coarse, rich men or elegant young wastrels. It was men of genius who attracted her, and aesthetically at least, the influence she had on them seems to have been wholly beneficial. As Mme Berton, whose husband had himself been one of her lovers, puts it, "To painters she would say: 'If you love me, then paint a masterpiece and dedicate it to me.' To poets she would say: 'If it is true that you love me, you will write a poem about me that will live when we both are dead.' " And the younger Dumas adds: "She drives me mad when I am with her. She is all temperament and no heart; but when she is gone, how I work! How I *can* work!" which hardly sounds like *la belle dame sans merci* or any other brand of *la femme fatale*.

Many have questioned that Sarah Bernhardt was ever very deeply in love with anything except the theater or anybody but Sarah Bernhardt, and Gamaliel Bradford was prepared to extend this even to her

[14] She was fond of describing herself as a vegetarian, but this seems unsubstantiated, and many observers record having seen her partake of various animal foods. Her usual drink seems to have been a little champagne, but Reynaldo Hahn describes one dinner before a performance: "She eats two poached eggs and a little cold roast beef, drinks Apollinaris and whisky, liking a frequent change of drinks." In her last years she was largely on a milk diet, but she still set a lavish table for her innumerable guests and was very particular about the preparation and serving of food. When Louis Verneuil read *Daniel* to her, she offered him lemonade and water.

[15] Verneuil (page 89) scolds Mme Berton for suggesting that Sarah seduced Francisque Sarcey to get good notices from him, then, when he had committed himself, dropped him. He might have attacked her even more severely, for she (a) asserts that Sarah never gave herself for interested reasons, (b) details a liaison with Sarcey in the terms reported by Verneuil, (c) quotes Sarah as denying that Sarcey was ever her lover, thus leaving the reader totally at sea as to what she imagines herself to be saying.

calamitous marriage: "the whole affair seems to have been mainly a conflict of sex-vanities, in which Sarah got rather the worst of it." Probably nobody knows much about any love-relationship except the people who participate in it; Robert Louis Stevenson says that some of the ugliest adulteries are committed in the bed of marriage and under the sanction of religion and law. Sarah Bernhardt was no exhibitionist, and she preserved the conventional nineteenth-century silence concerning her amatory affairs; consequently we do not really know very much about them. The number of liaisons in which she participated would certainly seem to indicate that she was a passionate woman, but if once we have allowed for the fact that she grew up in a circle in which chastity as an ideal was not cherished—until she got to the convent it can hardly even have been presented to her—we may perhaps avoid committing ourselves to the rash conclusion that she must therefore have been a monster of lust. Did the brevity of her attachments indicate mere fickleness, I wonder, or was she, as G. G. Geller acutely suggested, a nervous, or even neurasthenic, seeker, in love as well as in art?

She herself said that her days with Pierre Berton were like "pages from immortality," but if we are to accept the authenticity of the letters to Berton which Sylvia B. Golden published in 1930,[16] it would seem that if Sarah was the aggressor in this affair, she was also the victim, and the same thing may have happened elsewhere. The really interesting thing, however, is that, again and again, after the initial fire had burned itself out, she could retain the man involved indefinitely as a devoted friend, building on the old foundation a completely nonsensual relationship which enriched both their lives, and to this it should be added that there were also men like Jules Lemaître with whom her connection was of this character from the beginning. Not that Sarah could ever resist charming a man, but desire was not the only—or even the principal—spell which she employed. It is amusing that when she visited Edison at Menlo Park, she sensed that he was indifferent to her and bored by the necessity of showing her about; so

[16] "The Romance of Sarah Bernhardt," *Theatre Magazine* (July, 1930).

she deliberately set out to interest him and believed that she had done so. He explained everything, she says, and "I understood all, and I admired him more and more." She also admired Theodore Roosevelt, a friendly letter from whom she framed and hung in her house, and in one of her bursts of megalomania she exclaimed, "Ah! but that man and I, we could rule the world!" So they might have done if— well, if they had not been themselves, and she was far too sensible not to know that it would have been quite impossible to seduce such a man, even if she had desired to do so, or to establish any other relationship with him except the harmless, rewarding friendship which she enjoyed.[17]

As for the worthless, wastrel husband, Bradford may have been right, for he had challenged her by pretending indifference to her, and she herself is supposed to have said that she married because marriage was the only thing she had not tried. But if this is true, her behavior afterwards was certainly very curious, for the drug-besotted creature treated her shamefully and disgraced her before the world, and she accepted all the indignities he put upon her with a saintly patience worthy of a much better cause. Even after they had separated (they

---

[17] Verneuil believed that Sarah's amatory adventures ended as early as the death of Damala, denying that she ever had an affair with either Rostand or Lou Tellegen. He also takes the latter severely to task for the account he gives of Sarah's fondness for him in his really nauseating autobiography, *Women Have Been Kind* (Vanguard Press, 1931). Tellegen does not actually say he was Bernhardt's lover, however, nor does he seem to have claimed this on other occasions. I cannot now cite the item, but I read, years ago, in a cheap magazine, an article about Tellegen by one of his later wives in which she reports having remarked to him, referring to Sarah Bernhardt, "Of course, you were her lover," to which he replied in the negative, citing the great discrepancy in their ages. I believe this, if for no other reason because I cannot imagine Tellegen denying such an important conquest. In her autobiography, *Such Sweet Compulsion* (Greystone Press, 1938), Geraldine Farrar, who had the misfortune to be Tellegen's second wife, cites as one evidence of his moral worthlessness, "his supreme contempt for those great personages who extended a helping hand . . . all during his early career. Notably Sarah Bernhardt." There can be no doubt, however, that the aging Bernhardt was sufficiently taken by Tellegen to try to force him down the throat of a Parisian public which regarded him with contempt. Nowhere else in her career except with Damala himself did she ever make such a mistake.

were never divorced), the wretch had only to permit his excesses to bring him to the door of death for her to rush to him and care for him until the end. Legally she bore his name as long as she lived, mourned him a little ostentatiously, and cherished his family as if he had been the best of husbands. Sarah Bernhardt's loyalty always passed the bounds of quixotism in all family matters. She once told Lysiane that "the family that one has given to one is of no importance. The only people who count are those whom one loves and especially the family that one creates oneself." Her own conduct does not square with this. She practically brought up her half-sister Regina and looked after her devotedly to her early death, though she was well aware of her faults. The drug addiction of her other half-sister Jeanne, her mother's favorite, she faced with the same courage that she showed toward her husband. In so romantic a nature, the devotion to the practically unknown father might be dismissed as devotion to a dream, but Sarah did know her mother, and knew nothing good about her, at least in relation to herself, yet she loved her passionately. If we wish to understand how much better a woman Sarah Bernhardt was than her mother had been, entirely aside from her genius, and in spite of the irregularities of her life, we need only contrast Julie's treatment of her with Sarah's own unwise, infinitely indulgent treatment of her own illegitimate son: "He's a bad boy, but I like him." The joy of her life, Maurice adored his mother as much as she adored him, and after he was grown up, he was always ready to fight at the drop of a hat with anybody who had slighted her (they generally apologized and prevented a meeting). There is no indication that Sarah ever found her relationship with her son unsatisfying in any way, but an outsider cannot help wondering whether he would not have been even more useful to her if he had learned how to earn a living instead of quartering himself and his family upon her purse until she died.

Bernhardt's wild temperamental outbursts began in childhood and may well have begun as an unconscious protest against the rackety conditions under which she was compelled to live at that time. Inwardly, as she afterwards said, she was shy and afraid of everything; she always had a phobia for falling, especially downstairs, and she liked a hand or a shoulder to support her even before she began having trouble with her leg. Neither could she bear to be left alone in a room —"no one thinks of me any more!"—but if there were too many people around her she became uncomfortable. It is easy to see how a person with such a temperament would go to extremes to try to cure it or cover it up. When she was nine she hurt herself badly attempting an impossible jump over a ditch, and as she was carried away, she screamed that she would do it again *"quand-même"* if anybody dared her. Here, perhaps, was the origin of what Yvette Guilbert calls "her terrible yet magnificent motto." She used it all her life and had it stamped on everything that belonged to her. In the beginning it was a defiant proclamation of willfulness, but before she had finished it had come to symbolize indomitable heroism.

She never completely recovered from her early hysteria, though as she grew older she learned better how to control it. "There was no happy medium about me. I was 'too much' and 'too little' and I felt that there was nothing to be done for it." It did not always take the form of making scenes. In Baltimore, on her first American tour, the first New Year's Day away from home, "I wept all night and underwent that moment of discouragement that makes one wish for death," and she disliked St. Louis so much on sight that she wished to flee the city and pay an indemnity for not acting there. Sometimes it took the form of hauteur—she could always be very fussy about what she considered her dignity—as when, encountering the Prince of Wales, so soon to be her very great admirer, with his hat on in the wings of the theater, she curtly told him that gentlemen uncovered in the presence of ladies, or when, as a youngster, she refused to go to the house of even the aged and honored Victor Hugo for a rehearsal but made him come to the theater. Often, too, it made her unreliable about money and other social obligations, and she always had the tendency to promise to do anything anybody asked of her and then forget all about it. On her first visit to England, says Sir George Arthur, "she accepted invitations, and at the last moment failed to appear, or disturbed all arrangements by preposterous unpunctuality. She appeared irresponsible and intractable. She overrode convention and brushed aside remonstrance."[18] Sometimes she was melancholy or morbid. And sometimes, as with her fondness for keeping dangerous wild animals about her, she was just plain eccentric and unadapted to the world she lived in. "It's the first time in my long career that I've met the real actress of the novels," wrote Octave Feuillet to his wife, as Sarah began rehearsals on *Le Sphinx,* "the courtesan-actress of the eighteenth century, elegant, painted, eccentric, an insolent tomboy, la Desmares or la Duthé."[19]

Not that her outbursts were always without justification. It is difficult not to sympathize with her, for example, when, as a youngster, she precipitated a crisis at the Comédie Française by slapping an older actress after the latter had roughly attacked Sarah's little sister for inadvertently stepping on her train.[20] There was also the boorish German officer in a train compartment who would neither stop poisoning her with his vile pipe nor permit her to open the window, whereupon she triumphantly solved the problem by putting her elbow through

[18] "It is perfectly odious, I know, and yet I always accept with pleasure and intend to go; but when the day comes I am tired, perhaps, or want to have a quiet time, or to be free from any obligation, and when I am obliged to decide one way or the other, the time has gone by, and it is too late to send word and too late to go. And so I stay at home, dissatisfied with myself, with everyone else, and with everything."

[19] The words "painted" and "tomboy" in this statement sound strangely unreal today. When Sarah was rehearsing *Ruy Blas* with Victor Hugo, she sat down, at a break, on a table and began swinging her legs. Would anybody be offended by this now? Hugo was driven to impromptu verses to rebuke her:

Une Reine d'Espagne, honnête et respectable,
Ne devrait pas ainsi s'asseoir sur une table.

[20] It seems odd that in her later account of this incident, in *The Art of the Theatre,* Sarah leaves Regina out of it and says merely that Madame Nathalie "mercilessly ridiculed me because I was a young beginner, and continued to scold me so harshly that at length I boxed her ears."

it. ("As for me, I am not placid, I am active, and always ready for a fight, and what I want I always want immediately.") But there were other instances when she had no such justification, and in these cases the most one can say for her is that she was often ashamed and repentant afterwards and that sometimes she had the grace to apologize.

Sarah Bernhardt's unreliability in money matters needs qualification. All her life she supported everybody about her, and she herself estimated her earnings in the theater at about $9,000,000, yet she died virtually penniless. She was allergic to banks. As soon as she was in a position to dictate terms, she was paid in gold at each performance, and the gold went into her bag or box. Sometimes. She always lived beyond her means and was chronically in debt, and often what she received was earmarked for her numerous dependents and the creditors who were pressing her hardest even before she had got her hands on it. She paid wages generously but irregularly, and though there were some servitors she long retained, she changed her cook and kitchenmaid about twice a month. In the theater she was a good businesswoman in the sense that she knew how to drive a bargain, but she never had a strictly commercial outlook. "It may not make a sou," she said when she found *La Princesse Lointaine,* "but I don't care. I think it is superb."[21] She sank money recklessly into her summer home at Belle-Isle-en-Mer. Her shopping tours were orgies, and her unused purchases long outlasted her lifetime. When she was eager to have a letter delivered, she was quite capable of sending her secretary across France with it in person. In her last years she lived largely on the sale of her jewels.

[21] According to his brother, Maurice Grau, who long managed Bernhardt's American tours, never had a formal contract with her. "Moreover, although her understanding was that besides her stipulated guarantee she was to receive a share of the gross receipts, she had no representative at the 'count-up,' something wholly unusual and truly amazing for a foreign star. Madame accepted the box office statements as presented to her with the utmost indifference. In all the many years that my brother was her impressario they never had a quarrel." Robert Grau, "Sarah Bernhardt," *American Magazine* (February, 1913).

Bernhardt's love of animals was not eccentric in itself but its expression sometimes became so. Sometimes, as with her tortoise Chrysagère, it was harmless except for its extravagance.

> Its back was covered with a shell of gold, set with very small blue, pink, and yellow topazes. Oh, how beautiful it was and how droll! It used to wander round my flat, accompanied by a small tortoise named Zerbinette, which was its servant, and I amused myself for hours watching Chrysagère, flashing with a hundred lights under the rays of the sun or the moon.

But it was different with the wild animals which exposed her and others to danger and caused no end of trouble and inconvenience. Once, towards the end of her life, when an American reporter asked her if she had any animals with her, she blushed and said, "I only did those foolish things when I was a girl." Yet when a lion cub was presented to her on her last American tour, she dragged him over the country with her, at great inconvenience, and only gave him up when the hotels refused to take him in.

The charges of sadism which Sarah's enemies made against her in connection with her pets were quite ridiculous, but I think it clear that there was a streak of the primitive in her. It shows in her interest in the bullfight and her tireless passion for hunting.[22] When she came to Chicago she put herself through the horrors of a trip to the slaughterhouses, and that night she fainted on the stage. She took a whip to her sister Jeanne in a somewhat nonscientific attempt to cure her of drug addiction, and when her enemy Marie Colombier published her outrageous book, *The Memoirs of Sarah Barnum,* she not only

---

[22] As I have said elsewhere in connection with Theodore Roosevelt, I do not understand how one who loves animals, as I am sure both Sarah and T.R. did, can enjoy killing them. I don't know how many animals Sarah killed but she certainly tried. She habitually draped herself in furs, and the skins of dead beasts were as ubiquitous in her house as at Sagamore Hill itself. She gives me another problem in connection with her passion for games. I have always believed that the special devotees of games are people who enjoy playing with their minds rather than using them and who find life so dull that they cannot get through it without wasting it. Yet here was one of the most creative spirits who ever lived and she seems to have played everything that can

whipped her, which she richly deserved, but completely wrecked her apartment. There is a story about her feeding live quails to her tiger cub, and Mme Berton says she once threw a dog out the window of a hotel in a fit of annoyance, and five minutes later had her maid hold her out the window by her feet to rescue him from the ledge upon which he had fallen, after which she smothered him with love.

The morbid strain, however, cannot be denied. Sarah did have a rosewood coffin (she pawned the gold handles when she needed money and was buried in silver), and though she did not make a habit of sleeping in it, she was photographed in it, and there are reports of a mock funeral service and other excesses. She owned a skull or a skeleton. She witnessed executions and visited dissecting rooms (not wholly, I think, because of her interest in sculpture), and she is said once to have broken with a friend because he would not permit her to witness an embalming. On at least one occasion she expected to die on the stage (but found instead that her reckless emotionalism had greatly exhilarated her), and when she desired to become a nun she dreamed of dying while assuming the veil. Once, at the Odéon, she shammed death so effectively backstage that her demise was announced to the audience and a hearse sent for. There are even stories about attempts at suicide during the early years which fit in well enough with the twilight of nineteenth-century romanticism which was falling around her but which are hard to reconcile with the gallant courage of her later years. They may have been more theatrical than earnest, and in any case I think they indicate that her character developed more as she grew older than she is generally given credit for. It

be played, indoors and out, with the single exception of golf, which she regarded as idiotic. At games of chance, as she herself said, "I am a very bad player, and I hate to lose—it enrages me. This is ridiculous and silly, I know, but there it is! I can't bear to be beaten!" Generally, when she played with intimates and dependents, they saw to it that she was not. It is endearing to read that when young Harry Agate did magic tricks for her, she was so enthralled that she had to learn how to do "The Vanishing Penny" right away, and "went off with it in her bag . . . and in high fettle." On the whole, however, I cannot but feel that Sarah Bernhardt's activities in this area are another aspect of her restlessness and neuroticism.

must be remembered that Sarah's health was very bad in her youth and that she honestly did not expect to live long, and it may be that all this *memento mori* business had a therapeutic, though not, I think, a religious, value for her, in helping her to live with the thought of death and thus, paradoxically, to be drawn to life. For that matter, I doubt that the medieval *memento mori* was all religion; some of it must have been plain perversity and unhealthiness, and, to compare small things with great, I am not sure that Sarah's antics, theatrical as they were, were much more morbid than the impulse which inspired such great works of Bach's as *Ich Habe Genug,* which are much admired even today.

The theatrical note must indeed never be forgotten in dealing with her. "It is clear," says Max Beerbohm, "that even in her most terrific moments one half of her soul was in the position of spectator, applauding vigorously." I am sure this was true even in her attempts at suicide, so that in effect neither the universe nor the recording angel could "count this one," and I think again of Bradford's "When she was off the stage, she always seemed to be acting; she always seemed to be living when she was on it." Suze Rueff suggests that she could not always distinguish perfectly between herself and the characters that she played. And I am sure, too, that Lou Tellegen was right when he wrote, "She could fly into a rage about nothing, but that was only a necessary vent to her extremely dynamic and overcharged vitality."

VI

The gifted but crotchety American critic William Winter wrote of Sarah Bernhardt that "she could neither touch the heart nor kindle the exultant glow of the imagination. Therefore she was, by intellectual observers, viewed without deep feeling, and she is generally remembered without pleasure." He could hardly have been more wrong.

The secrets of Sarah's appeal were many. She had charm. She was a very great artist, and sensitive people could not fail to be grateful to her for the beauty she had brought into their lives. There was something childlike even about her excesses, and most normal people find it difficult to resist children. And in her old age she was increasingly a figure of heroism.

Those who knew Sarah Bernhardt during her later years found no suggestion of the wild woman of legend. "I have spoken of her caprices," wrote A. B. Walkley, "but really only by hearsay. . . . It is . . . our duty to speak of people as one finds them, and I am bound to say that Madame Bernhardt . . . as I knew her off the stage showed no caprice. She struck me as a sensible, shrewd, kind-hearted woman, with a keen sense of humour, and modest for all her fame." And May Agate, whose book about Bernhardt gives us, on the whole, the most winning picture we have of her, writes for herself and her family, "For us Madame Sarah had always represented the perfection of taste and good manners. We knew her as a devoted mother and grand-mother, who had watched over her grandchildren with tender protec-tiveness and solicitude. . . . Indeed, the fabulous, legendary Sarah was quite unrecognizable to us."

Essentially, then, people felt affection for Sarah because, beneath all her vagaries, she herself had a loving heart. Little as he had seen of her, her father showed real penetration when he wrote, "Sarah is a difficult child, but she has a sweet and very spontaneous nature." She was "sometimes hard," says Lysiane, "but never hypocritical or dis-loyal." "There was nothing crafty or cunning in her nature," says May Agate. She acted "always on impulse." When she did act un-generously, as when, once, arriving in New York, she denied ever having heard of Yvette Guilbert, it was so obvious that she was indulg-ing herself that she deceived nobody. And when she amused herself by telling wild stories, like the yarn she fed Reynaldo Hahn about the boa constrictor whom she bought to rest her feet on, but who came suddenly out of his torpor and began swallowing the sofa pillows, so that she had to shoot him dead, the artifice was so transparent that she cannot possibly have expected to be believed.

Childlike herself, she was never able to resist a child. She adored her own grandchildren, and her friends brought their children to see her as a special treat. Henri Charpentier as a child spilled hot consommé all over her dress; the dress gave her no concern, but she was desolated over his burned hand.[23] Once, at a rehearsal, she fondled and caressed a filthy child who had been brought in as atmosphere in a street scene. "I know he is horribly dirty, but I adore him just the same." As a teacher she was intolerant only of stupidity coupled with pretension, and when occasion offered she was not afraid to say, "My child, I can teach you nothing." (When May Agate used a chair in a scene from *L'Aiglon* because Bernhardt had used one, she asked, "Why do you need a chair? L'Aiglon was a youth, not an old woman like me.") She once stayed all night at the theater to take care of a workman who had been injured backstage, though there were others there to look after him. "I shall be sure if I stay here. If I go home I shall not." As she grew older she even learned how to tolerate fools gracefully. Once she attended a performance of *Fédora* which she thought so bad that she laughed till the tears ran down her cheeks, so that the audience supposed her to be weeping, and when she went backstage afterwards, she saved both the actress and herself by simply pointing to her face and saying, "Look at me!" Best of all, there was a silly girl who became so infatuated with L'Aiglon that she refused her suitors and reduced her parents to despair. "Send her to me," said Sarah. She received her admirer without make-up in an old dressing gown. "This," she said, "is what I am really like. There is no such person as L'Aiglon except on the stage." And the girl married and became a mother, and Sarah added the baby to her list of innumerable godchildren.

Yet she was still Sarah Bernhardt, still the French coquette who had enthralled and scandalized the world for half a century. She had developed superhuman power to work and such self-control that she could command sleep itself, under any conditions and at any time, and not only that but wake up at the exact moment she needed to

---

[23] "Life à la Henri: A Consommé for Bernhardt," *Saturday Evening Post* (April 7, 1934).

awaken. She was not a vain woman; her position being what it is, she was rather the opposite; as A. B. Walkley says, she took it for granted that she was "the greatest actress in the world" just as Victoria accepted the fact that she was Queen of England, but it did not seem to her anything to make a fuss about. In her autobiography she awards herself praise and blame as dispassionately as if she were writing about a stranger.[24] But she was always the center of her own world, the sun around which the others moved, and she could not have had it otherwise if she had tried. She dwelt in Liberty Hall, where everyone did as she pleased—so long as she provided the money. Ray Rockman, invited to Belle-Isle, was given to understand that she expected him to play tennis with her. "You play, of course?" He did not. "Then I will teach you."[25] Lysiane says that when she was living with her, Sarah took the greatest possible interest in her pretty frocks and hats, but did not bother to provide her with mundane things like underwear. The same attitude prevailed in more important matters. Having saved the Portuguese girl on shipboard and taken her under her wing, she decided that the baby would be a boy and that they would call him Robert, and they did. Many years later she wrote her daughter-in-law from America: "Terka, I've decided upon a name for my future grandson. He's to be called Louis." This time she lost. "He" was called Simone, and it may be that Terka was compelled to disappoint her in self-defense!

Lou Tellegen quotes Sarah Bernhardt as having once declared of herself, "From the profile, I look like a goat—full-face like a lioness!" and there certainly was a feline suggestion about her. She had the cat's grace and charm, her centrality and self-sufficiency, and her wonderful self-contained quality, but there was also the suggestion of claws. I think that her self-centeredness and her tact and her capacity

---

[24] Thus: "My débuts at the Comédie Française were only mediocre." But, on the other hand: "I took such a position, in a very short time, at the Comédie, that some of the *artistes* began to feel uneasy, and the management shared the anxiety."

[25] "Playing Tennis with Sarah Bernhardt," *Ladies' Home Journal* (February, 1912).

for quick adjustment to even the most embarrassing circumstances are nowhere better illustrated than in the story of the old friend who apologized for not coming to lunch on the anniversary of his wife's death.

"What?" exclaimed Sarah. "Your wife is dead? I never knew it. You never told me, your oldest friend. It's very unkind of you!" She was almost in tears.

"But, my dear Sarah, she died three years ago. You were at her funeral!"

Sarah never turned a hair. "I know, my dear," she exclaimed. "But I still cannot believe it to be true."

VII

I should like to close with two anecdotes in which it seems to me that a good deal of the essence of Sarah Bernhardt is summed up. When she visited Chicago for the last time during World War I, somebody had the asinine idea of having a number of young women wait upon her and pay homage as representatives of the various arts. Eunice Tietjens was Poetry, in which capacity she was required to read a poem to Sarah Bernhardt!

"She was looking at me intently," so Mrs. Tietjens afterwards told the story in her autobiography,[26] "with very bright eyes, and her player's mask succeeded in expressing a dozen different thoughts at the same instant. Predominantly she was amused at this young woman from *'la ville des porc'* who was so evidently embarrassed in her presence, and who dared to read aloud to the divine Sarah. She was also inclined to be sympathetic towards me. She couldn't understand a word of what I was saying, she was trying to size me up, and she thought that I was not doing so badly for a little provincial. They are extraordinary, these American women." But she smiled at the end, and when Mrs. Tietjens apologized for reading to her in a foreign language and handed her the poem, "she reached out, and with lovely

[26] *The World At My Shoulder* (Macmillan, 1938).

Gallic gesture she took poem and envelope from my fumbling hands and held them against her heart. '*Mais, mademoiselle,*' she said '*la poésie, cela se comprehend avec le coeur!*' "

Sarah Bernhardt's worldly wisdom and her humor and her charity are shown in this reply and—yes, her patience. For her heroism, for the power she possessed, during her last years, to fire the imagination by the thrilling expression of a courage almost surpassing human limitations, one must go to the infinitely more significant story which Dorothy Perrot sent Joanna Richardson for use in her biography. Miss Perrot tells of her appearance as a super in Cleopatra's death scene, as Bernhardt presented it in St. Augustine, Florida.

I was the first in the line of applicants, and I was chosen to stand at the head of the couch on which Sarah Bernhardt was to lie, while the others were grouped as far away as possible. The tableau being finally in order, the divine Sarah was brought on to the scene. She was carried on a sort of litter by two rather feeble little old men, followed by two women and a man who was evidently her doctor, and these removed her and placed her on the couch. It was obvious that she had no left [*sic*] leg for she wore no false one and the amputation had left only a stump. Her doctor and the two women arranged her robe and cushions, and the doctor gave her something she kept sniffing. It was the era of smelling salts and she was probably used to local "supers." She turned once and looked at me, and as I was beside her she gave me a sort of half smile which made my fluttering heart beat the faster. I remember that I had to hold on to the couch because my knees were shaking so violently.

It took rather a long time for her people to make her comfortable. One produced a little green rubber snake which they placed in the folds of her robe at the neck. She never spoke, and even to my worshipping eyes it was a very old woman lying there, restless and irritable and tired, under the heaviest make-up and loaded with a heavy scent. She finally waved the people away and they withdrew to the wings and the doctor gave a signal. After a moment the curtain went up. There was silence, and then she began to speak.

She has been called Sarah of the Golden Voice. She had suddenly come to life and I do not think it was because I was young and impressionable that there seemed to be a radiance about her. There is no description of that voice, its lovely haunting clarity and the purity of its cadence. It was the perfect melody of speech, and there was poetry in the gesture of her upturned hands and the floating movements of her arms.

It was the last scene she did. With the words *"Adieu, ma douce Charmian,"* she turned and addressed herself to me. This was a terrifying moment, and I fearfully bowed my head and wished that the world would swallow me. It was perhaps the best response. Soon she produced the rubber snake and brought it to fluttering life in her breast for the lethal sting. Antony entered the stage, and then the miracle happened. For she had nothing to hold, nothing to help her, and she rose from that couch, swiftly and without seeming effort, stood erect for a moment unaided, straight and firm and strangely beautiful, then collapsed into Antony's arms. She was an old woman and she had only one leg and a stump, but she had the quality of eternity.

There was tremendous applause and she took several curtain calls, leaning lightly on Antony, then the curtain went down for the last time, and he helped her again on to her couch. Every bit of life seemed to have left her. She lay there inert, and the attendants rushed on and placed her on the stretcher to carry her off.

I hurried to the exit and stood waiting until she should pass. As they carried her near me, she held out her hand and I kissed it, tears pouring down my cheeks. She patted my shoulder. *"Gentille petite fille,"* whispered the Golden Voice.

Commentary on such a story would be blasphemous, but surely "the greatest actress in the world" should have the privilege of drawing the curtain before her own portrait.

Life is short, even for those who live a long time, and we must live for the few who know and appreciate us, who judge and absolve us, and for whom we have the same affection and indulgence. . . . We ought to hate very rarely, as it is too fatiguing, remain indifferent a great deal, forgive often and never forget.

And what in the world better could she say?

· III ·

"The Shimmering

Iridescence That Was

ELLEN TERRY"

All divine things run on light feet.

FRIEDRICH NIETZSCHE

Ellen Terry is the most beautiful name in the world. It rings
like a chime through the last quarter of the 19th century.

BERNARD SHAW

If Miss Ellen Terry were possible anything might be possible,
including dragons and roc's eggs. The Gates of Elf Land had
been closing; Miss Ellen Terry flung them wide again: the Lady
Beauty had revealed herself just as I was about to say, "I don't
believe there's no sich a person."

W. GRAHAM ROBERTSON

A wind of spring that whirls the feigned snows
  Of blossom-petals in the face, and flees:
  Elusive, made of mirthful mockeries,
Yet tender with the prescience of the rose;
A strain desired, that through the memory goes,
  Too subtle-slender for the voice to seize;
  A flame dissembled, only lit to tease,
Whose touch were half a kiss, if one but knows.

HELEN GRAY CONE

She was a poem that lived and breathed, and suggested to us the
girl heroines that we most adored in poetry and the fine arts
generally. . . . Most of our favorite queens in verse were made
realities by Ellen Terry.

CLEMENT SCOTT

1 *Ellen Terry*

How GREAT BRITAIN FELT about Ellen Terry during her last years may best be seen in the graceful remarks of Sir James Barrie when she received her LL.D. at St. Andrew's University in 1922: "The loveliest of all young actresses, the dearest of all old ones; it seems only yesterday that all the men of imagination proposed to their beloveds in some such frenzied words as these, 'As I can't get Miss Terry, may I have you?'"

Those were the days when Englishmen rose to their feet whenever the old lady entered a place of public assembly, and we are told that when she last appeared on the stage, in 1925, in Walter de la Mare's *Crossings,* at the Lyric Theater, Hammersmith, "a long sighing 'Oh!'" arose from the entire audience. But such tributes were nothing new to her. Bernard Shaw said that every famous man of the last quarter of the nineteenth century who was also a playgoer was in love with Ellen Terry, and a Dublin University don declared publicly that "her genuis is fatal to criticism, for it transforms critics into lovers." The American playwright Channing Pollock saw her as Portia in an English provincial theater when he was eighteen and she was fifty. The next day he spent one-twentieth of his entire capital on flowers which he sent her without a card and dined that night on twelve cents. "No one else," he says, "was ever so radiant as Ellen Terry."[1] Women seem to have felt this charm as strongly as men and to have felt it off stage as well as on; thus Marguerite Steen speaks of "that faint and lovely perfume which clung to her through life: that fragrance as delicate as small flowers which was in her thick, silver hair, in her fine, healthy flesh, unblemished to the end, and in all the garments she wore."

Was Ellen Terry a beauty? Was she a great actress? Was she a good woman? These questions are not impertinent, though they may well

[1] "The Only Three Women I Ever Loved," *Good Housekeeping* (March, 1937).

seem to be, for if we would understand her, they must all be asked and answered. Her position as England's most famous lady of the theater was uncontested, but there were always distinguished critics whose admiration for her was carefully qualified and limited. Sir Johnston Forbes-Robertson, who greatly admired her and at one time wished to marry her, even said that "the man in the street" did not think her beautiful but considered her voice "hoarse and broken, and her movements uncouth." "During a long life," writes one friend, "I have never known a woman with a purer mind or a more stainless heart." "For unadulterated goodness," says another, "there's no one to match her." Her character, declares a third, "would do credit to many a saint." Yet she bore both her children out of wedlock, and there seems no serious question that she later sustained an irregular amatory connection with Sir Henry Irving.

The facts here recorded are incontestable, and the judgments expressed are not absurd. Moreover, Ellen Terry's character, however complicated it may have been, was remarkably consistent. Nor was there any conflict between the artist and the woman; both had the same strength and the same weaknesses. But we must look carefully to see how the picture was put together.

II

Ellen Terry, daughter of Benjamin and Sarah Ballard Terry, was born into a theatrical family at Coventry, on February 27, 1848. Her first appearance on the stage was made in 1856, as Mamilius in *The Winter's Tale,* with Mr. and Mrs. Charles Kean. Between then and January, 1864, she appeared in various roles at theaters large and small, but in that month she married the great painter George Frederick Watts, who was many years her senior. After the breakup of this union, she returned to the stage, but left it again in 1868 to live in Hertfordshire with the architect William Godwin, the father of her only children, later known as Edith and Gordon Craig. During this period she lived the life of a countrywoman, experiencing real physical as well as financial hardship. In 1874 Charles Reade lured her back to the stage to play Philippa Chester in *The Wandering Heir* at the New Queen's Theater.

In 1875 she created a sensation as Portia in *The Merchant of Venice,* under the management of the Bancrofts, at the Prince of Wales's Theater, but the production was not a success, due to the inexplicable and wholly unexpected failure of Charles Coghlan's Shylock. In 1878, under John Hare, at the Court, she first enacted the title-role in *Olivia,* W. G. Wills's dramatization of *The Vicar of Wakefield,* which she later did many times with Irving, and which was considered one of her great achievements and a prime expression of her tender and winning personality.

That same year Irving engaged her as his leading woman at the Lyceum, where she remained until 1902. Her first appearance under his management was as Ophelia in *Hamlet* on December 30, 1878. They last acted together at the Lyceum in *The Merchant of Venice* on July 19, 1902, and their final appearance together on any stage was made in the same play at a benefit performance at Drury Lane in July, 1903.

In 1902 Ellen Terry played Mistress Page in *The Merry Wives of Windsor* with Beerbohm (later Sir Herbert) Tree at His Majesty's Theater, where, in 1906, she was to be seen as Hermione in *The Winter's Tale.* In 1903 she took a lease of the Imperial Theater, where she mounted what turned out for her a financially disastrous production of Ibsen's *The Vikings at Helgeland* with very "advanced" settings by Gordon Craig. She starred in Barrie's *Alice Sit-By-the-Fire* and Shaw's *Captain Brassbound's Conversion,* both of which were written for her, and when she appeared as Juliet's Nurse with Doris Keane and Basil Sydney, they had to cut down her scenes before the second night to prevent the Nurse (and the affection which the public felt for Ellen Terry) from throwing the play hopelessly out of balance. Shaw had been quite right when, upon her asking him for a small part which an old lady could play, he had replied that it was impossible to cast a battleship as a canal barge. In 1916 she received a magnificent Grand Jubilee Testimonial at Drury Lane, at which so many distinguished artists wished to appear that the performance lasted more than six hours. This was important to Ellen Terry not only as evidence of the affection in which she was held but because it helped her to recoup her Imperial-shattered fortunes.

In 1911 she recited excerpts from *Hamlet, Romeo and Juliet, The Merchant of Venice, Much Ado About Nothing,* and *The Winter's Tale* for the gramophone, and in 1916 she appeared in her first film (there were to be two more, one of which was *The Bohemian Girl*). From *The Kid* (1921) on she was a devoted Chaplin "fan." *The Cabinet of Dr. Caligari* made her wish that Irving were still alive to create similar effects, and when she saw Valentino in *Blood and Sand* she wanted all young Romeos to come and study him to learn how to stand under a balcony.

Between 1883 and 1901 Ellen Terry made seven American tours with Irving; later she came on her own, both as actress and as a lecturer on Shakespeare, in which latter capacity she also toured Australia, which was a heroic undertaking in her then state of health.

She married Charles Wardell, known professionally as Charles Kelly, in 1878 and James Carew, an American many years younger than herself, in 1907. Neither marriage was successful. In 1925 she was created a Dame Grand Cross of the Most Excellent Order of the British Empire; King George V laughed merrily when after her investiture at Buckingham Palace she exclaimed, "Oh dear! I quite forgot to walk out backwards!" and Queen Mary herself tucked her into her wheelchair. She died on July 21, 1928, at Small Hythe, near Tenterden, in Kent.

III

When Irving first saw Ellen Terry act, he thought her "hoydenish." She probably was in her early phase; even at the Lyceum she shocked him by sliding down the banister. She herself placed her artistic awakening at her performance of Portia with the Bancrofts. But she also disclaims having been what it is now the fashion to call a "dedicated" actress at any period. "I have always been more woman than artist," she says, and she declares that when she was living away from the theater, first with Watts and then with Godwin, she did not miss it at all. She even disclaims ambition; the closest she ever came to it, she says, was to be passionately anxious to play every role that came to her in the best possible way.

> If it is the mark of the artist to love art before everything, to renounce everything for its sake, to think all the sweet human things of life well lost if only he may attain something, do some good, great work—then I was never an artist. I have been happiest in my work when I was working for some one else. I admire those impersonal people who care for nothing outside their own ambition, yet I detest them at the same time, and I have the simplest faith that absolute devotion to another human being means the greatest *happiness*.

I believe this to be a sound self-analysis as far as it goes. Ellen Terry retained characteristics which some persons took as signs of frivolity all through her stage career. She was often late; she forgot her lines; she laughed and cried too easily. But her habit of arriving on stage at the latest possible moment was deliberate—her nerves simply could not stand the strain of waiting in the wings for her cue—and she herself was of the opinion that her trouble with lines was not so much a mnemonic difficulty as a limitless capacity for being distracted; her own son called her "scatter-heart." He also says that she sometimes altered the text of the modern plays in which she appeared. At times she may have done this deliberately; more often, I should guess, she was improvising because she could not remember. Apparently she did it with great skill, so that the audience was not troubled by it, and her grasp of the character she was playing was so firm that she never struck a jarring note. When it happened in *Captain Brassbound's Conversion* Shaw told the troubled stage manager not to bother her about it, since she was speaking the lines he wished he had written.[2] She never quite got over the habit of occasionally playing tricks upon her fellow players on the stage. In one play she infuriated Charles Kelly by slid-

[2] Even in her old age, Harold Nicolson thought Ellen Terry's acting remarkable for

ing on the wig he had been required to cast down upon the boards, and when Harcourt Williams complained of a trick she had played on him in *Much Ado About Nothing,* she replied, "But you play the scene so much better when you're in a temper!" Except for such things as this, I should say that the unevenness of her acting was due not to carelessness but to her heavy reliance upon feminine intuitiveness and disdain of male schematization. She was well aware that her best effects, though cumulative, were not sustained. "On the stage, I can pass swiftly from one effect to another, but I cannot fix *one,* and dwell on it, with that superb concentration which seems to me the special attribute of the tragic actress." She was much the same off stage, and Clara Morris reports of her conversation that "she flashed brilliantly from subject to subject, from idea to idea—though they were the poles apart." Indeed she was quite the reverse of formal in all things, and the beauties of her art would find their natural affinity in a disorderly, old-fashioned English garden. Yet when she placed life ahead of art, it was not because she despised the latter. Herself the most womanly of women, she did not need to be taught that if the artist is only an artist, he is nothing. She encountered that kind of concentration in Irving and recognized it there as a crippling limitation, and she knew that in a woman it must be even more monstrous.

---

its spontaneity and pace; see his "Marginal Comment," *Spectator,* Vol. CLXXXVI (1951), 307–308. "I could detect no hesitation, no sudden pauses. . . . It was the actual speed of her performance, the vitality that she threw into it that caused exhilaration. There was about it an element of enthusiasm, in the Greek sense of the word, that rushed onwards, leaping over the rocks, as some fresh mountain stream." Off stage there was the same alertness. When he asked her about Tennyson, of whom he was writing at the time, "she responded vivaciously. . . . She described the terrace at Aldworth and the red geraniums in their terra cotta vases against the blue of the weald. She described his heavy brooding garments and his huge brown hands. She imitated for me his broad Lincolnshire accent and the deep grumbling overtones of his voice. She imitated for me, with spasms of her small clenched fists, the manner of his recitations. Off she thundered into the trochaics of 'Locksley Hall,' not speaking the words, but uttering the deep-mouthed tune of the thing." E. V. Lucas, "A Memory of Ellen Terry," in *Turning Things Over* (Methuen, 1929), gives an amusing account of how she turned restive and almost accusatory when he devised a means of having her appear on the stage without speaking lines in 1917.

Having grown up in a theatrical family, Ellen Terry was never stage-struck. She simply took the stage for granted and turned to it as naturally as, in some other great families, children have turned to the law, the school, or the church. But the theater did not mean less to her on that account. She resented the use of the word "theatrical" in a pejorative sense. "After all," she writes, "the life of an actress belongs to the theater as the life of a soldier belongs to the army, the life of a politician to the State, and the life of a woman of fashion to society." Sometimes she even felt that compared to the theater, the world was "sham—cold—hard—pretending. It's not sham here in our theater —here all is real, warm and kind—we live a lovely spiritual life here." She was known on occasion to sign private letters with the name of a stage character, and when she was called to Charles Kelly's deathbed, "I could not feel it was Charles, but I had the strangest wish to rehearse Juliet there by the bed on which he was lying!"

She used the theater to express the life values in which she believed. "I don't like ugly things," she told Shaw, and she explained why she could not play Julia in *The Philanderer*: "For three years I lived with a male *Julia*. He was my husband, Mr. Wardell ('Charles Kelly') and I'm alive!" Though she hoped posterity would remember to her credit what she had risked in producing *The Vikings at Helgeland,* compared to Shakespeare, Ibsen was nothing; that was why Shaw really never had a chance to lure her away from Irving. "I never said Borkman was a 'poor' play," she writes the dramatist. "I say the effect on an audience would be to depress, to make unhappy, to make less hopeful some of us who dream a little. I think the theater should gladden tired working people." "From my point of view," she told her lecture audiences, "no interpretation entailing a sacrifice of beauty, whether to mirth or to realism, can ever be satisfactory." On the title page of her Globe Shakespeare she wrote, "Sir, here is a poor friend of yours that loves you," and she once declared, not absurdly, that she thought Shakespeare the only man she had ever really loved. At his tercentenary in 1916 she called him "my friend, my sorrow's cure, my teacher, my companion, the very eyes of me." But if she loved Shakespeare she loved her audiences too and rejoiced in their love. "They love me, you know! Not for what I am, but for what they imagine I am." And Mary Anderson tells how when she and Geneviève Ward appeared with Ellen at the Drury Lane tercentenary pageant, Ellen restrained them from going out with the other actors. "Don't go with any of them. You, Ginnie and I will go out together and you'll hear something."

Her generosity to other players was never questioned. From Irving on down to the lowliest person on the Lyceum staff, nobody ever dreamed of complaining that Ellen Terry was throwing her weight about, or even assuming the advantages to which her status entitled her. "Like all great players," writes her kinsman Sir John Gielgud, "she listened beautifully, making the scenes alive for the other characters by the unselfish way she 'gave' to others." During a performance of *Becket* she once insisted that the spotlight operator take the "moon" off her and put it on Geneviève Ward. She encouraged Violet Vanbrugh, Lynn Fontanne, and Edith Evans early in their careers, and she discerned Laurence Olivier's talents while he was still a schoolboy.[3]

Above all, she worked. Other actresses dreamed of being "brilliant"; she wanted to be "useful." It would be foolish to martyrize her in her relations with Irving, for he gave her many opportunities that would never have come to her without him, yet one wonders whether any other actress of her eminence ever contented herself so long in what was, after all, a subordinate position.[4] It was her view that a useful actor ought to be able to play anything. She herself never saw a play without learning something, and she urged young actresses to understudy all the roles of the plays in which they appeared. "If only they

[3] Clara Morris, "The Dressing-Room Reception," *McClure's,* Vol. XXII (1903), 204–11, gives a good example of Ellen Terry's generosity to a fellow player. But she and Madge Kendal seem always to have disliked each other, and when they played *The Merry Wives* with Tree in 1902, Marguerite Steen reports that "the bickering of Mr. Tree's 'Ancient Lights,' as Cyril Maude wittily called them, afforded even more comedy than that of the text to privileged listeners behind the scenes."

[4] Bram Stoker lists *Romeo and Juliet, Much Ado About Nothing, Twelfth Night,*

would study," she lamented to Mary Anderson, and she poured scorn on Harcourt Williams when he complained of being tired at rehearsal. "One should be very much alone," she says, "and should study early and late—all night, if need be, even at the cost of sleep. Everything that one does or thinks or sees will have an effect upon the part, precisely as on an unborn child." Before appearing as Margaret in the Lyceum *Faust* she made valiant efforts to learn to spin. For Ophelia she went to the madhouse.

Moreover, though she knew that the actor's art "demands more instinct than intellect," she used her head. Even her love for Shakespeare was not blind, and she once wrote "FOOL" in her copy of Shakespeare over against Cordelia's refusal to express her love for Lear. Brandes was her favorite Shakespearean commentator, but the most valuable touches in her *Four Lectures on Shakespeare* come from her own shrewdness and penetration. She refuses to go along with the feminists of her time in becoming upset over Portia's surrender to Bassanio, for she understands (as the Court Scenes proves) that this is only a "beau geste." In judging the Portia-Shylock encounter, she steers a nice course between sentimentality, hardness, and sound knowledge of Elizabethan attitudes, which last comes to her aid again when she refuses to see Bassanio as stupid for his failure to recognize his wife, since "the impenetrableness of disguise" is a dramatic convention which must simply be accepted. Desdemona's unconventionality— "she is not at all prim or demure" (any more than Ellen Terry was)— plays into Iago's hands, and Cleopatra is a shallow woman with whom Shakespeare has, for once, told the truth about the wanton; actresses who idealize her keep the characterization from hanging together and ruin the play. By the same token, the producer who avoids having "that beastly *Do-er*" Fortinbras come in "all swelling and victorious"

Iolanthe, The Cup, The Belle's Stratagem, and *Olivia* as having been mounted at the Lyceum more for Ellen Terry than for Irving. Alice Comyns Carr says Irving often asked and followed Ellen Terry's advice in matters quite outside her own role. And Ellen herself writes suggestively in a private letter: "Henry *never* thought 'The Amber Heart' a good play—and never said so. But he and I think it an excellent vehicle for the display of certain qualities in an actress and the public thought so too."

at the end of *Hamlet* misses a contrast which was an important part of Shakespeare's idea.

She never ceased being critical of her own performances. Her Pauline in *The Lady of Lyons* was never really good, she says, because she could not sympathize with the character, and though she was satisfied with her Frou-Frou when she played it, she changed her mind after seeing Bernhardt. "No people in their right senses could have accepted my 'Frou-Frou' instead of Sarah's." She said that her face had never been "of much use" to her, and she told Clara Morris that she was flat and clumsy and had the worst figure in the world. She thought herself completely unsatisfactory as Queen Henrietta Maria her first night in New York. "When [as Lady Macbeth] I called on the Spirits to unsex me," she told Clement Scott, "I acted that bit just as badly as anybody could act anything." This role, understandably, was not considered one of her successes, but Ophelia was, yet she was almost in despair after her first performance of it. "I'm so unsatisfactory to myself as Ophelia. I imagine her so delicate, and feel myself old and frumpish in the part." Her Beatrice was considered incomparable, but she says, "I have played Beatrice hundreds of times, but not once as I know she ought to be played." She acted her best Ophelia, in her own view, one night in Chicago, and her best Beatrice in Leeds.

But if she knew her faults, she knew her gifts too. "An actress does not study a character with a view to proving something about the dramatist who created it," she told her lecture audiences. "Her task is to learn how to translate this character into herself, how to make its thoughts her thoughts, its words her words. It is because I have applied myself to this task for a great many years, that I am able to speak to you about Shakespeare's women with the knowledge that can be gained only from union with them." "Miss Angell was a very modern Beatrice," she writes of an early Haymarket *Much Ado,* "but I, though I say it 'as shouldn't,' played Hero beautifully!" She also played Desdemona beautifully "some nights," and after *Cymbeline* had got under way, she told Shaw that she had been doing Imogen beautifully "the last 3 or 4 nights now for a change, or it would kill me."[5] "Only I can do that bit properly," she writes him much later of a scene in *Captain Brassbound's Conversion*. She once fought Irving for a week over a tag he insisted on using at the end of the Church Scene in *Much Ado,* and though she was compelled to yield at last, it almost made her ill.[6] She does not hesitate to quote in her memoirs the praise which she received nor to speak of the criticism that has been accorded others. Much as she admired Irving, she did not care for his Othello ("he screamed and ranted and raved—lost his voice, was slow where he should have been swift, incoherent where he should have been strong") nor his Mephistopheles ("a twopence colored part, any-way"), and when he asked her whether it was true that he dragged his leg and said "Gud" for "God" she told him yes.

Ellen Terry's temperament being what it was, it was not (as I have already suggested) surprising that her Lady Macbeth should often have been rated a failure. Labouchère called it "an aesthetic Burne Jonesy, Grosvenor Gallery version of Lady Macbeth, who roars as gently as any sucking dove," Gordon Craig felt like saying, "Poor Ellen Terry—she is so sorry for the Thane of Fife's wife. . . . What a *nice* woman!" and even Christopher St. John admits that the sleep-walking scene was "pitiful where it should have been terrible." But her Juliet, too, though it was admired by Bernhardt, whose praise any sensible person would surely prefer to that of a whole bevy of critics, was generally felt to lack the requisite intensity, and though she was capable of encompassing the tragedy of *The Cup* on the same evening with the comedy of *The Belle's Stratagem,* she was certainly tempera-mentally a comedienne: "those emotional parts just kill me," she once wrote. But even in comedy her gentleness was sometimes a limitation. Tennyson thought she was not enough the "great lady" in the first

[5] Read Letters XXIV and XXXVI in her correspondence with Shaw (both written after receiving his detailed criticisms of her performance as Imogen) as an illustration of the perfect combination of modesty, discrimination, and independence which she manifested in rejecting or accepting suggestions even from him.

[6] See *Four Lectures on Shakespeare,* 95–96; *Ellen Terry's Memoirs,* 127–28; Laurence Irving, *Henry Irving,* 403.

part of *Much Ado*, and J. Ranken Towse considered her "Kill Claudio!" too tame. The same critic grants her *Madame Sans-Gêne* charm, humor, and hoydenishness, but finds it lacking in "the needed coarseness and dash of masculinity."

Like Maude Adams, Ellen Terry was a martyr to "charm"—only very charming women can afford to disdain it!—and when her Volumnia was called "sweet," it was hard to take ("*I* thought I was fierce, contemptuous, overbearing"). Theoretically she believed that the actor should lose his individuality on the stage and take on that of the character, but she knew, too, that an actor's conception of a role may be different from that which comes through in performance, for the simple reason that the physical resources are inadequate or the physical image gets in the way. Mrs. Siddons conceived Lady Macbeth as "a fair, feminine, 'nay, perhaps even fragile' woman," but, being what she was, she could no more have put this idea on the stage than Ellen Terry could have avoided doing so. "I myself love to take a part which presents immense difficulties to me, and to overcome them if I can. But I feel sure that I play better those characters that are easier for me."

> I can't play Lady Macbeth, of course, properly [she wrote a friend], but I do hope to play her much better than on Saturday before the next few hundred nights have passed. I have never had the passion of ambition, but watching my own mother, and some few friends of mine, all good women, I have wondered at the lengths to which ambition—generally for some son or husband—drove them and long ago I concluded that the Thane of Cawdor's wife was a much be-blackened person. She was pretty bad, I think, but by no means abnormally bad.

And she added to Clement Scott: "I do believe that at the end of that banquet, that poor wretched creature was brought through agony and sin to repentance, and was forgiven."

To a lesser degree, she handled other characters in the same way. Beatrice favored her beyond any other Shakespearean role she ever played—"there was a star danced, and under that I was born"—yet

Picture 1. Jenny Lind as she appeared in the romantic portrait
by Eduard Magnus, Berlin, 1846.

Picture 2 (*above*) recalls a historic moment in American musical history: Jenny Lind singing at Castle Garden, September 1, 1850.

Picture 3 (*right*). Jenny Lind at the age of thirty, from a daguerrotype taken in Philadelphia.

Picture 4. Sarah Bernhardt in street dress, from a photograph
taken in Boston on one of her American tours.

Picture 5. Sarah Bernhardt in her greatest role, Phèdre.

Sarah Bernhardt in three characters: Picture 6 *(above left)*, as Cléopâtre in Sardou's play of the same title; Picture 7 *(above right)*, as Marguerite Gauthier in *La Dame aux Camélias;* Picture 8 *(below right)*, as Doña Sol in *Hernani.*

Picture 9 *(left)*, *Head of a Young Girl*, by George Frederick Watts, showing Ellen Terry in her youth. Picture 10 *(below)*, Ellen Terry in later life.

Ellen Terry in four Shakespearean characters: Picture 11 *(top left)*, Katharine of Aragon; Picture 12 *(top right)*, Mistress Page; Picture 13 *(lower left)*, Beatrice; Picture 14 *(lower right)*, Lady Macbeth.

Picture 15 *(left)* shows Julia Marlowe in her youth, as she appeared as Parthenia in *Ingomar*. Picture 16 *(below)* is a theatrical publicity photograph, taken at the height of her career.

Picture 17. Julia Marlowe as Mary of the Highlands in
For Bonnie Prince Charlie.

Julia Marlowe in three Shakespearean characters: Picture 18 *(above left)*, Imogen; Picture 19 *(above right)*, Juliet, on the way to the Friar's cell; Picture 20 *(lower left)*, Viola.

Picture 21. Isadora Duncan, from a photograph by Arnold Genthe.

To Edward Wagenknecht
with warm Regards
& Greetings —
Mary Garden
1951.

Picture 22. Mary Garden on an American lecture tour.

Mary Garden in three operas by Massenet:
Picture 23 *(top)*, *Le Jongleur de Notre Dame;* Picture 24 *(lower left)*, *Thaïs;*
Picture 25 *(lower right)*, *Sapho.*

Picture 26. This happy photograph of Marilyn Monroe, taken early in her career, shows her in the first bloom of her youthful beauty. Note the inevitable terry robe.

Picture 27. Marilyn Monroe
in her soubrette aspect,
a publicity shot for *Gentlemen Prefer Blondes*.

Pictures 28 *(top left)*, 29 *(top right)*, and 30 *(center)*,
taken near the end of her life, show the wistful, *spirituelle* kind of beauty that Marilyn
had by then developed. *(Center)*, with Wally Cox in the film that she never
completed, "Something's Got to Give."

it might reasonably be argued that her Beatrice was a "nicer," though not a nobler, woman than Shakespeare's; there is an element of vulgarity in some of the early sparring scenes with Benedick that Ellen Terry simply chose not to grasp. Charles Hiatt doubted whether even in *Henry VIII* "she was not a trifle too winning, too graceful, too obviously attractive," and John Gielgud says of her Nurse in *Romeo and Juliet*, "I suppose it was not a great performance of the Nurse. There was too much of Ellen Terry's own sweetness and personal charm, but now and again there were superb hints of character." I think Gordon Craig betrays the citadel from within and reveals an inhuman conception of acting when he says, "She played but one part—herself; and when not herself, she couldn't play it," but I am sure Richard Jennings was right in judging that "she 'spoke in tenderness,' always; even when she ought to have been speaking with tragic force."[7] There may be actors who disappear completely into their roles; it is impossible to tell, for if there are, nobody ever remembers or discusses them. When you go to see a great personality in the theater, you are always conscious of *both* the character *and* the actor, and it is only when the two clash that the total result is unsatisfactory. This is what George Edgar Montgomery means when he ends a fairly severe description of Ellen Terry's limitations[8] with the words, "But, on the other hand, one may say of Miss Terry that she remains in the memory, as some ravishing dream of youth, beauty, and sweetness remains there." If you do not wish to have the actor interpret the dramatist (which he can do only by passing the character through the alembic of his own personality), then you must not go to the theater; you must stay at home and read the play. That is the only way you can prevent another human personality from coming between you and the character. "Mere intellect, histrionic ambition, fine technique could never have produced these women," said Kate Douglas

[7] "Ellen Terry, 1848–1928," *Spectator,* Vol. CXLI (1928), 124–25.

[8] In Brander Matthews and Laurence Hutton, eds., *Actors and Actresses of Great Britain and the United States: The Present Time* (Cassell, 1886). See also the analysis of J. Ranken Towse, "Ellen Terry," *Nation,* Vol. CXXVII (1928), 133–34.

Wiggin of Ellen Terry's Shakespearean heroines; "they could only have been conceived in love."

IV

Such was Ellen Terry on the stage. What, now, was she off, and what were her interests?

For politics she cared little—she was too gentle to be a good partisan in any cause—but she read her newspaper with care and took an intelligent interest in public affairs. She had no sympathy with either the Boer War—which she considered a disgrace—or with World War I, whose horrors "for a few minutes now and again make me crazy, when I dare think, but I daren't"[9] She thought Shaw's *Common Sense About the War* "splendid," which was not the adjective generally applied to it at the time, and when she gave her Shakespeare lectures in wartime, she went out of her way to "pay my tribute" to Germany's contributions to Shakespeareana, "although you don't want me to, I can see."

Nature she loved as the English poets have loved her. Despite her sunny temperament, she was a moon worshiper, and she once spent a whole night lying out of doors watching the pageant of the heavens until it faded into the light of day. Once at least she kissed the trees in her ecstasy, and I know no more sensitive record than hers of the varying responses of a human being to the wonder and terror that is Niagara. "I hardly know when best I love the woods: at all times there is great mystery in a wood, a great kingdom in them by night—invisible but audible, all fulfilling their wonderful part." She could declare that "the weather and I are friends" even when it was what people call "bad" weather, but perhaps because she had lived in the country and knew country hardships, she did not read ineffable meanings into nature. Once at least she wondered "that beautiful places don't

---

[9] It is interesting to note that Ellen Terry, England's most distinguished actress during World War I, was out of sympathy with the conflict, and that during World War II, England's most distinguished actress at that period, Dame Sybil Thorndike, was a committed pacifist.

make the people beautifuller in mind and body too. The beauty of Durham Cathedral which I saw the other day, for instance. I never did see such ugly folk as the Durham. I think they are all sense less."

We have here passed from the beauty of nature to that of art. Ellen Terry had no education whatever, but she was early thrown much into the company of painters, writers, and other creative spirits, and, as Marguerite Steen says, she "mopped up literature and history and archaeology like a sponge." She was the great actress of the "aesthetic" movement, and the pictorial element was always very strong in her acting. Even Henry James comments on her Pre-Raphaelite quality, though he did not think she could act, at least not until he saw her Imogen. "Aided by draperies arranged with the most singular skill," wrote the critic of *The Academy* of her Camma in *The Cup*, "the figure in its freedom and suavity, recalls the Elgin Marbles and the designs of the artist who has learned the best use from them—Mr. Albert Moore. In hue and line the actress is a realization of Mr. Moore's paintings."

Ellen Terry recognized her own knowledgeability in these matters. Her children were brought up very "aesthetic." They wore Japanese kimonos and Viollet-le-Duc tabards in Bloomsbury (their mother herself always dressed in complete disregard of current fashions); they had Blake and Japanese prints on their walls; Crane, Caldecott, and du Maurier illustrated their books for them; if anybody gave them anything ugly, it was burned. When Forbes-Robertson first went to see Ellen, she had bamboo chairs with matting on the floor and a cast of the Venus de Milo in the middle of the room with a censer of incense on its pedestal! In general, however, I should say that she liked plain, sound, old-fashioned things. She "collected" old country cottages and at one time owned six of them, and one day when she looked up at the lovely village church and saw "a bright and shining NEW CLOCK . . . stuck upon its sweet face," she almost had a fit. "The beasts, the idiots! Just two new cogs would have put the old clock right." If one compares the simple good taste manifested in the pictures we have of her interiors with the heterogeneous accumulation of rugs and skins and feathers and bric-a-brac with which Sarah Bernhardt surrounded herself, it is difficult to believe that both women lived in the same period.

As a matter of fact, the painter's eye was a comfort to Ellen Terry even in sorrow:

> The Earthly Paradise was coming out at the time my children were born. I lived in the country—in the middle of the common—and I forgot my pangs whilst reading The Watching of the Falcon on a certain bitter-sweet night in December when Edy, my first child, was born. They were playing in the church "O Rest in the Lord." I heard them as I passed through the village—alone,—feeling frightfully ill and afraid. I could never forget that music and that poem. It was all lovely—and awful. I am growing quite George Moore-ish.

She knew and loved Dante, Newman, Tennyson, Browning, the Rossettis, Dickens, Disraeli, Tolstoi, and many more, and, rackety though her memory became, she found comfort in her "bad times" remembering the poetry she had learned. Occasionally you may raise your eyes at a literary judgment, as when she tells Wills that nothing more beautiful has ever been written than the last five pages of *Charles I,* but an actress should not be criticized for being kind to one of her playwrights! (But when she writes of the Russian ballet that it has delivered dancing from Renaissance standards, and that "there is a deadness about all Renaissance things, whether in architecture or dancing," one cannot but wonder whether she means her "all" to embrace literature, and if so, what becomes of Shakespeare.) She loved Bach, Handel, and Chopin (especially Bach), and her son says she played the piano well. She did not care much for opera as a form, but she found an effective union of music and drama in *Carmen* and *Otello,* and she praises such artists as Calvé, Garden, and Maurel. "When jaded ill-treated, *cheap*-treated Italian opera was at its lowest and dullest, Wagner ... made the air shimmer with ravishing, expensive exhilaration." Notice that she does not sell out the Italian opera *as such* to Wagner, as it was once the fashion for musical snobs to do.

As a businesswoman, Ellen Terry would not have ranked high. She could drive a bargain when she needed to: when Charles Reade begged her to return to the stage, she held out for £40 a week and got it. Irving paid her £200 a week, and $1,000 on the American tours. But her personal tastes were few and simple, and her principal interest in money was to have some to give away, which she did to people who had not the remotest claim on her; for years she supported the sisters of Charles Kelly's first wife! In her old age her finances got into such a mess that they finally had to be taken in hand by others and straightened out for her.

v

But Ellen Terry was a woman, and women cannot live wholly on art and beauty, either off the stage or on it. Her marriage to George Frederick Watts was arranged for her when she was not yet sixteen and he was forty-seven. She was married on a January morning in an ice-cold church, without flowers or music, to a bridegroom who told her to stop crying because "it makes your nose swell." Before going to church she had bathed her younger brothers and sisters and brushed their hair, but her father was the only member of her family who bothered to go with her. Yet she thought she was "in Heaven, for I knew I was to live with those pictures. 'Always,' I thought, and to sit to the gentle Mr. W. and clean his brushes, and play my idiotic piano to him, and sit with him there in wonderland (the Studio)."

The bridegroom's thoughts were somewhat more realistic: "To make the poor child [he got that much right] what I wish her to be will take a long time, and most likely cost a great deal of trouble, and I shall want the sympathy of all my friends." It does not seem to have occurred to him that she would need any.

She posed for her husband until she fainted from fatigue but found it impossible to do anything else for him. She was a person of no consequence in her own house, whose management was given over into the hands of others. When Tennyson came to call, she played with his children instead of talking with him. Finally, she quite innocently offended her husband, and he made up his mind that he was not going to be able to make the "poor child" into what he wished her to be, and that it would be better to be rid of her. So that was arranged too, just as the marriage had been. But he would not give her a divorce because that would reflect adversely upon him.

Understanding nothing of what had happened to her, she returned home, desperately unhappy, barely upon speaking terms with her conventionally minded older sister. "This was the period when, though every one was kind [a typical example of Ellen Terry's almost foolishly unfailing charity], I hated my life, hated every one and everything in the world more than at any time before or since."

From this misery she went to Godwin and motherhood and the years in Hertfordshire. She loved Godwin, more probably than she ever loved any other man. But again she had chosen a self-centered egotist who was totally incapable of understanding her. The scales fell from her eyes when, one day, while she was carrying Ted, Godwin found her harnessing the pony to take him to the station and burst out, "Haven't you cost me enough money already, without obliging me to fetch a doctor for you?" "I nearly left him then," she said. Later she added, "You cannot go on caring about somebody in whom you no longer have faith." But in the end it was he who left her for another girl.

When she married Charles Kelly, she was a famous actress with suitors by the dozen, Johnston Forbes-Robertson among them. "Most of the letters written to me I destroyed long ago," she says in her memoirs, "but the feeling of sweetness and light with which some of them filled me can never be destroyed." Among other things, she wished to marry again to give "my poor children," as she always called them, a father, and her brother Fred says that she put the names of all her suitors into a hat and drew out Kelly's. Whether this is literally true or not, one cannot but wonder over a woman who might have married Forbes-Robertson and chose Charles Kelly instead. Like her final husband, James Carew, he was what is now called a "he-man," and, after Watts and Godwin, it is not difficult to understand why she may have thought she needed a change. Kelly had his virtures, but when Ellen Terry told him she would marry him, he celebrated his victory by getting drunk. She later said that she left him because she could not live with a steam roller.

Laurence Irving seems not to admit that his grandfather was ever Ellen Terry's lover in the technical sense, though he does say that at one time he wished to marry her.[10] If there was a liaison, they must have been very discreet, for there was no contemporary scandal. But Miss Steen says that in reply to her direct question whether she was ever Irving's mistress, Ellen Terry replied, "Of course I was. We were terribly in love for a while. Then, later on, when it didn't matter so much to me, he wanted us to go on, and so I did, because I was very fond of him and he said he needed me." This rings true to me, and this is just how I should have expected Ellen Terry to behave for the reasons stated. But once more she had chosen a man whose concentration upon himself and (what was in this case the same thing) his art was almost pathological, and being older and more sophisticated now, she understood his shortcomings as she had not understood Watts and Godwin in the days of her youth. Her private notes on Irving's character, printed in the revised edition of her autobiography,[11] are penetrating indeed, and she was equally sensitive to his faults and his virtues. "I have contempt and affection and admiration. What a mixture!" As early as 1896 she told Shaw that the "silly old cautious thing" was "such a dear Donkey! Darling fellow. Stupid Ass!" but the next year, when the playwright seemed on the verge of precipitating an out-and-out quarrel with Irving over *The Man of Destiny*, she wrote, "If you worry (or try to worry) Henry, I must end our long and

---

[10] Irving had a wife, but he had not lived with her for a long time. As they were riding home together after his first great triumph in *The Bells* (1871), the thoughtful and affectionate lady made her loving contribution to the most important night in her husband's life by asking him, "Are you going on making a fool of yourself like this all your life?" Facing up to the inevitable, Irving did not reply. Instead he told the driver to stop and got out of the brougham. He never returned home and never spoke to his wife again.

[11] Pages 268–74.

close friendship," and Shaw backed down. By 1898 she was writing Shaw that "Henry is so nice to me lately that I'm convinced he has a new 'flame,' " and in 1900 she was "so certain Henry just hates me! . . . We have not met for years now, except before other people, where my conduct exactly matches his of course." Miss Steen quotes her as having said, about 1921, that Irving "began to get tired of me and pay attention to other women. I wasn't jealous, but I said, 'I love and adore you, and while you wanted it everything that was mine was yours. But when you ceased to want it—"No." ' " Professionally there was never a "break" between them; they just drifted apart. It was not entirely Irving's fault, for Ellen Terry was no longer young enough for all the roles she had once played, but he does not seem to have made any effort to hold her. Before he produced *Robespierre*, he told her that his plans did not include her "for the present," but when he learned that the syndicate taking over the Lyceum would withdraw from the deal unless she appeared, he sent Comyns Carr to enlist her aid, and she yielded of course, as she always did when anybody needed her.

About Ellen Terry's final marriage to James Carew it does not seem necessary to say much, nor is there anything to say against Carew except that the match between them was completely unsuitable. Ellen thought her husband "a child," which, since he was younger than her own children, ought not greatly to have suprised her, and wished she were twenty years younger, "and could grow to him." But she couldn't, and they quarreled, about everything and nothing, and finally parted. "You must not treat any woman the way you have treated me," she said grandly, but when she was questioned as to the meaning of this cryptic statement, it appeared that he had kicked her dog! "I felt I could not live alone," said Ellen Terry. "Afterwards I thought it better to live alone, apart from Jim, for we do not suit each other. We are better, and happier apart, and now we *like* each other very much."

That was the authentic Terry note. She forgave everybody—Watts, Godwin, Kelly, all. "I wish I could have made his Sun shine," she wrote wistfully of her first husband, "but I was so ignorant and so young, and he was so impatient." In his case at least, it is good to know that, astonished by her development in later years, he wrote her and begged her to forgive him, and of course she replied that there was nothing to forgive. In her memoirs she spoke of his "chivalrous assumption of blame." He knew better, and thanked her for making it possible for him to leave the world without the sense "that any malediction will follow me now that you do not think unkindly of me." After Godwin was dead, she wrote of him to a friend of the old days, "The times of which you were part, were my best times, my happiest times. I can never think of him but at his best, and when he died, he thought only so of me. I could never suffer again I think as I have suffered, but I joy in the remembrance of him."

VI

It is a strange story, but I repeat one absolutely consistent with her character and temperament as a woman and as an artist. Marguerite Steen writes of Gordon Craig that "he was utterly charming, utterly without principle—in the common interpretation of the word; he admitted no moral obligations apart from those he owed to his work." Then she adds that he was "the true projection of Ellen Terry's soul. Had she been a man, she would have been a Gordon Craig; hers was that same happy levity, that wildness of creative spirit, that reaching out towards far horizons."

I am not concerned with the justice or injustice of Miss Steen's judgment of Gordon Craig. As to Ellen Terry, I think she is wrong. To her she attributes a callousness and lack of consideration for others of which I do not believe she could have been capable under any circumstances. Yet I think I know what Miss Steen is trying to say.

A lady of very rigid principles once declared indignantly that Ellen Terry was never immoral, but only illegal. Exactly! Very few women have legal minds, and women like Ellen Terry behave themselves (when they do) because good behavior is practical, or because it serves the needs of life in the particular situation by which they are confronted, and not because they feel bound to obey a preformulated code.

Insofar as Ellen Terry had "views" on these matters, they were conventional views, during her later years at least. She wanted everybody to behave himself in quite the conventional way and thus stay out of trouble. But her views were not really very important. "You see I have no lovers," she once wrote, "only loves," and this was not far from the truth. She could find nothing of the South in her own temperament. "Not a bit. Northy, Northy-Polish. (That's where the true fire burns, in the North, I'm sure.)" She couldn't understand "kissing in conservatories." "Very many women kiss 2 men at the same time. Pigs!" She was horrified when Lewis Carroll told her that a little girl whom he had taken to see her in *Faust* was disturbed by the scene where Margaret begins to undress. "I thought you know only *nice* children," she told him indignantly. "It would have seemed awful for a *child* to see harm where harm is; how much more so when she sees it where harm is not." But Ellen Terry could never play that scene again without shame.

When Shaw wrote her about the green-eyed Irish heiress whom he wasn't sure whether he wanted to marry or not, she exclaimed, "How very silly you clever people are. Fancy not knowing! Fancy not being sure!" And then she let him have it:

> One thing I am clever enough to know (TO KNOW, mind. I know few things, but I know what I know). It is this. You'd be all bad, and no good in you, if you marry anyone unless you know you love her. A woman may *not* love before marriage and really love afterwards (if she has never loved before). We all love more after union (women I mean, and surely, oh surely men too). *But a man should know.*

A few days later she spoke of Irving's having married a woman he didn't love because he thought he ought to, "and he had better have killed her straight off."

But Ellen Terry also believed that women have more moral courage than men, that the worst woman is better than the best man, and that what women like most is to give. One would suppose that this element must have been very important in her own love affairs. There was certainly a malleable element in her. When she returned from her second American tour, she was accused of playing Portia with an American accent, and she may well have done so, though it would probably have been said of her whether she had done it or not. She herself said that she had a heart of wax—"no impression lasts long"—for which reason she did not take much credit to herself for her ability to forgive. Told that someone hated her, she replied, "I know there is a good deal hateable in me." In this incapacity for resentment alone, I think she resembled her great friend Bernard Shaw, in so many ways her temperamental antithesis.

Her lack of interest in scandal went almost to the length of having no curiosity, and though it is not true that she was always happy—she was, on the contrary, capable of great depression—it is true that she always tended to forget the bad things and remember the good. She loved people and she loved animals; she once tried to be a vegetarian, but it upset her digestion! She was famous for the time and interest she wasted on insignificant people, and her sympathy was easily enlisted in humane causes or in those in trouble, even if it was altogether their own fault and they were totally unknown to her.

Yet she could be stubborn and difficult, especially in her later years. Her difficulties with her daughter—"Edy's a devil"—whose apparent coldness and unwillingness to be touched, even in childhood, and inability to express affection were a great trial to a demonstrative mother, may have been three-quarters Edy's fault, but Ellen Terry cannot be acquitted of all responsibility since we are told that she broke up two love affairs for her daughter because the man was "not good enough." She could be wildly impulsive also, and her near-blindness in her old age was largely due to her having impatiently torn off her bandages after having been operated upon in New York for cataract.

Moreover, for all Ellen Terry's kindness and tenderness, there have always been those who believed that she loved the earth and the sky—and poetry—even more than she loved people. She was good to everybody, but few persons were really important to her. "Things, thoughts, dreams, memories," says Graham Robertson, "seemed to affect her more." It is interesting that her earliest memory was not of people but of her little room and the things she could see from the window when she was left alone there. "What did it matter to me that I was locked in, and that my father and mother, with my elder sister Kate, were all at the theater? I had the sunset, the forges, and the oak bureau." We know that there were times when she needed to be left alone, and once when a friend came to her between the matinee and the evening performance and offered to read to her, she said, "Oh, do leave me alone, my dear child, and try to exercise your sympathy with understanding." But after the evening performance she came to the girl with tears in her eyes: "I was a pig, a hideous pig to you today. Will you forgive?"

Shaw reports Ellen Terry as once having said that what had supported her through all her trials was the consciousness that she had never done anything wrong. Whitman, it may be remembered, made similar claims to Bronson Alcott, and I suppose that the opposite extreme temperamentally is that type of over-sensitive conscience which we find in Mark Twain and, among the persons treated in this book, in Marilyn Monroe, the yellow-dog conscience which, as Mark Twain makes Huckleberry Finn say, goes after a person when he does right just as hard as when he does wrong. Ellen Terry was fond of quoting from *John Ingelsant:* Nothing but the Infinite Pity is sufficient for the infinite pathos of human life," upon which she commented that "everyone must some time or other, feel that tremendous need of Divine mercy and pity." She can hardly, then, have meant whatever statement Shaw had in mind to be taken literally; for all that, I think she might, in some moods, have made it. There is an interesting passage early in Ellen Terry's memoirs: "I tried to learn to smoke, but I never took kindly to it and soon gave it up." There is no indication that she considered the morality or the desirability of the habit at all. Much later she wrote Shaw from Monte Carlo: "The Tables here don't amuse me. I play 2 or 3 francs each eve—win 2 or 3 —lose 2 or 3, and then come out on the Terrace!" But what would she have done if she had taken kindly to it, or if she had been amused? I do not gather that she was a woman of principle in the sense in which her two great successors among English actresses—Dame Sybil Thorndike and Dame Edith Evans—are women of principle. For the most part, I should guess, she kept free of evil because evil did not tempt her, and a finished perfection, developed according to preconceived an established standards, did not interest her much more in life than in art. In the last analysis, it was not her principles but the kindness of her heart that made her a good woman.

Lovers of the eighteenth century may be reminded at this point of Fielding's famous goodness of heart and of the debates occasioned by this criterion after the publication of *Tom Jones*. Whatever may be said against such a temperament, the beauty of it is the spontaneity it can achieve. This shows in Ellen Terry's art, and it shows too in her religion. "I seldom talk on sacred subjects," she told Shaw. But she thought of them all the time, because her heart went out to God in joy and gratitude, and when she did speak of them, she spoke to good purpose. Though she loved to study her roles in churches, I doubt that the church meant much to her as an institution. God, on the other hand, meant everything. The supernatural side of religion presented no problem to her mind, for as she saw is, life itself was a miracle. "All that God does is a miracle—I *couldn't* doubt our Savior's miraculous birth, it seems to me in the supernatural order of things connected with the Son of God—the miracle of the Sacraments." She believed in and practiced prayer, alone and with others, and she thought of her art as a means of serving God. "If you don't act for the whole glory of God," she told an actor, "the sooner you leave the stage the better." On the flyleaf of one of her lectures she wrote: *"Gloria in altissimis Deo, et in terra pax hominibus bonae voluntatis,"* and she loved Portia's Mercy Speech and put her whole heart into it because of its affinity with the Lord's Prayer. How touching is her reply to the friend who told her of some scandal that had been circulated about her:

> M. dear, it's nought but the idle tongue that says those silly things. —— is far from vicious or malign. I know your, and G.'s dear hearts are generously wounded for me, and because you love, you grieve and take to heart. But God forbid that I show any difference to ——. So much

of the wisdom and true Christianity of Shakespeare was derived from his Maker. "Use every man after his deserts," which comes to this: Did God treat us as we deserved, we should hardly escape hell! *But,* God so loved the world! And then dear Tommy Kempy[12] amplifies: "Thou ought'st not to take to heart if some think ill of thee." You mustnt, either of you, talk of my being forgiving. Oftentimes I have said, dear M., we should not withhold our love. Call it forgiveness if you will, but I prefer not to. Forgiveness seems to imply *we* are in the right, and as often as not, we are the stumbling blocks ourselves, only we dont know it! Oh do let's try, like the dear Saviour, to be *dumb* when we fancy we are injured, you and I and G. That's the way to love Him who loved us.

Much in the same vein is the testimony of a young actor who appeared with Ellen Terry in the Doris Keane production of *Romeo and Juliet.* Her kindness, he says,

was as real and impartial and personal as the sunlight, but it was a human sun that seemed only to see the things one wanted seen. The rest werent there, or it didnt matter in the least if they were. If that is not theological charity, what is? It is the greatest virtue, and only saints and very great artists can possess it. It makes life possible.

When Ellen Terry died, the men in the Kentish fields left their work and came with their tools in their hands to stand as a guard of honor while her coffin was carried into the church. On the gate in front of her cottage passers-by read these words which had been found after her death in her copy of the *Imitation:*

No funeral gloom, my dears, when I am gone;
Corpse-gazings, tears, black raiment, graveyard grimness.
Think of me as withdrawn into the dimness,
Yours still, you mine. Remember all the best
Of our past moments, and forget the rest.
And so, to where I wait, come gently on.

[12] Her pet name for Thomas a Kempis.

JULIA MARLOWE

The Actress

as Idealist

Long had I loved this "Attic shape," the brede
  Of marble maidens round this urn divine:
But when your golden voice began to read,
  The empty urn was filled with Chian wine.[1]

HENRY VAN DYKE

Make way for Julia—Julia of "the mighty line"!

JAMES HUNEKER

Duse is the soul made flesh, Réjane is the flesh made Parisian, Sarah Bernhardt the flesh and the devil; but Julia Marlowe is the joy of life, the plenitude of sap in the tree.

ARTHUR SYMONS

1 *Julia Marlowe*[2]

MORE THAN ANY OTHER famous actress of her time, Julia Marlowe enjoyed a deliberately self-directed career. Mrs. Fiske turned to Ibsen because he seemed, better than any other of the moderns, to suit her particular style. Ethel Barrymore played everything from *The School for Scandal* to *The Kingdom of God*. Even the association of Maude Adams with Barrie and with Rostand was due more or less to managerial exigencies. But Julia Marlowe knew from the beginning that what she wanted to do was to interpret grandly the heroines of Shakespeare. To this aspiration she dedicated all that there was of her, and after years of struggle in the face of terrific odds, she won through by sheer force of perseverance and talent, bringing her girlhood's dreams at last to a richer, fuller realization than even she could have dared to hope for.

Sarah Frances Frost was born at Caldbeck, in Cumberlandshire, on August 17, 1865. Her father was a shopkeeper, a bootmaker, an enthusiastic amateur sportsman, and apparently something of a ne'er-do-well. Her mother was a devout Wesleyan, a lover of the Bible and of Burns's poetry. While Sarah was still a very small child, her father gaily flicked a whip at a neighbor during a race, and resting thereafter under the wholly erroneous impression that he had put out the man's eyes, he took his family and fled to America, where he changed their name to Brough. They lived first in the frontier town known as Lenasee, Kansas, and then came east to Ohio. Finally the parents were divorced, and the mother married a German baker named Hess, whom her children loathed.

Fanny Brough, as she was then called (when she first went on the stage, it became Fancy Brough), made her first vital contact with Shakespeare by buying an edition of his plays illustrated with portraits

[1] "Reading Keats's 'Ode on a Grecian Urn,'" from *The Collected Poems of Henry van Dyke* (Charles Scribner's Sons, 1911).

[2] This portrait was published in *Modern Drama*, Vol. I (1959), 244–55, and was copyrighted in 1959 by the magazine's editor, A. C. Edwards.

in character of various famous actors and actresses from a traveling book agent, and paying for it on the installment plan with her twenty-five cents a week allowance. When she saw, in the lobby of a theater, a large photograph of Adelaide Neilson as Imogen, she made up her mind that she too would play this role.

Her first appearance on the stage was at Vincennes, Indiana, in 1876, in a juvenile *Pinafore* company. In 1884 she formed an alliance with an actress, Adah Dow, with whom she went to live in New York, where she spent the next three years in seclusion and constant study. In 1887 there was a two-week tour of small New England towns in *Ingomar, Pygmalion and Galatea,* and *The Lady of Lyons.* On October 19, she hired the Bijou Theater, New York, for a special matinee of *Ingomar,* and it is one of the most picturesque legends of the metropolitan stage that after the second act the audience slipped out and stripped the neighboring florist shops quite bare of bloom.

In December she found an opportunity to permit Gothamites to see her as Juliet and Viola. She obtained financial backing from the photographer B. J. Falk, and though critical counsels were somewhat divided, she found herself embarked as a "star." She added Rosalind, Beatrice, and Imogen to her repertoire, as well as several non-Shakespearean plays, but though her reputation increased steadily, she still earned only a bare living.

In 1894 she married her leading man Robert Taber, with whom for a time she co-starred. Taber proved a better actor than husband; they parted three years later, and commercial considerations forced Miss Marlowe to relinquish Shakespeare for a time. In 1904 she formed a professional alliance with E. H. Sothern; their first performance together was in *Romeo and Juliet,* at Chicago, on September 19. With Sothern, Julia Marlowe first appeared in *Hamlet, The Merchant of Venice, The Taming of the Shrew, Antony and Cleopatra,* and *Macbeth.* In 1907 they appeared in London in their own productions of *Romeo and Juliet, Hamlet, Twelfth Night,* and *As You Like It,* besides Hauptmann's *The Sunken Bell,* Percy MacKaye's *Jeanne d'Arc,* and *When Knighthood Was in Flower.* In 1909 they opened the ill-starred New Theater in New York with *Antony and Cleopatra*. In 1911 they were married.

The ten years from 1904 to 1914 and the five years from 1919 to 1924, when postwar economic conditions dictated an emergence from retirement into alternate seasons of Shakespearean repertoire, saw the greatest triumphs of their lives. No longer was it necessary to appear in meretricious plays, salving their consciences by trying to read into them a spiritual significance their authors had never dreamed of. Now their repertoire was exclusively Shakespearean, and to each production they brought the same intelligence, the same scholarly care, the same superb artistry. Increasingly, as time went on, they were recognized as distinguished artists and as distinguished citizens who had made an important contribution to the life of their time. They won the plaudits of Duse and of Bernhardt. In 1921 George Washington University conferred the degree of Doctor of Letters upon each of them. Miss Marlowe received a gold medal for her diction from the American Academy of Arts and Letters in 1929 and another doctorate from Columbia in 1943.

The last Sothern-Marlowe tour occurred in 1923–24, Miss Marlowe's final appearance on the stage being made in Pittsburgh. After their retirement they lived much abroad, in Egypt and elsewhere, but they were making their annual visit to New York when Sothern died at the Plaza Hotel on October 28, 1933. In 1939 Miss Marlowe returned from Europe for the last time and settled down at the Plaza until she herself died there on November 12, 1950, at the age of eighty-five. Her retirement was broken only in 1943 when she presented her costumes, photographs, and theatrical memorabilia to the Museum of the City of New York and recited Sothern's ballade, "Fair Ladies I have Loved and Lost." During her latter years she was an active member of St. James Protestant Episcopal Church and was also greatly interested in welfare work for the blind.

II

When one looks for the elements of success in so deliberate an artist, one finds first of all, as might have been expected, a tremendous capacity for work. As a girl Julia Marlowe studied in seclusion for three solid years the five roles in which she had decided to prepare herself. Her voice was trained scientifically, as a singer's voice is trained. To keep her body supple she took up fencing. She was willing to practice half a day if necessary on the tone quality of a single word. Her texts she studied in the light of all the commentaries, reading as widely as possible in the backgrounds of the period involved. She made herself a miniature theater, with dolls for actors, so that she might visualize the entire production from start to finish, giving it actual body before her eyes. In all this she was aided notably by unusual powers of concentration, frequently becoming so absorbed in her task that she would be oblivious to everything else going on around her.

These heroic methods were not confined to her youth. For every play she made her own prompt books, marking every stress, indicating each minute bit of "business" not for herself alone but for every character in the play. Not for her the sloppy reliance upon "inspiration" which is the last resort of the lazy and the unprepared. When she stood on the stage she knew exactly what she was going to do and she knew exactly how she was going to do it. One dress rehearsal of *As You Like It* lasted sixteen hours. She studied Beatrice all through one summer, and then when autumn came, being still dissatisfied with her interpretation, postponed her production of *Much Ado About Nothing* for another year. Lady Macbeth got twenty years of conscious cerebration before she was exhibited on the stage, and elaborate and detailed preparations were made for both *Measure for Measure* and *The Winter's Tale,* neither of which ever materialized.

This spirit of devotion extended even to mechanical, purely external matters. Salome's dance in *John the Baptist* called for days of grueling work before the phonograph, and when she was preparing to revive *King Henry IV* she wore her armor at home until she got so that she could move about in it easily and naturally! For years she had publishers send her proof sheets of forthcoming novels, and she and her staff would go through them diligently in the hope of finding the idea for a new play.

Along with this capacity for work she had superb self-confidence. "I have never known what is called stage fright, or any sensation of it, even on the first night of a difficult play." As for the critics, she soon learned to regard them purely from the business point of view. "I was assured that my acting . . . was satisfactory because my reason told me I had done it well." When she was praised, she was "not in the least surprised. That sounds egotistical, but what I mean is that I was so certain of success that these tributes all seemed natural and no more than I had expected." And when she was censured she took it in the same way. "I knew I was right and he was wrong."

She was almost equally independent toward the public for whose suffrages she must bid and upon whose favor she must rely. "I am grateful for whatever commendation the public has given me, but, as far as applause is concerned, I have always for the love of my work and for the honor I bear it, played as well to twenty people as before a full audience." She had something to give, and she knew its value; the others were there to receive. Her joy in her work she sought "in the study, the plotting, the thinking out and coordination of its innumerable details, quite as much as in the public exhibition of the finished product." It was almost as if in her eyes the creation of beauty was worth while for its own sake even if nobody ever came to see it. "Except for a shallow or vain nature there is nothing in the rewards of this profession commensurate with its pains; but in the very labor of it there's joy, if you're born to know it, that nothing else can approximate for you."

The dangers of such a temperament in the theater are obvious, and Miss Marlowe did not escape them all. That she succeeded as well as she did was due, I think, to the unusual amount of what I may call spiritual ballast that she carried about with her. Indeed she was in every aspect a woman of such strongly marked, such strikingly positive qualities that just a shade more emphasis on any one of her salient characteristics would have been enough to throw the whole personality off balance. Deliberate as she was, she still realized that though acting must be self-conscious, it should never appear so. "In the theater, you should approach a play with your heart, not your head." Her motto "Leave nothing to chance" did not mean that the characterization once established was never varied. On the contrary, none of her portraits was ever completed; she altered, deepened, and enlarged her characterizations as long as she continued to present them. When she called her work good, she did not mean that she was satisfied with it, or that she had nothing more to do in connection with it. She simply meant that she had achieved the goal she had set up for herself thus far: her dream for the future was something else again. When she returned to *As You Like It,* for example, after not having presented the play for some years, it was almost as if she were creating a new role. "The words of Rosalind are all clearly in my mind, but I have a richer conception of their meaning than when I played it last; so I must say them over and over until they have filled me with that added richness." And when a critic really had something to say he was sure of a hearing, as when she was censured for not beginning to weep early enough in the church scene of *Much Ado.* "You don't begin until Benedick says: 'Lady Beatrice, have you wept all this while?' Not only that, but you say then: 'Yea, and I will weep a while longer.' Why don't you weep sooner?" To which she replied, promptly and simply, "I shall, after this."

Her "inwardness" saved her spontaneity also. She was never a "versatile" actress, and she ranked the generally much overestimated flair for impersonation in its proper subordinate place among the actor's endowments. She never wore a wig on the stage; she used very little make-up. She did not change her features; what she did try to change, from play to play, was her soul. "I don't look in the remotest degree as Ophelia must surely have looked. She was a Dane. I couldn't look like her if I tried; and I wouldn't try. I only try to be as she was, to do as she did." As Rosalind she used to turn pale at the sight of Orlando's "bloody napkin," and her audiences would wonder if she had used white powder on her face. She did not need to. "I feel that if . . . I act

Rosalind skilfully enough, the idea of her pallor will so take its place in the minds of the spectators that they will not concern themselves too much with the actual color of my face."

III

This is clearly the idealist in the theater. Julia Marlowe had the unpopular idea that the actor's business is not to exploit his own individuality but to interpret the dramatist. Rant goes. Sound and fury go. "Points" are ruthlessly sacrificed. As Arthur Symons notes when she plays in England, she has "none of the attractiveness of excess."

I know of no better illustrations of her ability always to concentrate on the role rather than the actress than two simple stories which Elizabeth McCracken tells of her.

She never cared much for the role of Portia in *The Merchant of Venice,* yet she costumed it more elaborately than any other part she played. When Miss McCracken asked her to explain the paradox, she immediately replied, "Portia was very rich—richer than anyone else I ever played. She had such things and quantities of them."

Once she showed Miss McCracken a rose-colored, green-brocaded cloak that she had prepared for Juliet to wear to the Friar's cell. Miss McCracken remarked that she preferred the simple dark cloak that had formerly been used in this scene. "So do I," said the actress, "but Juliet would not. . . . This combination of colors is in many of the Italian portrait paintings of the period. In soul, Juliet is universal; but outwardly she was not different from other Italian girls of the Renaissance."

At their best, then, her productions were not only intelligent but scholarly. She carried a set of the "New Variorum" Shakespeare around with her until she wore it out. Nor did she neglect her non-Shakespearean interpretations. In her investiture for *Romola* she must have the peculiar deep brownish red that she had noticed in the paintings of Filippino Lippi. As Yvette in Mary Johnston's play of the French Revolution, *The Goddess of Reason,* she carried a tiny gold heart marked with a fleur-de-lis, admitting that the audience would not be able to see it, "but I shall like having it in keeping." And when *For Bonnie Prince Charlie* was in preparation she went into the problem of Scottish plaids in the minutest detail: all the clans must be exactly right, though it took endless time and trouble and worry to make them right.

It is beginning to sound a little as if the woman were a pedant. She was not, but she might very easily have been. Here again she knew just where to stop, and whenever the stage and the study came into conflict, it was the stage that won. Her reverence for Shakespeare did not mean that she treated him like a dead thing. The heavy hand of tradition rested but lightly upon her. With the actual text as her authority, she tried to work out her interpretations as freely as if she had been studying a new play. Perhaps this appeared most clearly in her interpretation of *The Taming of the Shrew,* which she and Sothern presented as a boisterous farce with a very knowing Katherine, tamed with her tongue in her cheek, a procedure for which they were roundly censured by all the learned Elizabethans whose knowledge of Shakespeare consisted largely in having seen somewhere a very solemn portrait of Edwin Booth as the Prince of Denmark. Miss Marlowe replied with a lengthy statement which, though it did not convince all the dissenters, at least made it clear that she had not acted perversely or with any thought of playing to the gallery.

IV

Not only was Julia Marlowe devoted to her work—she believed in it. To her the theater was a great institution, one indispensable at its best to the spiritual life of mankind. Had it been otherwise, she could hardly have cared to identify herself with it, for she was a very serious person always. There had been little in her hard austere youth to encourage frivolity; neither did she have any intention of devoting herself to frivolity when she was older.

She hungered for beauty always, and to her the theater was beauty. The Wordsworthian loveliness of those Cumberland hills had got into her blood somehow, and no work of art that was not fundamentally beautiful ever made a very strong appeal to her. After her debut in *Ingomar,* the managers besieged her with offers to appear in modern realistic plays. Unhesitatingly she rejected them all. It was the poetic drama that she must have. Let others play the realistic pieces if they chose: there was merit in *Magda,* and there was merit in Ibsen. But they were not for her. "The modern unpoetic plays tie the actor down. What I want is sweep—a great wonderful outlet for the imagination and the soul."

Perhaps there is no better test of an actor's loyalty to his art than his willingness to make financial sacrifices for it. Had she been willing to relinquish her ideals, Julia Marlowe might from the beginning of her career have played to enormous receipts. As a classical actress she had to fight her way through eleven years before she could come to the end of the season with a surplus. There came a time when, as we have seen, she was compelled to drop Shakespeare temporarily: managers were unsympathetic, and the public would not pay its money to come to see her in his plays. Even then she significantly chose romantic, not realistic, material, and light as *Barbara Frietchie* and *When Knighthood Was in Flower* may have been, she managed somehow to put beauty and sincerity and moral earnestness into them, by the mere fact of her presence to touch them with faint vestiges of poetic glories. "More than once in the course of last year I have all but wept for the memory of my gentle Rosalind and Viola; I so do long to play them again."

Equally cogent testimony to her idealism—and Edward Sothern's —came in connection with their appearance at the New Theater. For years they had longed and begged and pleaded for a subsidized playhouse. When, finally, they were asked to join the company at the New Theater, it seemed as if their dreams were about to be realized at last. Unhesitatingly they disbanded their fine company, gave up their personal plans, and devoted all their best efforts to the success of the new venture. Disillusionment followed swiftly. Their prompt books were cast aside and the terms of their contract violated. The director was basically unsympathetic to their aims and ideals. What had been designed as a great democratic institution was changing, under their very eyes, into one more plaything for New York society.

All the rules of the theater would seem at this point to have called for a series of temperamental outbursts and stormy denunciations. Only, they did not occur. Quietly, Sothern and Marlowe informed the management that they would withdraw from the New Theater as soon as the opening production of *Antony and Cleopatra* had run its course. In public, they refrained meanwhile from speaking a word which might prejudice the success of the enterprise. Indeed they even went the length of rehearsing two modern plays in which they had not the slightest intention of being seen.

The theater was beauty to Julia Marlowe. The theater was something more. The theater was righteousness. Acting was "a great moral force"; on her own part she felt an obligation to keep it so. Asked whether an actress must have "lived" to portray great emotions in the theater, she replied dryly that it was possible to play Lady Macbeth without having first committed a murder. "No dramatic artist that does not follow the common-sense laws of health and right living can ever hope to penetrate to the heart of an audience." And the artist who does follow these laws is of necessity much more than an entertainer. "What is after all the most difficult thing in life? To keep always fine in one's inside dwelling place, whatever that may be called, isn't it? Nothing helps that so much as the exalted feelings that belong to a great work of beauty."

With such convictions, it was natural that she should be careful not to associate herself with the portrayal of base emotions in the drama. What interested her was "the dramatic attraction of the woman that stays pure." She conceded that "a woman of moral depravity offers the modern playwright greater scope than a good woman because her life is full of incidents that are dramatic." Yet she was convinced that "it takes a greater artist to make a good woman interesting than to make a base woman sympathetic and thrilling." For all that, she was not a prig. As I have already pointed out, she was not unfair in her judgment of modern realistic plays. "I am far from saying that many of the fin de siècle playwrights have not treated these stern questions of morality in a convincing manner; but after all is said, what do they really achieve, except to enforce the rather self-evident proposition that fire burns and that the piper must be paid?"

Twice in her career Julia Marlowe herself appeared in plays which some persons found objectionable. One was a very minor episode, a play by Henry Esmond called *Fools of Nature* about which she does not appear to have felt very strongly one way or the other. But her Salome in Sudermann's *John the Baptist* was another matter. She earnestly believed in this play, and, in sharp contrast to her usual position, she maintained strenuously against all comers that, unsavory as the subject was, the play still abundantly justified itself as a work of art.

Salome was the exception that proves the rule. With her rich, ripe womanhood, Julia Marlowe might, had she chosen, have put forth an intensely sensuous and, to her, immensely profitable appeal. She chose not to do this, chose to try instead for a different kind of beauty, the beauty of the spirit. Many years ago, when the Puritan mistrust of the theater still lingered in the land, the great preacher Theodore T. Munger attacked the drama upon the ground that, no matter how pure a play might pretend to be, no sinner was ever reclaimed through its influence. Unfortunately for the argument, it does not happen to be the business of art to reclaim sinners, yet I think Munger might have been interested in the story of the gambler Jack Oakhurst, who happened to stroll in one evening on Miss Marlowe's *Twelfth Night*.

It seemed to him [writes Charles Edward Russell], an expression of purity, goodness, and ethereal beauty all new. The farther the play went the more he was engrossed with it and the more he became conscious of the difference between the world that this signified and the world in which he moved. . . . Anyway, he said that the sheer and pure beauty of that performance touched something in him that needed to be touched and when he walked out of that theater he was done with the old way of livelihood and never went back to it.

v

Because she lived her life in art, because her work was not simply her method of making a living but rather the supreme expression of her own highest ideals, we experience no change, no precipitous descent as we pass in Julia Marlowe from the professional to the personal aspect. She refused to be exploited either in the parlor or in the press, disliked reporters in their professional capacity, discouraged all sensational publicity, and always refused to discuss her private concerns. Once a persistent newspaperman tried to goad her into talkativeness by reminding her that he represented a syndicate, so that whatever she said to him would be printed next morning in 117 newspapers. "That," she replied, "is one hundred and seventeen reasons for not saying it."

The same love of beauty that she manifested in her professional devotion to Shakespeare comes out again, naturally enough, in her judgments of art and literature generally. As a child she used to shut herself up in a closet and pray for books. They came—when she was too busy to find time to read them!—and she began praying for leisure, retirement, freedom. During her very early years she was a devotee of Deadwood Dick, but Dick was soon replaced by Sir Walter, and as a woman she could find time only for literature of quality. Carefully excepting free verse, which she detested, poetry was always her first choice. But she did not confine herself to genteel writers: Whitman, Thoreau, and Balzac were among her favorites. She loved good music and good pictures; she tried to keep in touch with the nonaesthetic aspects of contemporary civilization. She had a healthy interest in woman suffrage. And just as she stopped gracefully short of priggishness in her dislike of problem plays, so she was careful not to be absurd as she sought to foster idealism through reading. When Charles Edward Russell objected to the revelation of Stevenson's weaknesses in William Ernest Henley's account of him, she took issue directly:

> A biography that pictures a man as all of a piece is no biography at all. . . . If we knew the truth about any man or woman we call great, we should find exactly such slips as Henley tells. The fact that we have these complexities and still go on and win in spite of them is much more important than the every-day virtues that some biographers make so great. . . . Pedestal worship is not biography and does the world little good.

These remarks come from her with more than ordinary fitness, for the serenity, the poise, the atmosphere of high-minded quietude that she presented to the world often deceived people. They assumed that because she indulged in no temperamental outbursts, she had no temperament, that because she kept her name free of scandal, she had no passions. Nothing could be more absurd. Women without temperament do not have important careers—particularly in the theater; women whose virtue is negative, not positive, never make themselves symbols of moral beauty and encouragement to mankind. In her early days Miss Marlowe had a high temper; she was prone to brooding, discouragement; girl-like, she suffered from fits of the "blues." Not being able to afford these luxuries, she got rid of them, and in later years her temperament was always her slave, not her master.

I am not quite sure what to say about Julia Marlowe's health. She herself always regarded it as precarious. As a girl she was pale, sallow, anemic. More than once her career was broken into by serious illness. When she was playing in *For Bonnie Prince Charlie,* which was an adaptation of François Coppée's *Les Jacobites,* she used to leave the stage every night feeling that something had given way in her chest, and she always liked to spend the day in bed after having acted Lady Macbeth. Certainly she always took the best possible care of her health in the way of exercise, diet, and regular habits. Yet she lived eighty-five years, and at the end of her life she went through a series of strokes and other maladies which might have been expected to finish off a weak woman long before they finished her.

If Miss Marlowe had a serious fault, it was along the lines that have already been suggested; she was somewhat overdisciplined. In later years, her interpretations—beautiful, charming, intelligent as they were—seemed at times overelaborate, overconscientious. Her biographer speaks of her "almost morbid hatred of slang. She would not use it herself and if in conversation someone else used it, the clouds would begin to gather on her black brows." Or, as she herself puts it, "I always insist that every thought, whether I voice it or not, shall be well-rounded and couched not only in language clear to me but in the best words I can find." The ideal could hardly be better stated, yet I think one sometimes feels a certain lack of spontaneity in those who conduct their conversation upon such austere principles.

Like many persons who have fought a hard fight with themselves and with the world, Julia Marlowe was not given to sentimentality. As a girl she had no recreations and no intimate friends; she had to stand absolutely on her own feet. One cannot feel that her family ever helped her very much. So she developed a seriousness, a self-confidence, an independence of judgment without which she could hardly have gone as far as she did, and the natural result was that the light give-and-take of ordinary social intercourse never became altogether easy for her. Even her sports and exercises seem to have been approached from the business standpoint; one feels that she took up swimming, for example, because she thought it good for her rather than because she particularly enjoyed it. Sometimes her own struggles even influenced her attitude toward the roles that she played. How revealing is her comparative indifference to Bassanio's Portia on the ground that Portia was too rich; she had always had everything given to her! When her future biographer was first introduced to her on a train he found her distinctly disinclined toward idle chatter. "She gave me the tips of her fingers, an icy response to my congratulations, and I think about one-fourth of a glance of austere regard. Then she disappeared behind her book covers." Even in her full maturity he writes of her, "Her confidence was extremely hard to gain, for she was always reticent and wary."

For all that, she was never unsympathetic or unkind. She simply realized that her contribution to society must be made through her art, not in casual social contacts, and she saved her strength and conserved her energy toward that end. The friends she did make she cherished deeply, and—as is so often true of artists—she had an intuitional understanding of human problems even when she had not come into direct contact with them or familiarized herself with all their details. She was democratic in her manners, thoughtful about the theater, and particularly kind to stagehands and other subordinates. She made it a point never to leave a letter from a child unanswered. There are many stories of financial assistance to unfortunates and kindnesses in the way of birthday cakes and other remembrances. When she went to Europe in 1903, she was much concerned about the steerage passengers, herself took food and other comforts to them, and at one point paid the ship's band to go down and play for them. As for intruders, she did her best to protect herself against them, but once they had penetrated her barriers, she was quite incapable of the severity with which Jenny Lind, for example, could rebuke them. "Oh, well, I suppose it is a real joy to them, and none of us has so much of that that one can afford to be miserly about giving it to somebody else if one can."

In more intimate matters, such as the failure of her first marriage, Miss Marlowe characteristically kept her own counsel, but it is clear that her humanity and self-respect did not desert her. When she married Robert Taber she actually considered dropping her own name and appearing with him as "Mr. and Mrs. Taber." Fortunately this absurdity was not perpetrated, though she did call herself Julia Marlowe Taber, greatly to the disgust of her managers. In several cases she subordinated herself to her husband, notably in *Romola* and *She Stoops to Conquer,* and outstandingly in *King Henry IV, Part I,* in which Taber appeared as Hotspur and actually persuaded his wife that Prince Hal was a wonderful role for her! When the break came, she tried her case in the courts, not in the newspapers.

She had decided views on the matter of race prejudice, and I do not know where in her life her courage, earnestness, sincerity, and kindliness were better exemplified than in the visit she and Sothern made in 1920 to a Washington high school for colored pupils, where, speaking and reading, they consciously challenged racial snobbery and made a profound appeal to the imagination of the Negro race.

> I do not know [writes Mr. Russell], that she ever seemed greater and I do not know that at any moment of her career she was creating a more profound impression. I need not say that the familiar lines took on new meanings as she read; that they always did. But what seemed still more a thing for memory was the effect upon the children, overcome at once with two subduing sensations, the beauty of the thing they heard and the novel beauty of the thought that famous white persons had cared enough about them to visit and read to them.

How could it have been otherwise? This woman had given her life to Shakespeare, to the spirit of dramatic art in its noblest, most reverent, most utterly charming manifestation, the only force in the whole world, as Galsworthy once declared, "that consciously works for unity and destroys the barriers between man and man." So too she generously accepted the homage of Emma Goldman and sent flowers to her at a time when all "right-thinking" people regarded her as a red female devil. An actress capable of such deeds as these does not need to preach sermons to her audiences; she has no use for the "horrible example." Rather she gives her powers to the creation of "a perfect ideal of beauty," and such an ideal, as William Winter remarked of Julia Marlowe's Viola, "sinks into the mind, remains in the memory, and beneficently influences the conduct of life."

VI

To my portrait of Julia Marlowe I should like to add a more personal postscript. In the mid-forties, twenty years after I had last seen her on the stage and long after I had ever expected to see her again, I learned of her residence at the Plaza and wrote to her. She read and liked what I had written about her, in 1945 I dedicated *The Fireside*

Book of Christmas Stories to her, and when I was in New York in the summer of 1946 she entertained me.

In spite of her eighty-one years, she was still a beautiful woman. I do not mean that she was beautiful for a woman of eighty-one; she was beautiful judged by any standards. The face and the figure were much as they had always been, and the magnificent voice was largely unimpaired, but the hair had been dyed a golden blonde, which was the more startling because when I entered her rooms, I found her sitting under the well-known painting of herself by Irving R. Wiles, in which the brunette beauty of her stage years has been so well preserved.

I am aware that this may sound grotesque as I tell it; I must insist that the effect was nothing of the kind. The blonde hair was completely becoming to her, and no doubt gave a softer effect to her face at this stage than dark hair would have given.

It was clear that her interests and loyalties lay in the past, as at her age they had every right to do. She did not like the Brave New World any better than I did; she mistrusted the New Deal and all its heritage; she decried the spirit of an age which she characterized by quoting the words recently uttered by her banker: "O Mrs. Sothern, it's all conniving!" For all that, she knew what was going on, and I thought she showed her age most in her complete lack of interest in the contemporary theater, which seemed quite unable to meet her strenuous idealism at any point.

Perhaps the high moment of the afternoon came when she turned to me suddenly and exclaimed, "I wish Edward could have known you!" which I accepted gratefully as the highest compliment she could have paid me. Her apartment was filled with photographs, including one of an old servant, now dead, whom she evidently remembered with great fondness.[3] She was now served by a French maid who struck me as extremely efficient, but I judged that her relations with Miss Mar-

[3] There is a good deal about this woman in E. H. Sothern's *Julia Marlowe's Story,* where she appears invested with picturesque idiosyncrasies of her own, of which I caught no inkling in what Miss Marlowe told me that afternoon in 1946.

lowe were pretty much upon a business basis. Mary's photograph became the occasion for a description of what good care her old servant used to take of her. When she got a very good notice, she said, she would always hand it to her to read; Mary would go through it unmoved and then hand it back to her with "It isn't half what you deserve, Madame." And she was very proud of the fact that when Mary was once asked whether she hadn't ever thought she would like to have a home of her own, she replied in amazement, "A home of my own? Why, *this is my home!*"

Finally, as I was standing at the door, ready to go, Miss Marlowe picked up a small framed picture of a little dog from the bookcase where it had been standing and passed it to me with "This is ———" (I am sorry that I have forgotten the name of the animal). But I had already heard much about him, correspondence-wise, for he had recently died, and she had written about him almost as though she had lost a child. I held the picture as reverently as possible and finally, not knowing what else to say, I asked her if she planned to get another dog. At this point she placed her hand on my arm, and glancing toward the kitchen into which her maid had just disappeared, replied in her best conspiratorial stage whisper (we might almost have been doing *Macbeth* together), "No. *She* doesn't like dogs!" It was a touching moment, and I could not help thinking of Mary, for whom home and Julia Marlowe had been spelled the same way and for whom nothing could ever be good enough for Madame.

V

The Dance of Life
       as Art and as Orgy

ISADORA DUNCAN

In our flesh grows the branch of this life, in our soul it bears
   fruit.

ROBERT BROWNING, "Saul"

We then, who are this new soul, know
   Of what we are composed and made,
For the atomies of which we grow
   Are souls, whom no change can invade.
But O alas! so long, so far,
   Our bodies why do we forbear?
They are ours, though they are not we; we are
   The intelligence, they the spheres.
We owe them thanks, because they thus
   Did us, to us, at first convey,
Yielded their forces, sense, to us,
   Nor are dross to us, but allay.

JOHN DONNE, "The Ecstasy"

These women—such women—can sometimes love so well that
no man's nature can contain all that they have to give. There are
men like that, too. And it is not a light love. The light lover has
many, and rapidly shifting aims, but never two loyalties at once.
But these others may love once, or twice, or often, but change-
ably. They do not love unworthily—it is lamentable when they
love unworthy men.

JOHN DRINKWATER, *Mary Stuart*

1 *Isadora Duncan*

It was Isadora Duncan's conviction that "you can't do a half truth about a great being. The entire value is in telling the absolute truth of every side of her character, good and bad." When she wrote her autobiography, she tried to apply this principle, telling the exact truth about herself, without apology or concealment of any kind. She was apparently not familiar with the journal of Marie Bashkirtseff, and she was under the impression that nobody had ever tried to do this before. Frankly unveiling the soul of one woman, she hoped to illuminate all womankind.

In this aim I believe she fell far short of the distinguished success which some of her admirers have claimed for her. To begin with, she herself was not a typical woman. It is true of course that in his work the artist speaks for mankind, expressing its emotions, interpreting its aspirations, but this does not in itself make him personally or temperamentally representative of humanity in general. Dr. Johnson imaged even the lexicographer as a harmless drudge, shut out from the ordinary experiences of human life, and if this is true of scholars, it is even more true of artists. For that matter, Isadora herself was less representative than many artists and less qualified to allow for the differences between herself and others. Even with regard to the events of her own life she was not always either accurate or clear-sighted. She worked without reference to accurate records of her past, and though she was often eloquent, she was not, as she well knew, really a writer. "What is the truth of a human life," she asks, "and who can find it? God Himself would be puzzled. In the midst of all this anguish and delight; this filth and this luminous purity; this fleshly body filled with hell fire, and this same body alight with heroism and beauty—where is the truth?" It is not wonderful, then, that the fashion of telling "all" which the sensational success of *My Life* inspired should have produced more exhibitionism than illumination.

Born in San Francisco on May 27, 1878, Isadora Duncan passed her girlhood in what might be called an atmosphere of impecunious enthusiasm. Her father was something of a ne'er-do-well whose operations finally brought him within the clutches of the law, though he was never convicted. He was also, however, a man of some aesthetic sensitiveness. In 1898, many years after having been separated from his wife and family, he was killed in a steamship disaster.

Themselves still children, Isadora and her sister gave dancing lessons, after their own method, to the children of San Francisco society; then, impelled by Isadora's faith, they drifted first to Chicago and New York, then to London, Paris, and Berlin. Isadora was associated with the Wagner festival at Bayreuth; at Grünewald she established a dancing school for girls. She won personal triumphs in all the great centers of Europe; in Germany they spoke of her as *"die göttliche, heilige Isadora."* She toured the United States, arousing enthusiasm by her dancing and shocked astonishment through her unconventional views and habits.

Her life was smashed on April 13, 1913, when Deirdre, her daughter by Gordon Craig, and Patrick, her son by Paris Singer ("Lohengrin"), were drowned in the Seine in a runaway motorcar. The rest of her days she spent in frantic efforts to forget the grief that consumed her, and as time went on she became increasingly less able to discriminate between the distractions that she chose. In 1921 her extravagant idealism was fired for the last time, and she went to Moscow in the hope of establishing a dancing school under the auspices of the Soviet government. Here she contracted her mad marriage with the unbalanced young Russian poet, Sergei Essenine, a harrowing experience which contributed still further to wreck her life. After the inevitable separation she continued her mad career, more and more losing control of herself, until at last fate once again took charge of a motorcar and ended her life at Nice on September 14, 1927.

It should be understood at the outset that Isadora Duncan was not the kind of celebrity whose work in the theater would not have been noticed except for the elements of sensationalism in her private life. Before all else this woman was an artist, a very great and very original

artist; we must not allow the hysterical rhapsodies of her more un-
critical admirers to blind us to that. For this is a matter on which those
best qualified to speak have spoken—Stanislavsky, George Grey Bar-
nard, Yvette Guilbert, and many more—and their testimony leaves
no doubt that she touched something in them that only the elect can
touch. I can conceive of no sensitive reader, however shocked or disgusted he might have been by her autobiography, who, passing on to
The Art of the Dance, could fail to be other than profoundly moved.[1]

---

[1] Elie Faure found in Isadora's dancing "the certitude that the day is near when we
shall once more come in fecund contact with instinctive life." Edith Wharton "beheld
the dance I had always dreamed of, a flowing of movement into movement, an endless interweaving of motion and music, satisfying every sense as a flower does, or a
phrase of Mozart's." Lorado Taft saw "Poetry personified. She is not the Tenth Muse
but all the Nine Muses in one—and painting and sculpture as well." "The soul becomes drunk," said Ernest Newman, "with this endless succession of beautiful lines
and groupings." Lola Kinel's first impression of Isadora was that of "a fat, middle-
aged woman. . . . She had a small head with Titian curls, a beautiful but cruel mouth,
and sentimental eyes." Miss Kinel never saw her practice during the weeks that preceded her first recital while she was living with her as her secretary; neither did she
diet nor do anything else that a dancer is supposed to do. Yet when the dance came,
the secretary found "a sort of religious exaltation" in it. "All the different emotions
through which a human being, or humanity itself, passes in a lifetime" were revealed.
When in her Brahms waltzes, she strewed flowers over the stage, "I could have sworn
I saw children on the stage—there where I knew was nothing but the bare rug. . . . It
was pure magic."

Of course the magic did not work for everyone. Though Carl Van Vechten appreciated Isadora Duncan, he thought one of her Gluck dances "more or less a sacrilege"
and a Beethoven number "a perverted use of the *Seventh Symphony.*" "I distinctly
recall," writes Merle Armitage, "many measures where lack of discipline, uncertainty,
and unrealized intention intervened. There were holes and blanks in Isadora's art . . .
at least for this observer." But no dissenting opinion has impressed me more than that
of the not at all conventionally minded Margaret Anderson, who complained of Isadora that she "ran, jumped and skipped and stamped and swooned about the stage,
dragging with her a body that was never meant to move in rhythmic line . . . using the
same gestures for the sweetness of Schubert as for the sacraments of César Franck,
moving always inside the music, never dominating it. . . . If the music made a wide
swinging curve she made a cramped sudden curve; if it made a descending line she
interpreted that, for some mysterious reason, by reverently clutching her abdomen
and looking to God." See *The Little Review Anthology* (Hermitage House, 1953),
80–81.

As she conceived it, dancing must begin with the awakening of the dancer's own spiritual nature, but this, taken by itself, was not enough. From here one must go on to a harmonious adjustment of the me to the not-me, merging the soul of the individual with the soul of life. What she wished to develop, in herself and her pupils, was "the highest intelligence in the freest body," and it was on the basis of these preconceptions that she set out to discover the source of power and motion, to lay bare the first movement from which all others must proceed.

> Every movement that can be danced on the seashore without being in harmony with the rhythm of the waves, every movement that can be danced in the forest without being in harmony with the swaying of the branches, every movement that one can dance nude, in the sunshine, in the open country, without being in harmony with the life and the solitude of the landscape—every such movement is false, in that it is out of tune in the midst of Nature's harmonious lines.

To achieve this harmony she must use music, and herself she would have none but the greatest. She detested contemporary music, even the best of it. "The music of today . . . only makes the nerves dance. Deep emotion, spiritual gravity, are entirely lacking." She also disliked many modern dancers. "Their movements are all *down*, groveling on the earth. They express nothing but the wisdom of the serpent, who crawls on his belly." And when she comes to the stilted inanities of musical comedy and the appalling sensualities of modern jazz, she will give no quarter whatever.[2]

She thought and functioned not in terms of the theater but in terms of life. Her primary interest was never in building a career. What she wanted to do was to awaken a sense of beauty in people, to restore to

[2] "An entire audience of so called respectable people, who would leave the theatre if anyone appeared to blaspheme or to use indecent words, will sit through a performance in which someone makes indecent movements which, if translated into words, would make the audience rush from the theatre. A seemingly modest young girl would not think of addressing a young man in lines or spoken phrases which were indecent and yet the same girl will arise and dance the phrases with him in such

the world the glory of a lost art. And for all the wonder of her individual performances and all the praise that she received, solo dancing was a very subordinate part of her work. Her hopes and dreams were all for a symphony of the dance, a symphony which should bind all the girls of the world together in their worship of beauty. Art "which is not religious," she said, "is not art, is mere merchandise." Surely nobody ever brought more religious enthusiasm to it than she.

This element of mysticism in Isadora's art and life is all the more interesting in view of the religious nihilism on which she had been reared and from which she never recovered. Her mother had been in earlier days an Irish Catholic, but when she divorced her husband she felt it necessary, for some mysterious reason, also to divorce God, and from then on she attempted to nurture her children's souls on a crude, ill-apprehended rationalism. "There is no Santa Claus," she told them, "and there is no God, only your own spirit to help you." The Humanists should put up a statue to her in the park.

Isadora's mind assimilated this point of view, but her spirit never did. As in the case of the youthful Shelley, as so often in naturally devout persons under similar handicaps, her religious feelings, balked in their natural channel, expressed themselves in a passionate, self-immolating worship of beauty, and she speaks of herself as "I, who by my work have always tried to preach that Joy is stronger than sorrow; that Death is but a door that leads us to the Eternal Harmony of the Universe; that the fearsome appearances of physical suffering and matter are merely an illusion that the initiated know how to interpret."

She knew that religion in some form is necessary to mankind, that the soul of man cannot live without it. When the Bolshevists turned a cathedral into a Communist club, she warned them that it is dangerous to destroy religion without having first devised a substitute for it. It

dances as the Charleston and Black Bottom, while a negro orchestra is playing *Shake that thing!*" But even here she is far from being consistent. Sewell Stokes reports her as denouncing modern music one minute and the next "staring into space, humming: 'I wonder if my baby does the Charleston.'" She once precipitated a scene with Paris Singer by doing a particularly sensual tango with Maurice in a café.

was she who arranged the ceremony for the first famous secular christening in Moscow, where she danced to the music of Schubert's *"Ave Maria."* If men could only learn to love as Christ loved, as Buddha loved, all our problems would be solved, and there would be no further need for art. Love was indeed the heart of the matter, and when it was present—or she imagined it was—she was not inclined to be anxious about other things. When she was asked how she could be so enthusiastic about Lenin when Lenin did not believe in God, she replied, "That is simply a phrase. Lenin was God, as Christ was God, because God is Love and Christ and Lenin were all love," which is surely an original interpretation of Lenin.[3]

So it was not enough for her to create beauty; she wanted to share it with all mankind, and especially with the underprivileged, with those for whom there were none to care. And she would not stop with the beauty she herself had created. When at one time it seemed possible that a theater might be built for her in Paris, her imagination was fired by the thought of what Duse might play there, what Mounet-Sully might bring forth within those walls, quite as much as by anything that might proceed from Isadora Duncan.

This superb generosity stamps Isadora Duncan as a great humanitarian as well as a great artist. Not that she was free from the ordinary vanities of humanity. She had them all. Unlike most women, she expressed them frankly and freely. But few great artists have ever been so unselfish. Clothes? She cared nothing for clothes. Paul Poiret is an artist if you like, but his is profane art, not sacred, and as such it does not appeal to her. She could tear up a contract to accommodate a recalcitrant manager. She could leave her own house and go to a hotel rather than eject an unwelcome guest. Moreover, she was fired by the ardor of great causes, touched by the appeal of humanity in the mass quite as deeply as she was moved by individuals. Her sympathy

---

[3] Here, again, Isadora is inconsistent. Max Eastman tells of her rapt absorption in the ouija board. But Lola Kinel reports how she once argued violently with Essenine in defense of the proposition that there was no god except Beauty and Love. The argument culminated when she pointed to the bed and cried, "There is God!"

for Russia all dated back to the day in 1905 when, entering St. Petersburg, she met the funeral cortege of the workmen who, coming to petition the Czar for redress of grievances, were shot down in cold blood before the Winter Palace.

Even to the supreme and most intimate aspects of life she carried her noble idealism. Passionately as she loved her children, she did not think mother love the greatest thing in life. "The future love will be not 'my family,' but 'all humanity,' not 'my children' but 'all children,' not 'my country' but 'all peoples.' " When her own children were killed she sent for the chauffer, telling him that he must not worry, for she did not hold him responsible in any way. And as they were carried to the crematory she turned to Mary Desti at her side: "No tears, Mary—no tears. They never had a sorrow, and we must not be sorrowful today. I want to be brave enough to make death beautiful, to help all the other mothers of the world who have lost their babies." This was perhaps the one incident in her life when universal sympathy was felt for her. "My friends have helped me to realize what alone could comfort me—that all men are my brothers, all women my sisters, and all little children on earth my children."

II

It is clear, then, that, for all her faith in instinct and intuition, Isadora Duncan was a completely conscious, indeed self-conscious, artist. She herself was profoundly convinced that she was a great intellectual; instead she was in many ways extraordinarily naïve. To be sure, she was seduced by the glamour of great names, hypnotized by the magic of the past, but her rapturous absorption in the treasures of the Louvre or the British Museum suggests the bright sophomore's puppy love of learning, never the sustained scholarly interest which Isadora thought she possessed. Mabel Dodge Luhan, who admired her greatly, says bluntly that "she had not enough mentality to estimate correctly the value of anyone's poetry." In the early days, before she discovered more exciting pastimes, she would go home after a performance to read Kant's *Critique of Pure Reason* far into the night, hoping—

145

"Heaven only knows how," as she herself expresses it—to find there some inspiration for her work. That "Heaven only knows how" is profoundly suggestive. She liked to have heavy philosophical tomes about her; somehow or other she even managed to derive a kind of emotional excitement from them; but I doubt she would have been able to pass the simplest kind of examination on the concepts involved. When she was a child in Augustin Daly's company, she used to go about backstage with a volume of Marcus Aurelius under her arm, but as William Bolitho remarks acutely, it would be a fairly safe bet that she never read that Marcus Aurelius quite through.[4] With her free-thinking predelictions, it was natural that she should conceive a wild admiration, first for Nietzsche, then for Haeckel, but she understood the latter so little that she invited him to Bayreuth of all places, and she was surprised and troubled that he should be bored amid all the mystical subtleties of *Parsifal*. Surely she was right when, being asked to interpret the meaning of the Russian revolution for the French press, she wrote, "I can only give you my impressions as an artiste, and these impressions are more felt than reasoned."

Even the things she fought for, the causes she championed, were chosen purely on the basis of their emotional appeal. She repudiated the ballet before she understood it, and years afterwards, when she saw Pavlova, she was unable, despite all her theories, to resist that great dancer's appeal. She took part in a Sacco-Vanzetti demonstration in Paris without knowing anything about the circumstances of the case. Even her spectacular Russian adventure used ignorance for its fuel. When she went to Moscow, burning her bridges behind her, she was so uninformed concerning what had happened in Russia that she was actually under the impression that the word "Bolshevik" meant "big"! For all her experience of life, for all the disillusionment she had experienced, she still believed—this divine madwoman—that

---

[4] On the other hand, Macdougall reports that "the copious marginal notes in the handwritings of Isadora and of Gordon Craig" in the margins of her copy of Gilchrist's *Life of Blake* "attested to a diligent study, not only of the text but also of the illustrations."

she was going to utopia, that human nature had changed overnight, and that every Russian officer was a baby Tolstoy.

Even after she had lived in Russia she could not give up her dream. On her last American tour she was continually in hot water for her prorevolutionary utterances. Really they did not mean a thing except that she was disgusted with what she saw in America. She had a "fuzzy" mind which saw ideas in a penumbra of emotion. If you had asked her how Communism was going to remedy the conditions she complained of, she could not for the life of her have told you. Here, indeed, is the root of the inconsistency involved. She could make wildly inflammatory speeches at the close of one of her programs, and then, when she was called to account for it, she could declare, with complete sincerity, that she was purely an artist, that she knew and cared nothing about the political aspects of the Russian situation, and that she had had no idea whatever of speaking disrespectfully of the American government.[5]

But if Isadora Duncan was not an intellectual she was something much better. She had the uncanny, intuitive gift of the artist for seizing atmosphere; by a sudden leap of the imagination she could grasp something that it would have taken a mere scholar many months of patient labor to study out. Once she argued with Cosima Wagner concerning the proper interpretation of one of the dances in *Tannhäuser*. Cosima went home, studied patiently among the master's papers, and came back to tell Isadora that she had been perfectly right. Much later, when she and Harold Bauer studied music together, the

[5] None of her performances along this line are more peculiar than her exhortation to an audience in Symphony Hall, Boston, to knock down the statues in the balcony because they were "not real," not "real Greek gods." They are all copies of masterpieces of classical sculpture, the precise kind of thing which Isadora journeyed to Greece to see and by which she professed to be inspired. Moreover, all the male figures are stark naked, a circumstance which has inspired many ribald jokes down through the years, with many speculations as to how and why the supposedly proper Bostonians chose these particular decorations. The statues stand very high up in Symphony Hall, and I cannot help wondering how good Isadora's eyesight was at this period and how clearly she was able to see them from the stage.

great pianist told her that she had uncovered the meaning for him in many phrases of Bach, Chopin, and Beethoven that he had never been able to understand. Nor was this sympathetic insight wholly confined to aesthetic matters. One would not accept her authority on any practical aspect of the Russian situation, but the force behind the revolution, in its idealistic aspect at least, she understood as well as anybody in the West.

III

So *"die göttliche, heilige Isadora"* hardly seems an exaggeration until we remind ourselves that we are thinking about a woman who made shipwreck of her life. If Isadora Duncan had been merely a promiscuous and intemperate woman, this phase of her experience would have little serious interest and were much better forgotten. But it is impossible to take this line with her.

She seems never to have had any sense of shame in connection with sex, any shrinking from sexual experience, any instinctive desire to protect her virginity. But one cannot rashly conclude that she was a wanton by nature, that her soul was consumed by lust, that she was like the girl who becomes a harlot from choice. The young Isadora was anything but a wanton. What wanton ever reverenced life as she did? ever so passionately yearned for motherhood? so gladly embraced pain? The wanton sins gladly, deliberately, as Byron flaunts his sins and glories in them. Isadora was rather (insofar as a woman can, in these matters, be compared with men) the Shelley type of sinner, who cannot do what the world calls wrong except he first convince his own conscience that the world's standard is false and that his own particular code is, in this matter at least, higher than that of the world. I agree with Lloyd Morris that though her love affairs sprang from passion, she "conducted them on principle." And this preoccupation with theory in the realm of the emotions strikes me, I must confess, as far more masculine than feminine.

With Isadora, I should say, theory came first, practice afterwards; her sensual nature seems to have awakened late. Long before she had any definite desire for personal experience in this area, she had formulated her rebellion against marriage, and it was on the somewhat flimsy basis of her mother's unhappy marital experience, plus the sad fate of Hetty Sorrel in *Adam Bede,* that she made up her mind to champion the right of women to be free and bear their children, if they chose, out of wedlock. I do not believe that she acted instinctively in these matters, though I am sure she thought she did. She was far too civilized for that; she was born too late. She *tried* to live instinctively; she had a deliberately cultivated spontaneity; and that is a very, very different thing. Her young head was full of Rousseauish nonsense, of half-baked rebellions that nobody had ever taken the trouble to think through. When she was a young girl, she tells us, Rodin once made advances to her. Frightened, she repelled him. This she did spontaneously. Later she regretted that she had not yielded, mourned the puritanical misconceptions which had lost her the honor of giving up her maidenhead "to the Great God Pan himself." Behold what a marvelous thing is theory!

The time came, however, when she gained the courage to carry her theories into practice. At first she encountered difficulties, for her admirers respected her, and they did not wish to take advantage of her. But finally the Hungarian actor, Oscar Beregi ("Romeo"), proved accommodating, and Isadora was transformed with the ecstasy of love and felt that at last she had really begun to live.

Neither then nor at any other time did she feel in this connection any sense of wrongdoing. Her considered word is "I am not conscious of having sinned." She scorns the "virtuous": they have a single-track mind, or they have never met temptation, or they live in a vegetative state. Ultimately she became so expert that she was capable of attempting to seduce Stanislavsky, and then, when he refused her, of relating the whole story, quite calmly and objectively, to his wife. Yet I cannot help wondering why she was always so disgusted by the sight of other people's "petting." She was not incapable of jealousy. She proved that when one of her lovers fell in love with one of her pupils. But I do not think that jealousy wholly explains her reaction. It seems more likely that when she was set free from the emotional excitement that accompanied her own love-making, she found the bare, unglorified sexual impulse, as observed from the outside, a somewhat unlovely thing, or, in other words, that the puritanism which was, after all, one phase of her complicated character expressed itself here once again.

But, you may say, however mistaken all this may have been, it was naïve, unsophisticated, and idealistic, far removed from sensuality in the ordinary sense of the term. So on first view it seems, and so in a way it was. She was in the mood of Donne's poem "The Ecstasy." "This was not a young man making love to a girl. This was the meeting of twin souls. The light covering of flesh was so transmuted with ecstasy that earthly passion became a heavenly embrace of white, fiery flame." And every time she had another lover she made herself believe that this was Love Himself at last. All the others had been mere ambassadors, and now the hour of supreme fulfillment, so long postponed, was at hand.

Only she could not keep to that level. I wonder if any *grande amoureuse* has ever been able to do so. In theory, Isadora Duncan wanted the soul to be awakened so that, even in the dance, it "can completely possess the body." In love this proved impossible. In her own words, she learned that love can be a pastime as well as a quest; if she could not have eternity she would at least seize the pleasure of the moment. You were bound to experience a certain amount of physical pain during the course of your natural life. That being so, why should you not also make the body yield the maximum pleasure of which it is capable?

With sexual indulgence there went, as there so often does, the stimulation of alcohol. It was not new to Isadora: as far back as 1902 she would keep liquor in her dressing room and fortify herself before her dance. As time went on, she learned, more and more, to drink for pleasure, and after she had lost her children, she learned too what it means to drink for grief. Her union with Essenine plunged her inevitably into frightful excesses, though it does not appear that she ever took part in his indulgences, and by the time she gave her last recital in Paris she was lamenting that her admirers had sent her flowers instead of champagne. George Seldes draws a dreadful picture of her toward the end, in "a Greek robe lovely on a slim goddess, but revealing rather than concealing the enormous breasts, the distended stomach and the wide hips of a woman prematurely distorted by drink and carelessness."

In all this one wonders about the nice question of loyalty. Herself she always claimed it. When she gave her love it was forever. She never left her lovers; they left her. There can be no doubt as to her entire sincerity in this claim. Certainly she showed the patience of a saint toward her sodden husband. For all that, one cannot take her claims quite literally. She was a connoisseur in love, an epicure, and I for one cannot believe that under any circumstances she would—or perhaps could—have confined herself permanently to one man. Herself she admits as much when she compares a woman who has known only one lover to a musician who has listened to but one composer. Toward the end of her life she met a man whom she had liked in her youth, and she was shocked and somewhat disgusted to learn that he was still in love with the simple woman he had married long ago.

Whatever her loyalty to men, she was completely unscrupulous toward other women. She used married men and affianced men to satisfy her needs, or tried to, and there is no suggestion that she was ever conscious of the slightest impropriety in so doing. Marriage was nonsense anyway; what her lover gave her was clean and decent; what objection could there possibly be?[6] In her youth she greatly admired a woman, a librarian in Oakland. Later she learned that this woman had been her father's mistress.[7] One might suppose that a sense of loyalty to her mother would here at least have awakened a feeling of disgust. On the contrary, she senses a mysterious bond binding her father's daughter to his paramour.

[6] However, Sewell Stokes does quote her as saying of D'Annunzio: "I never loved him as I might have done, it wouldn't have been fair to Duse, who was my greatest friend at the time."

[7] Macdougall says this woman was Ina Coolbrith.

Isadora Duncan's palate was not jaded, and there is no indication that twisted sex relationships ever attracted her. But she did not lose her "liberal" attitude as she confronted such things, though I think her extravagant loyalty to "nature" wavers somewhat at this point. When she first encountered homosexuality she was inclined to be shocked, but remembering her Plato, she was soon able to adjust herself to a universe in which such things exist. When she was living with Gordon Craig they both felt the kinship of their spirits so strongly that the bond between them seemed an inappropriate one. "Often he cried to me, 'Ah, you are my sister.' And I felt that our love was some criminal incestuousness." One does not gather that she enjoyed it less on that account.

There are other slight suggestions of abnormality. When she held her first baby to her breast its cruel little mouth reminded her of the mouth of a lover. And one does not know quite what to say when she excuses her infatuation for the youthful Essenine on the ground that he reminds her of her lost Patrick. Why should a woman conceive sexual passion for a man because he recalls her dead child? But the resemblance must have been pretty farfetched to begin with, and there was certainly a strong maternal element in Isadora Duncan's feeling for Essenine.

Having said the worst that can be said of Isadora's sensuality, one is immediately constrained to add the best—that there was little selfishness or self-seeking about it. She never victimized her lovers. When she gave herself to love, she surrendered everything, absolutely and without reserve. And when she was refused or deserted, she seems— save on one terrible occasion, of which she herself speaks frankly and fully—to have been remarkably free from rancor or bitterness. In this sense her claim of perpetual fidelity *is* a just one; few women can ever have hated so little and loved so much.

Nevertheless this was the tragic flaw, the heel of Achilles, the place where the lime-leaf clung to Siegfried—and this was what destroyed her in the end. Mary Desti realized it, for all her admiration: "Had it not been for her sense-loving body dedicating itself to the worshipful service of Venus as well as art, Isadora's life would have been very different." And Isadora herself knew it also, learned to her cost that a man—or a woman either—cannot serve two masters:

> I believe that in each life there is a spiritual line, an upward curve, and all that adheres to and strengthens this line is our real life—the rest is but as chaff falling from us as our souls progress. Such a spiritual line is my Art. My life has known but two motives—Love and Art—and often Love destroyed Art, and often the imperious call of Art put a tragic end to Love. For these two have no accord, but only continual battle.

IV

A fundamental instability appears, then, in Isadora Duncan, almost a note of hysteria, and this is by no means confined to her emotional life. Her admirations are often so violent that they become ludicrous. She came before Carrière as she imagined she might have felt in the presence of Christ; she saw Podovsky "with an infinite love and clairvoyance in his eyes, such as one does not meet in the eyes of a human being, but only dreams of in the eyes of a God." When her crazy husband threatens suicide (which he finally achieves, though not until after they have separated), she is more than ever convinced that he must be a genius. And what a giveaway is her admission that she thinks all sympathetic persons must be a trifle mad!

Perhaps this instability shows best of all in connection with money. She was magnificently, appallingly generous always. What she had belonged to anybody who might ask for it; it is no wonder that Communism as she understood it held no terrors for her. But if she sometimes refused what was rightfully hers, she was also quite capable of demanding that over which she possessed no shadow of a claim. The world owed her a living, no matter how she might choose to conduct herself in it. She would throw legal communications into the wastebasket without reading them and then consider herself cruelly persecuted when action was taken against her. Consequently she was a beggar all her life. As a child she begged from butchers and grocers in San Francisco. When she wanted to go abroad she begged from wealthy women before whom she had danced. And in later years she would take money from anybody without any sense of shame or even of obligation. It was quite impossible to help her. As soon as she felt money between her fingers she would spend it, wildly, extravagantly, for others quite as much as for herself. The only way anybody could have put her on a sound financial basis wold have been to treat her like a child, taking charge of her affairs and paying all her bills for her.

Hysteria showed up too in quite impersonal matters, as in her plans for the common good. It comes out clearly in the Russian adventure, even more clearly perhaps in the earlier visit to Greece. When the Clan Duncan arrived in that sacred country, they astonished the stolid natives by kneeling down piously to kiss the soil. Publicly, tearfully, they embraced each other. Discarding modern clothes, they marched through the streets in the tunic and sandals of the classical age. Finally they bought a hill near Athens, for no reason under heaven save that it was on a level with the Acropolis, and here they proceeded to build a temple on the plan of Agamemnon's palace. Not until building operations were under way did they notice that no water was available.[8]

Insincerity? Exhibitionism? Yes, if this were your portrait or mine. Hardly, since it is Isadora's. She really was quite as enthusiastic as she seemed, and she never went out of her way to shock public opinion; she simply disregarded it. "We were all very emotional and refused to be repressed," she writes of her childhood days. She might have said the same of her whole life. And here is the element in her that wrecked, and must inevitably have wrecked, that great dream of her existence, her school. Unquestionably she caught a great vision here,

---

[8] Max Eastman's paper on Isadora Duncan in *Heroes I Have Known* (Simon and Schuster, 1942) is very good on this hysterical element in her. The confusion in which she lived during her later years cannot be described briefly, but the reader can get a very good idea of it from such books as Sewell Stokes, *Isadora Duncan: An Intimate Portrait* (Brentano's, 1928), and Lola Kinel, *This Is My Affair* (Atlantic-Little, Brown, 1937). See also M. R. Werner, *To Whom It May Concern: The Story of Victor Ilyitch Seroff* (London, Jonathan Cape, 1932), and Mabel Dodge Luhan, *Movers and Shakers* (Harcourt, 1936).

conceived a great creative design, capable of exercising far-reaching beneficent influence on the youth of the world. But say what you will about the stupidity of governments and the shortsightedness of capitalists, the fact still remains that the greatest obstacle in the way of Isadora's school was Isadora. Her private life being what it was, how could she for a moment have imagined that the mothers of the world would be willing to entrust the training of their children to her? And even if we leave her private life out of it, she still could never have mustered the stability necessary to manage a school. Again and again, she wantonly, needlessly antagonized those who might have helped her. She did this even when she had nothing to gain by such conduct. Paris Singer is an example. Mayor John Purroy Mitchell is another. She could have given Edgar Allan Poe information about the imp of the perverse. She simply would not face the fact that it takes more than good will to engineer a great beneficent enterprise. Love is necessary, but love is not enough. And this woman could not possibly stay put under any circumstances; in success as in failure, she must everlastingly be dashing off somewhere to new and untried experiments. "Nietzsche says, 'Woman is a mirror,'" she writes, "and I have only reflected and reacted to the people and the forces that seized me and ... have changed form and character according to the decree of the immortal gods." Woman is a mirror? Ask Alice Freeman Palmer. Ask Susan B. Anthony. Ask Jane Addams. Ask any of the women who have actually carried through the kind of enterprise of which Isadora Duncan could only dream.

v

One phase of Isadora Duncan's emotional life was as pure as her art, as aspiring as her humanitarianism, and this was her motherhood. I have already spoken of her love for children. "Beauty is to be looked for and found in little children; in the light of their eyes and in the beauty of their little hands outstretched in their lovely movements." When her first baby lay in her arms, she felt that even art was of no consequence compared to this. "Once you are interested in shaping children's lives you will never be interested in anything else again. There is nothing greater."

Yet in her strange life, it turned out that this, even this, was to work against her, and doom her and crush her and kill her in the end. What happened in 1913 can only be understood by those who have had to endure something like it. Human sympathy unaided is not yet strong enough to encompass such an experience. Isadora's own view was that the calamity marked the end of her spiritual being. She tried to save herself, to catch hold of life once more by bearing another child. But here again fate struck at her cruelly. The baby died at birth, and all the old agony was simply renewed and intensified. For fourteen years she carried it about with her. Work could not kill it. Drink could not drown it. The strange wild adventure of Russia could not blot it out—neither the hope of building a new world in that incomprehensible country nor the vermin that nearly ate her alive when she went there to try. Almost on the day of her death she cried out, "Mary, if you have the slightest affection for me, find me a way out of this cursed world. I cannot live in it another day, in a world filled with little golden-haired children."

In the midst of such agony, it was not unnatural that her thoughts should often turn to suicide. But she seems to have attempted it only once, not very seriously, by wrapping her mantle about her and stalking out into the sea. Often, she tells us, she would swim out toward the horizon, hoping to go so far that it would prove impossible to return, but always the will to live conquered and she turned landward in time. In spite of all her suffering, the will to live was not destroyed in her.

Yet even here with the children you catch the suggestion of hysteria, and you think of Constance in Shakespeare's *King John*. Constance is sometimes cited as a perfect presentment of mother love. To me this is absurd; there is entirely too much selfishness, too much ambition and self-seeking about her. Isadora had none of this, but she did share the hysteria of Constance. After all, though it may seem cruel to say it, other women have lost children, untold thousands of them in the long, heartbreaking centuries, and it would be ridiculous to suppose that none of them loved their children as much as Isadora Duncan loved hers. But they did not all permit the blow to destroy their spiritual being.[9]

"Genius of flesh and blood, human superhuman, may Olympus greet you!" With these words, Yvette Guilbert, who appreciated her genius, sympathized with her aspiration, and understood her tragedy, hailed the liberation of Isadora Duncan from the prison of the flesh. But Isadora herself had a certain clear-sightedness despite all her vagaries; she should be allowed to pronounce her own valedictory:

> No one has understood since I lost Deirdre and Patrick how pain has caused me at times to live in almost a delirium. In fact my poor brain has more often been crazed than anyone can know. . . . I have reached

[9] "All the bare-legged girls," writes Max Eastman, "the sun-tanned, assured, and natural girls with strong free steps wherever they go, owe more to Isadora Duncan than to any other person. And the boys that are unafraid of such girls and unafraid of their own instincts—all who have escaped in any degree from the rigidity and prissiness of our once national religion of negation—owe a debt to Isadora's dancing." In a world in which every girl and young woman is free to go bare-legged wherever she may choose, it is difficult to understand the consternation which Isadora awakened when she began to dance in her bare feet, with bare legs, and I think there is much in what Eastman says; from this point of view, Isadora Duncan may well have had a larger influence upon life than she ever exercised on art. Yet judging by the shock which greeted Marilyn Monroe, when she emerged in the fifties, one would be tempted to believe that Duncan had exercised no influence whatever.

By the time Marilyn arrived, it is true, pin-up girls had lost their daring; her special appeal was due to her own personality, and not to her doing something different from what others were doing. Isadora would not have approved of pin-up girls as such; she might even have been sincerely shocked by them. On the other hand, Marilyn was never, like her predecessor, a sensual or dissolute woman; neither did her life give occasion for scandal. She was self-disciplined, financially responsible, and dependent upon her own resources; whatever problems she may have had, they were certainly not occasioned by self-indulgence. As an artist, she had less vision than Isadora; as a woman, she had incomparably more decency and common sense. Instead of conceiving wild-eyed theories and then trying to match her life to the theories, she submitted herself to experience itself, in the age-old way of woman, and proceeded to make the best she could of the materials which life brought her.

such high peaks flooded with light, but my soul had no strength to live there—and no one has realized the horrible torture from which I have tried to escape. Some day if you understand sorrow you will understand too all I have lived through, and then you will only think of the light towards which I have pointed and you will know the *real* Isadora is there.

· VI ·

The World and

MARY GARDEN

Who is 't can read a woman?

WILLIAM SHAKESPEARE, *Cymbeline*

Lo, whiche sleightes and subtiltees
In wommen been! for ay as bisy as bees
Ben they, us sely men for to deceyve.

GEOFFREY CHAUCER

[Maeterlinck] is devoted to his camera. The last time I saw him, he said to me: "Come into my dark room. I want to photograph your soul."

He was entirely in earnest, and a lock of white hair like a secretive curtain hung over his left eye. I shook my head at him.

"I should say not. Everything about me the world seems to own. That is the only thing that belongs to me and I can't let it go on a plate."

MARY GARDEN, 1930

1 *Mary Garden*

JENNY LIND had P. T. Barnum to create a public image for her. Mary Garden needed no Barnum; she was abundantly capable of doing the job on her own. Like Bernard Shaw, like Sarah Bernhardt, like Barnum himself, she understood the value of publicity and used it for everything there was in it. The mere sight of a reporter seemed to stimulate her. For a quarter of a century and more, she regaled Chicago, and the nation, with many wild tales. She was in love with Lindbergh, or Gene Tunney, or William S. Hart, or Al Smith, or the Prince of Wales (she changed pretty often), or she had discovered some marvelous pink pills by means of which she had regained the figure of her youth, or she had taken up sun-bathing in the Mediterranean, or she had become a convert to Émile Coué and his autosuggestion, or she considered prohibition the best thing that ever happened to the United States, though as for herself, perhaps some kind soul would give her a nice cold drink of champagne now and then, or she thought Madame Jeritza a fool because she hadn't bobbed her hair, or almost anything else you can think of. Has there been a single fad in all these years that Mary Garden has not sometime sponsored? Has there been even one star to which her wagon has gone unhitched?

She has made many an exhibition of prima donna petulance, often paraded hurt pride or wounded vanity. In her late autobiography, she describes with obvious self-satisfaction how she blocked Lina Cavalieri from singing Thaïs for Oscar Hammerstein in New York many years before. (She even goes on to tell how she attended Cavalieri's debut in *Carmen,* "and my, it was awful!" though she adds that in *Tales of Hoffman* the singer was radiant, "full of diamonds and beauty.") She has aired her prejudices. At times, despite her intelligence, she has descended to rank banality. So she has perhaps impressed you as a frivolous, undisciplined, terribly spoiled woman, who has used her gift to buy exemption from the sensible, serious things of life, as you, I, and the readers of newspapers know them, and who sails along outrageously, knocking her head against the stars.

Why did Miss Garden build up such a picture of herself in the public mind? Partly, no doubt, because she knew that she was living in a world in which most persons were comparatively indifferent to art but tremendously interested in absurdity. Many great artists with really great gifts never come into their own because, with all their ability, they have never learned how to dramatize themselves. She had no intention of remaining in obscurity. Moreover, she had something new to offer, something that she believed in with all the fervor of an evangelist. Her material was unique; her method was unique; she was the creator, the exemplar of a new school. Her art was more exotic, more intellectual, more limited in its appeal than that of the Melbas, the Tetrazzinis, and the Galli-Curcis. Coloratura *Traviata* trills were not for her, though she had produced them often enough in Paris. Take Strauss's *Salomé,* for example. *Salomé* was something new under the sun, a work of genius, representing a great step forward in the creation of a vital music-drama. Perhaps the public would not come to *Salomé* on that account alone? Perhaps the public is indifferent to such considerations? Very well, then. There are some things to which the public is not indifferent. There are some things for which the public will come. Sin, for example. So we must have mysterious whispers of dreadful naughtiness and startling disclosures in the Dance of the Seven Veils which neither Mary Garden nor anybody else ever had any idea of making. Crazy Mary Garden! Yes! Crazy like a fox!

Of course that is not all. To explain the motives of a great woman artist is inevitably to falsify them, translating them into masculine, analytical terms. With her all was feminine, intuitive. She has temperament, great stores of nervous energy often overlooked by those who were bewildered by her. Even during her last very successful lecture tours of America in her seventies, she fairly sparkled with the zest of life. "Please God," she once prayed, "I shall never be a cynic." I can think of nobody who is in less danger.

When she had ensnared her captive, when he came to the opera house on a Mary Garden night, came to see the phenomenon—what then? She had made it difficult for him in all conscience. Especially if he found her in one of her more serious roles, he had much to unlearn before he could even begin to understand what she was doing. For there were many Mary Gardens. He had been attracted by Mary Garden the press agent. He had encountered Mary Garden the artist.

II

Mary Garden was born in Aberdeen, Scotland. The official date is February 20, 1877, though there are those who would place it three years earlier. As a very small child she came with her parents to the United States, finally settling in Chicago, where her musical education began. She sang in church choirs. She appeared as Angelica in an amateur production of Gilbert and Sullivan's *Trial by Jury* on the South Side. Toward the end of the century, she went to Paris to study for an operatic career. She tried many famous teachers, rejecting each in obedience to an inner prompting which told her, she knew not how, that this one was not for her. One of the most famous of all, Mathilde Marchesi, could not have failed her more completely if she had been a teacher of engineering rather than singing. When her patroness, senselessly crediting ridiculous stories about her, suddenly cut off her means of support, she faced real want. But Trabadello and Lucien Fugère stood by her, and Sybil Sanderson generously took her into her home and introduced her to Albert Carré, director of the Opéra-Comique.

Carré employed her as a kind of hanger-on about the theater and told her to study the role of Louise. One night in 1900, according to the accepted story, Marthe Rioton broke down in the middle of a performance. Garden went on before a hostile audience, with a conductor distinctly unfriendly to the musical aspirations of American girls; after the final curtain, the audience went wild with enthusiasm, the composer cried, "Brave, Mademoiselle Gardenne!" and the orchestra stood to honor her.

She sang *Louise* at the Comique between two and three hundred times. She sang *Thaïs, Aphrodite, Chérubin, La Reine Fiammette, Pelléas et Mélisande*, and other operas. In 1907 Oscar Hammerstein brought her to the Manhattan in New York, where she introduced modern French opera and fought a bitter fight to establish a new type of art in a city still largely committed to the thesis that the mad scene in *Lucia* represented the pinnacle of operatic glory. Three years later she came to Chicago, perilously introducing herself to her home city as Mélisande. Until 1931 she was the most conspicuous member of the Chicago Opera Company under its various names (she had functioned as general manager in 1921–22); then she decided she had had enough and left the city without bothering to tell anybody that she had retired. She sang a while longer in Europe, and when Riviera society began to move around cocktail parties, which she loathes, she removed herself to Aberdeen. After her retirement from singing, she made two American lecture tours and also acted as a talent scout for both Metro-Goldwyn-Mayer and the National Arts Foundation.

Miss Garden's operatic repertoire was largely, though not exclusively, confined to the works of the modern French school. Sometimes she sang German and Italian operas—*Salomé, Tosca, Resurrection*—in the French language. Though the wits have often twitted her about speaking French with a Chicago accent, I should say that the spirit of her art was decidedly a French spirit. Yet she can hardly be called narrow in her artistic sympathies. In *Faust*, old-fashioned as it is, she finds "a human story that can never grow old and music that will live when many modern works have been forgotten." That she should speak of her Parisian performances of *La Traviata* as among her most cherished memories will surprise nobody who knows her brilliant old Columbia recordings of *Ah! fors e lui* and *Sempra libera*. She never cared for opera in English, but when Victor Herbert's *Natoma* came along, she gave her best to the creation of the title role. Among singers she has responded enthusiastically to artists as unlike herself as Destinn, Fremstad, and Ternina. She speaks of Mozart's "heaven-kissed melodies," and as for Wagner, "sometimes I have been so Wagner-hungry that I have not known what to do." When she was a busy prima donna at the height of her career, she decided that she knew too little of Wagner and the Russian composers, whereupon she had a phonograph installed in her Chicago quarters and proceeded to buy all the records she could find.

In any case, Mary Garden has been less interested in the opera of a particular country than in that of a particular method, period, or point of view. Operatic artists themselves she divides into two classes—the singers and the creators—and she was fond of lamenting that America worshiping the Golden Calf must at the same time worship the Golden Voice. It would be difficult to sum up the difference between the old school and the new more effectively than she did it:

> Today we see the beginning of the great modern school, the music which deals with and carries to the hearts of its audiences great human truths. This modern music aims not wholly at the senses, but also at the mind. It does not aim merely at producing a vehicle for the production of glorious tones. It goes deeper than tone. It strives for a musical interpretation of the impulses and motives of the human mind and heart and soul. It represents not persons, but passions.

This possibility was what she found in *Louise,* in *Thaïs,* and in *Pelléas et Mélisande.* To this she dedicated herself, and on it she staked her career. Not that she always felt she had ideal material. Even Massenet seemed to her "one of those passive musicians who sacrificed conscience to the inflection of popular theatricalism." With great honesty she wrote on the eve of her American debut that the opera *Thaïs,* in which she proposed to introduce herself to New York, did not represent the new school at its best. "Other, greater operas would be too difficult for the public now." Massenet's *Cléopâtre* she bluntly calls a poor opera. Always it was the developments of the future upon which her eyes were fixed.

Once she caught the future and held it in her hands, and this was when she was called upon to evoke the soul of Mélisande. Here was a great stage in her development. "To be an originator and not merely a repeater of the ideas and achievements of someone else is . . . the highest goal of every artist." There was an unearthly beauty about her Mélisande that I have never seen duplicated in kind: she was like a remembered vision of a medieval dream-world. "We worked and doubted and labored together. Every one of us was something bigger than ourselves—part of an immense dedication. Something was being preserved here and we were needed for it." Surely, even if she had never done anything else, she would still deserve to be remembered as one of the great artists of her time.

Yet she could be equally creative with much less splendid material. Pitts Sanborn thought her Monna Vanna even greater than her Mélisande. I cannot speak to this point myself, for I never saw her as Monna Vanna, but Sanborn's description well reveals the quality which made a Garden performance such an unforgettable experience:

> It has been said in Boston that Miss Garden's conception of the second act contradicts her conception of the first. This contention seems absolutely to miss the point of Monna Vanna's character. In the tent Miss Garden makes her, with the exchange of memories, the girl she has in fact always remained. Her spontaneity is wholly natural. Her kiss is no betrayal, no adulterous sharing, because it comes partly from pure gratitude and partly from a kind of love which, so far as her own experience teaches her, is not wifely.
>
> The way she subdues her shudder at the contact when Prinzivalle first touches her, her humble willingness to go to the couch, her trance-like, anaesthetized willingness for anything that she must suffer and respond to, and then the release and the childlike abandonment to the good she finds and to the old playmate who for her becomes at once what he used to be, all these are portrayed with a sureness and finesse rarely seen on the stage. Her *"Tu n'es pas revenu"* is something never to be forgotten.
>
> Pictorially, in her flaming robe and filmy blue veil, the Monna Vanna of the second act suggested a type into which the Judith of Holofernes fame was developed in the art of the Renaissance. There is the same suggestion of stealth—as in the wonderful sidewise advance of the entrance —and of self-sacrificial beauty of the flesh.

III

In all this, how much of music? I have no intention of reviving the tiresome old discussion of whether Mary Garden was a singer or only a "singing actress." If any pioneer ever suffered from the brutal stupidities of criticism it was she, nor has the myopia of the academicians ever done them a greater disservice than when it led them to disregard the unified perfections of the various portraits that she has limned. The music-drama is an expression of life, and singing and acting are component, complementary parts of it. Carl Van Vechten was perfectly just when he pointed out that Miss Garden did much of her finest acting with her voice.

She did not work from score. When she was preparing a new role, she would have the opera played for her; she listened and tried to follow the notation. "After a few repetitions, the rhythm of the part gets under my skin; the whole thing passes into some white-hot moment of illumination, and before I am aware of it, through some occult instinct, the whole composition is mine—accurately placed, understood, fixed in mind." This is a highly individual, perhaps eccentric, method. It could hardly be taught or widely communicated. But he who thinks it shows that she is not "musical" does not understand the English language. She herself has always found the spoken drama inadequate because here the music is missing; she needs the background and the stimulus of music to create and to communicate a mood. Indeed she goes so far as to say, "Poetry alone has never touched me, except to make me restless and nervous." For this reason, no doubt, the legitimate stage has never tempted her; probably it was on this account too that her films proved so disappointing.

She herself is of the opinion that the character of her voice depended upon what she was singing.

It was a brilliant voice and it cut through an orchestra like steel. It was both big and piercing. I did what I liked with my voice; I was always its master and never its slave. It obeyed me, and not I it. And I used it as freely as a painter uses his brush. But, then, I never thought of my voice as distinct from the rest of me. It was never a thing apart. My voice, my acting, my whole personality were one.

She even thought that the opera singer must be master of silence as well as sound. "I've had more power over an audience with a silence than I ever had with a note. That's where I would look if I went into an opera house hunting for a genius—I would look into their silences."

When Oscar Hammerstein brought her to New York in 1907, the New York critics at first said of her substantially that though she was a great artist, she could not sing. James Gordon Bennett gave her a page of the *Herald* to reply to them, and the onslaught made musical history. She has never since retreated substantially from the position she took up then:

> I have sung *Louise* between two and three hundred times, and I should like to go on record now as saying that you have to know a little bit about singing to do that—and survive it; you have got to possess the voice fundamentals. I doubt very much if Melba could sing *Louise* two hundred and fifty times and save her vocal cords in their incomparable perfection. I doubt if God made her throat strong enough.

In contrast to such confident pronouncements, it is interesting to catch her off guard occasionally, as when she remarks that she would like to try the old Italian roles, believing that she could infuse human reality even in them, except that here the public demands "the very high notes, the perfect coloratura."

Like Julia Marlowe, and unlike Sarah Bernhardt and Ellen Terry, Mary Garden was blessedly free of stage fright. Even that first night of *Louise* in Paris, she knew no fear. "I never leaned on anything but my own backbone, and that stood so upright it never bent." When Samuel Goldwyn approached her about motion pictures, he found "not one moment's doubt on her part that she could do pictures. Her only misgiving, frankly revealed, was that I might not pay her enough to justify her in making them."[1] She resented it when reporters came

[1] *Behind the Screen* (Doran, 1923), Chapter X.

to her more interested in her sun-bathing in the Mediterranean than in "how splendidly I had sung the season before at the Opéra-Comique." And she speaks of her grandmother, who "bore somewhere about her body the accent of genius," and whose reading of poetry revealed flair and style. "I have often wondered just how much of her I appropriated."

But along with this self-confidence, there went, again as with Julia Marlowe, a tremendous capacity for work. In the early days in Paris, she rehearsed months on end in a single opera, under the very nose of the composer. Work on *Pelléas et Mélisande* continued every afternoon except Sunday for four months, including forty orchestral rehearsals! In preparing her roles Miss Garden left no stone unturned, but she always remembered that intelligence was more important than industry. When she was working on *Thaïs* she wasted no time on Anatole France's novel, for she realized that the psychology of the woman in the opera was not that of the woman in the book. Instead, she read her way diligently into the history of the time, using materials quite unconnected with either the opera or the story. In *Salomé* she was the first singer to undertake the Dance of the Seven Veils, which—climax of the opera though it is—had hitherto been entrusted to a professional dancer.

Nobody who has seen Miss Garden on the stage needs my testimony to her ability to evoke atmosphere and period. Carl Van Vechten remarks that having seen her as Mélisande, as Fiora, and as Monna Vanna, one is tempted to conclude that "she is at her best in parts of the middle ages, until one reflects that in early Greek courtesans, in French cocottes of several periods, in American Indians, and Spanish gipsies she is equally atmospheric." But as an illustration of how thoroughly she could enter into the character she was portraying—and of what it cost her to do it—a single reference may not be out of place. When she came off the stage after the last act of *Louise*—so she declared—she was a physical wreck, her emotions strained to the breaking point, her face covered with tiny wrinkles. *Thaïs* had no such effect upon her, for *Thaïs* was a professional courtesan who knew that her face was her fortune and therefore controlled it, while Louise was only a poor working girl and not so clever! What she felt she expressed. "It was foolish of her, I know; but I can't prevent it." Indeed the singer even insisted that when she played Mélisande she really died, but she died as Mélisande, not as Mary Garden.

Seeking to define her appeal in the theater, one immediately runs into paradox. It was characteristic of her work that one should always be conscious of the controlling intelligence behind it. "She is a 'cérébrale,' " wrote her great admirer James Huneker, "and a cerebral is defined by Arthur Symons as one who feels with the head and thinks with the heart." It is here that the oft-cited comparisons between Mary Garden and her chief contemporary rival in the business of humanizing and electrifying opera in America, Geraldine Farrar, begin to have some point. I should say that the difference between Farrar and Garden was the difference between Berlin and Paris, or between Boston and Chicago; to put it differently, I should say that it was like the difference between painting and sculpture. Miss Garden reaches the heart through the mind. You are moved by the sheer beauty of the thing that she has created; it stands before you like a perfectly chiseled piece of marble. This I have felt in every role I ever heard her sing, but only once—as Mélisande—did she make a direct emotional appeal. Now this is the one thing that Miss Farrar never failed to do—on the operatic stage, on the concert platform, in her films, even (I must insist) in her records. Of course this does not mean that Miss Farrar is less intelligent than Miss Garden. It certainly does not mean that she was less beautiful. It does mean that she had an emotional directness which Miss Garden lacked. In comparison, Garden was an exotic, a hothouse flower; Chicago might call her "Our Mary," but you can hardly think of her being called "Gerry" whatever her name might have been. Hence, on the one hand, the unutterable poesy of her Mélisande; hence, too, her scarlet ladies of sin. Farrar scorned Mélisande: "I cannot say that I am much in sympathy with the vague outlines of the modern French lyric heroines: Mélisande and Ariane I think can be better entrusted to artists of a less positive type." Yet she had a role which was to her in a way what Mélisande was to Mary Garden; this was the Goose Girl in *Die Königskinder*.

With what exquisite charm Miss Farrar was likely to invest so romantic a heroine [wrote Henry Edward Krehbiel], the artist's admirers might easily have guessed; but it is doubtful if any imagination ever reached the figure she bodied forth. She was a vision of tender loveliness, as perfect in poetical conception as in execution. Memories of the picture which she presented walking through the massive town-gates followed and surrounded by her white flock will die only with the generation that witnessed it.

The tone is very different from that of Pitts Sanborn's description of Garden's Monna Vanna; is it not? Surely the Goose Girl is as poetic as Mélisande and as exalted, but it is both in a somewhat different way. There is a touch of homeliness in its poetry and more than a touch of morality. It lies closer to the center of our emotional life. Farrar, again, had her scarlet ladies, but here again she differed from Garden. Far more brutal in her realism at times, she was never decadent. No matter how bad the woman she was portraying might be, the singer never forgot her essential humanity, and one can hardly imagine her writing of any of her roles what Garden wrote of her Salomé: "Everything was glorious and nude and suggestive, but not coarse." Nor can one imagine an admirer describing any of her work in the terms which Huneker chose to apply to Miss Garden: "The Infernal Feminine. A vase exquisitely carved containing corruption. Sculptured slime." Which is more important in these differences—the personalities of the two women or the respective materials which they employed? (In some cases, the materials were the same.) Can it be that we are, in any sense, under the spell of the somewhat flamboyant newspaper portrait which Miss Garden created of herself? Or was her expression of emotion merely too Gallic to touch us directly?

One explanation must be instantly rejected, and this is that Miss Garden did not herself feel emotion and that she did not wish to communicate it to us. In life she does not strike me as a highly emotional person, but she has always been more than commonly susceptible to the expression of emotion in art. When Debussy first played *Pelléas et Mélisande* for her, she sobbed like a child. "When I began to study it, it was weeks before I could sing it with dry eyes. Even today there are little phrases in it that, when I sing them, make the tears come." And even in *Faust,* she tells us, she is often so overcome at the death of Valentine that she fears the control of the effect will pass beyond her.

A new form of art is, of course, always likely to take on a touch of exoticism. It demands a certain background, a certain intelligence, and the problems involved in presenting it are not lessened when it has to be presented to a public which has been seriously debauched by the meretricious. But Miss Garden never aimed at the exotic for exoticism's sake, and there is plenty of evidence to show that she has a heart. She used to say that if she was ever tempted to do less than her best at a performance, she only needed to remind herself that there was somebody in the audience who had made a real sacrifice to come and hear her.

> We cannot hope for the highest and best until the so-called common people have had their art sense awakened; until we have a jury of the whole, which shall decide what is good and what is bad; what we will and what we will not accept. Give me the approval of the masses and I can survive without the aristocracy or the critics.

Elsewhere she expresses it more mystically: "All who love music are brothers and sisters to me."

IV

Mary Garden the showman. Mary Garden the artist. There is yet another Mary Garden: Mary Garden the woman.

It was once remarked of Mary Austin that she was not merely a great woman but a great person who happened to be a woman. This is all very well so long as we do not allow it to cause us to forget that women can never achieve greatness by repudiating their sex. Certainly Mary Austin never did this, nor did Mary Garden.

Consciously, deliberately, she places herself on the common human level. "Why is it you find Mary Garden exciting? If you only knew it, any woman in a truthful mood would be equally as interesting." She claims no exemption from the cares of other women. "I have had many sorrows and disappointments in my life—intimate things, such as your sorrows and disappointments have been." Great prima donna though she was, she did not pretend to possess any sources of comfort that were not available to other women also. "I try to keep my mind forever off the things I have longed for and could not have, and on the few people whom I care for, who care for me."

Of the common interests of womankind, the greatest, the most impelling, the one about which she has talked most and on which she has been listened to most eagerly is love. She is quite clear on the importance for women of their contacts with men. "The hidden springs of a woman's character are moulded by her contacts with men. This influence commences early in childhood. Sometimes the hand that does it is a brother—or a father—or a relative, but always a man." She herself had a wise, understanding father, but she had no brothers; what she learned of the youthful male she had to gather entirely on the outside.

Marriage she early rejected, having made up her mind that it was incompatible with a great career. One woman could not be equal to both, and it was unthinkable that one could permit one's children to be brought up by strangers. Yet she tells a good many anecdotes about her love affairs. There was the teacher of whom she was desperately enamored in the early days, and "although I was in perfect health, I managed to faint dead away at his feet one day in the hope that he would take me in his arms." But alas! he never did. There was the ardent Russian prince who once, as his motorcar lurched suddenly, lay sprawling ridiculously at her feet, thus destroying any spell that he might have had for her, and whom she never saw again. There was the Parisian of noble family whom she ran away from because he loved her so much that he threatened to kill her, and who lived out his life alone in Paris, believing that some day she would come to him. And of course there were men like Oscar Hammerstein and Clarence Mackay, with whom she enjoyed an association which was not amatory in any sense but which had much nourishing food for the mind and the spirit in it.

But if marriage is not for the great artist, the great artist is still a woman with a woman's needs. Mary Garden is full of passionate protest against the wrongs of womankind, and she makes without qualification the statement that she does not believe men capable of genuine fidelity, but she is somewhat vague when it comes to suggesting remedies about any of these things. Once at least she suggested that there was a special law for women of genius. "There has always been a *lex femina* for them. . . . Each one possesses some powerfully adequate means of inducing the world to accept them on their own terms. The George Sands, the Ellen Terrys, the Sarah Bernhardts have never forfeited the respect of it by the courageous phrasing they have put on love."

And Mary Garden? She does not actually tell us. When *Mary Garden's Story* was about to be published, there was a good deal of rather distasteful publicity according to which Miss Garden was about to tell "all." These hopes were not destined to be fulfilled, and as soon as the book was available it became perfectly clear to everybody that Miss Garden had, in the Isadora Duncan sense, very little to tell, and that even if she had had, she would have been too much a lady to tell it. Smile as much as you like at such naïve statements as "Nobody with a brain like mine can ever do that"; "Most of my beautiful jewels are in Scotland, and most of them were gifts from my many admirers"; and (above all) "I sometimes think I am really a very spiritual person." Spiritual or not, there can be no doubt that she *is* a very highly disciplined person. The passion for possessions has never had much power over her. She eats as little as a human being can eat and stay alive, and nothing else bores her so much as a long sitting at table.

After her performances she drinks milk. She claims to have tasted cocktails only once in her life, when she was immediately prostrated with alcoholic poisoning. There are passages in her autobiography in which she seems to wish to convey the idea that she was completely a virginal spirit, incapable of real passion, and she thanks God that she was made so that no vice ever tempted her. "As I often said to Mother, 'Nobody will ever believe what my private life was really like.' "[2] It is interesting that the year she was director of the Chicago Civic Opera Company, she never had any trouble with another prima donna; all her troubles were with the men. But though she is unequivocally clear that she never had any kind of an affair with Debussy, she seems to me somewhat vague about her relations with André Messager, Albert Carré, and the one man she thinks she might have married if conditions had been different.

v

The artist, the woman—is there still another Mary Garden? James Huneker wrote: "In the kingdom of the mystics there are many mansions, and Garden lives in one—at times." Yes—with Mélisande and with Jean, *"le jongleur de Notre Dame."*

Miss Garden rejects "luck" and "fate" as the excuses of the lazy and

[2] This view is supported by Merle Armitage, who managed Miss Garden's "concerts and tours over a span of years" and had "countless hours of conversation with her." "For Mary Garden, far from being an audacious, promiscuous, and morally unregenerate wanton, as thousands believed, was actually one female who succeeded in sublimating every sex urge and instinct into her performances, plus arduous rehearsals, and other high tension functions endured by a world celebrated prima donna." Again he writes: "Despite the fact that she was critical of all vice to the point of being provincial in her manifest attitude, she certainly was intrigued with the subject to an amazing and naïve degree. Any 'affairs' which I was able to relate, any so-called perversion of which I had a scant knowledge, even the most ordinary amatory experience, would be received with absorbing attention, and requests for more. Her questions, demanding details, were often embarrassing, until I realized with some astonishment that this sophisticated woman was actually as ignorant of most facts of life as a little girl." See Armitage's very sympathetic portrait of Miss Garden in his *Accent on America* (New York, E. Weyhe, 1944).

the incompetent, but she has always retained her faith in intuition. "Life is like leaves; blown by winds—not by chance, but all with a premeditated plan and purpose. You wonder what the plan is, but it is there. I am as certain of it as I am of the air that gives me life." In this confidence she has always looked forward, not backward: the best of life is yet to be. "As a child my mother taught me about God, and the simple teachings of the Christian faith. For that I am glad. I think it a criminal thing for a mother to bring up children without religion. That rudder is necessary in life."

In her eyes, "the only enduring work of the race is done by the artists, and the only real morality is that of accomplishment, of work and achievement." The artist must discard "set ideas, inflexible morals and fixed formulas for life." Unconventionality is simply another name for creative behavior, stepping out of the old grooves, refusing to be driven with the herd. Of course, "no one obtains freedom by breaking a good law—you only become a fool." The casino at Monte Carlo means unconventionality to most people. "This? What a farce! Why this is only a madness!" Yet she lived for a long time at Monte Carlo, finding stimulus, rejuvenation in what Katherine Mansfield saw as the very image of hell, and sometimes she even consented to participate in its life, mad as it is. Even then, one may be sure, the pilot light never ceased to burn. "I've seen so many fine careers snared and caged and laid low by desires; they are insidious things, and danger-ous. . . . Watch them, seize them, bind them, strap them down with iron clamps."

There is a paradox here, but in some form the paradox is inescap-able by any who seek to live in this world without being wholly con-formed to it. Mary Garden's explanation of the conversion of Thaïs as symbolizing everywoman's fear of age is almost shockingly worldly and unspiritual. "Thaïs . . . succumbs to the fear, and finds peace only by retiring from the world. Another woman—perhaps most women today—would subdue the fear and conquer the future." And when an interviewer asked her whether she might someday emulate La Vallière and end her days in a convent, she was emphatic in her denial.

"No. That would be beautiful, but not for me.... What I shall do, I do not know, but it will be something to surprise the world." Yet it is clear that the conflict between human conduct and human aspirations has often troubled her. It troubled her in Debussy, for example. There was never any question in her mind that his treatment of his first wife was profoundly wrong, and she suffered with Lily in her suffering and for him that he should have degraded himself. To explain such things to herself and make it possible for her to accept them, she sometimes committed herself to what might be called a kind of refined Gnosticism:

> The gift at no time comes into conflict with the tenement of flesh known as the body. That is preserved inviolate by another power, outside of itself. What that body does—how it acts—its pettiness—its meannesses— its desires—its passionate hungers—destroys nothing but itself. It cannot touch the flame, the life, the torch, because, you see, that is part of God itself.

There is a sense in which all this is true; there is even a sense in which it may be taken as the expression of a noble, unconquerable idealism. But its dangers are obvious, and Miss Garden can hardly be said to have lived by the sentiments here enunciated. In her heart she knew that in this life the gift and the body are very closely connected. That is one reason why she guarded her body as she did.

The essence of her religion and her morality was connected with her basic conviction that there were two kinds of people in the world —the builders and the destroyers. "Destroy with deliberation, and nothing about you will survive—not your beauty, your success, your health, your charm, your position. This is one of the inexorable laws you and I live under." For her the unpardonable sin is "putting pain in the world." Once she met the test in her own life. There was Mr. X, a great soul, unawakened. Through her he came to know himself. Through her he entered into music, art, literature. Through her he came to understand what friendship means.

But there are certain barriers in life you cannot cross. You cannot build on the pain of others and survive yourself. It was a tragedy in his life that he was not free, and it was my tragedy that my nature would not consent to him freeing himself. . . . So the division in our friendship came irrevocably and finally, and when you have sacrificed something that was as close as your breathing—more than your career, more than your gift, more than anything this stunning universe makes an offering of— when you have done this you will find yourself mentally sitting framed among the astonished stars and nothing shall by any means hurt you.[3]

But whatever may be said of any of these matters, one thing—and this is the important thing—is abundantly clear: the real passion of Mary Garden's life went into her art. She knew what it meant to be a great artist, she knew what it costs, and she gladly paid the price. She achieved "complete obliteration of self" that the character she had created might live, and while she was on the stage the role completely absorbed her. "I was never myself on the stage," she says, "except, in a certain sense, in *Louise*." Again and again she expressed emotions which she had never felt as a woman. "I never felt the lust of Salomé in my life. And I was never drunk, yet there was Katusha in Alfano's *Resurrection,* hiding her bottles in her prison bed and getting drunk on vodka. At that moment I *was* drunk." She is a small woman—only five foot, four—yet her Thaïs was tall because she thought her tall and used immense gestures, and the audience saw what was in her mind, as the audience always does with a great stage artist. She herself did not think of the audience. "The audience never existed for me till the curtain was down and the spell was off." But her understanding of the woman whose embodiment she took upon herself always came in the last analysis from within. She had no patience with singers who cannot play a death scene until they have seen somebody die. "Why don't these singers have the imagination to see it

[3] In her autobiography, Chapter XIII, Miss Garden gives a somewhat different account of this matter, indicating that this man had shortcomings which would have made it impossible for her to accept him even if he had been free. Readers of Arthur Meeker's not always discreet memoirs, *Chicago, With Love* (Knopf, 1955), cannot help wondering whether J. Ogden Armour was not the man in question, but I cannot of my own knowledge make the identification.

themselves?" Whatever mystification Miss Garden may have created in the course of her career, and however the world may have enthralled her, I am sure she is telling the literal truth, or coming as close to it as one can in addressing the uninitiated, when she tells us that her work "drained off so much of me that by comparison my private life was empty." "The others 'acted' a role," she says again: "I *was* the role. She who was Mary Garden died that it might live. That was my genius ... and my sacrifice." And surely this is a spiritual as well as an artistic triumph.

· VII ·

MARILYN MONROE

Rosemary

for Remembrance

Thou wert the morning star among the living,
  Ere thy fair light had fled;
Now, having died, thou art as Hesperus, giving
  New splendour to the dead.

PLATO-SHELLEY

Once in a while one meets with a single soul greater than all the living pageant which passes before it.

OLIVER WENDELL HOLMES,
The Autocrat of the Breakfast-Table

Why should a dog, a horse, a rat have life,
And thou no breath at all?

WILLIAM SHAKESPEARE, *King Lear*

A rosemary odor,
  Commingled with pansies—
With rue and the beautiful
  Puritan pansies.

EDGAR ALLAN POE

The last night that she lived,
It was a common night,
Except the dying; this to us
Made nature different.

EMILY DICKINSON

But those fine spirits which do tune and set
This organ, are those pieces which beget
Wonder and love; and these were she; and she
Being spent, the world must needs decrepit be.

JOHN DONNE

1 *Marilyn Monroe*

In the year 1962 there were two very exciting Sunday mornings. The second of these was a happy day. This was the Sunday in October when word came over the air that Chairman Khrushchev had committed himself to a course which seemed to promise a peaceful settlement of the Cuban crisis. But the first Sunday in August was all desolation, for that was the day we learned that Marilyn Monroe had been found dead in bed at her Brentwood home from an overdose of sleeping medicine.

I have juxtaposed these two wholly dissimilar events for a definite purpose. We live in an age when we have been so sated with mass murder and destruction that private calamity has almost lost its ancient power to move us. We open the newspaper or switch on the radio trembling lest we should learn that some fool has undertaken an enterprise calculated to menace all our lives and the civilization in which we live, and if what we hear of is only small-scale disaster—slaughter on the highways or an explosion taking, say, a score of lives—we breathe a sigh of relief. It is a sign of the moral deterioration which mankind has suffered during our lifetime that this should be the case, for we can all remember when such headlines would have robbed us of our sleep. Industry talks of "hands," and the state prates of "man power." When we ride in a Pullman car we become "this space." To be sure, the state also makes elaborate plans for our "welfare" and "insures" our future in a manner we never dreamed of when we were young. But somehow these plans seem curiously unrelated to us as individuals, and when we come across Cardinal Newman's statement that it would be better for the world to be destroyed than for one soul to sin, we seem to be listening to a voice from a world so alien to our own that we can only with difficulty make out what it is saying.

The death of Marilyn Monroe was the exception to all this. Many distinguished persons died in 1962, but I can think of none whose passing caused quite such sorrow in kind. The death of the young is always bitter because one cannot but feel that they have been cheated out of what life promised them, and that, deprived themselves, they have also deprived us of what they might have continued to give us down the years. Then, too, Marilyn was very beautiful, and brightness falls from the skies when beauty dies. So *Life* cried out that "her death has diminished the loveliness of the world in which we live," and the editors of *Vogue* found the "waste" by which they were confronted "almost unbearable." "I think my response to her death was the common one," wrote Diana Trilling: "it came to me with the impact of a personal deprivation but I also felt it as I might a catastrophe in history or in nature; there was less in life, there was less of life, because she had ceased to exist. In her loss life itself had been injured." It was interesting, too, that though Miss Monroe was an American, her press coverage should have been even more impressive in Europe than it was here. Every important European picture magazine gave her a feature and a cover; where *Life*'s memorial issue devoted eleven pages to her, *Paris Match* gave thirty-six to *"la plus grande star du monde."*[1]

Movie careers are proverbially short, and most stars long outlive them. It is very unusual for a great star to die on the heights. To find anything approximating Marilyn's death I think you would have to go back to the death of Rudolph Valentino in 1926. And 1926 was the year Marilyn was born.

But this was only the public tribute. The private tribute was far more impressive, and of course it cannot be charted. How many tears were shed, how many prayers murmured nobody will ever know. We can only guess from how we felt ourselves and what we heard from our friends. Myself, I kept finding evidences of grief for months, in the most unexpected places, and among people whom I should have thought the unlikeliest Monroe fans possible. And all this was the more remarkable because Miss Monroe was generally thought of as

[1] *Life* (August 17, 1962); *Vogue* (September 1, 1962); *Paris Match* (August 18, 1962).

having functioned during the film star's *Götterdämmerung*, and few persons believe that either the movies or the people who appear in them were anything like so important in the emotional life of the American people in 1962 as they had been in 1926.

It was not Valentino's fault that his funeral was a macabre circus or that women who had never seen him off the screen made a mawkish spectacle of themselves to dramatize their grief over his passing. But all this was in harmony with the mood of the time. Thanks to the good taste of Marilyn's former husband Joe Di Maggio, she was interred with simple, quiet dignity in the presence of only a few close friends (the sister of the President of the United States crossed the continent to attend the service—and was refused admission), after a ceremony that was in harmony with what she was rather than what many ill-informed persons mistakenly believed her to be. What was more surprising was that Di Maggio's good taste should have rubbed off on the public to the extent that it did. Marilyn's death caused easily as much grief as Valentino's, but the people who expressed it were in general easier to respect than those who demonstrated over him, and the "mob" that the police were prepared to "handle" on the day of her funeral did not materialize at all, for the people who came to stand quietly outside the church to watch and to wait were simple, sad, quiet people who obviously had no thought in mind of any emotional orgies but had come instead to pay a sincere last tribute of respect to a girl whose beauty of face and figure and whose sweetness of spirit had brightened the world for them and whom they had loved. All this, I think, was heartening not only to those who care for films but even more to those who care for human values. It showed that a motion-picture actress can still be important to the world, and it showed too that we have not yet become collectivized to such an extent that personality has wholly lost its power to move us.

Of course there were other reactions also. From the Vatican to the Kremlin Marilyn's poor corpse was used as a stick to beat Hollywood with, though since she herself had, from time to time, said everything that can legitimately be said against that community, much of this seemed without point.[2] And though there had never been any scandal in her life, there were others who could find only an opportunity for cheap moralizing in the event, and one well-known religious leader rushed into print to proclaim that if this girl had been a Christian, she could not have made such a bad end, which was exceptionable not only because Christians have met much worse ends but, more importantly, because the gentleman in question knew nothing whatever about Marilyn's spiritual condition, and when he presumed to judge her, he put himself in the place of God, which is blasphemy. Goethe says:

> *Eines schickt sich nicht für alle:*
> *Sehe jeder wie er's treibe,*
> *Sehe jeder wo er bleibe,*
> *Und wer steht, dass er nicht falle!*

The peculiar horror which most normal people feel for suicide is, I suppose, due basically to the feeling that the suicide has turned against life itself. In the only completely convincing fashion, he has proclaimed that he has found the game not worth the candle, and because we know that he was a human being like ourselves, we feel that he has in a measure passed judgment upon our lives also. In the nature of the case, nobody will ever know positively whether Marilyn Monroe took her lethal dose of sleeping medicine intentionally or accidentally. But in view of the evidence available, the suicide theory seems very weak. She was one of the worst pill-eaters on record and

---

[2] See the editorial in *The Christian Century*, Vol. LXXIX (1962), 977: "Marilyn Monroe was accountable before God for her life and for choosing, if that is what she did, to escape from it by an overdose of sleeping pills. . . . But Hollywood and Americans who live everywhere else were and are also accountable before God for the elevation and eventual destruction of this woman. Hollywood made her a sex symbol, and kept her in roles which magnified sex in spite of her struggles to develop abilities of a higher order. . . . In the interview whose publication in *Life* magazine shortly preceded announcement of her death, Miss Monroe pointed to Hollywood as a city without monuments because everybody in the film industry grabs his profits and runs. The indictment will not soon be forgotten."

habitually depended upon barbiturates to control her chronic insomnia. We know that on her last night she had been asleep and was awakened to talk over the telephone; she probably, therefore, had to take more medicine to get to sleep again. After being dropped from the never-completed film, "Something's Got to Give," she spent most of her time, during the last weeks of her life, being interviewed and photographed; consequently we know a good deal about what was in her mind, and there is no indication that there was anything there that was not sensible and normal. That she had great problems is undeniable—when had she ever been without them?—but all that she said and did would seem to indicate that she was facing them courageously. She had purchased and was furnishing a new house. She had—and discussed—multitudinous plans for the future. She went to bed on Saturday night having made an engagement for Sunday. In her two last massive interviews with Richard Meryman and Alan Levy[3] there is nothing visible except sound common sense and a completely reasonable sense of values.

If Marilyn's death was not the result of an overdose, taken accidentally, then there must have been a sudden (and, no doubt, temporary) psychic collapse or breakdown, for which she had no responsibility except in the sense that we are all responsible for everything that happens to us through the mere fact of being ourselves. Either way, it would seem to have been a misfortune, not an act of guilt. All things taken into consideration, it is not within reason to suppose that Marilyn *committed* suicide; the worst that can possibly have occurred is that it happened to her. We do not call people murderers unless they kill deliberately and with premeditation. Is it not high time to begin to use the word "suicide" with similar humanity and intelligent discrimination?

Marilyn's first film of any importance, *The Asphalt Jungle,* was directed by John Huston, who also directed her last completed film, *The Misfits,* during which she became so ill that he sent her to the hospital

[3] Respectively, in *Life* (August 3, 1962) and *Redbook* (August, 1962).

for a rest. When an interviewer asked him whether he had acted out of consideration for her or in the interest of the picture, he replied indignantly, "The *picture?* The hell with the picture! The girl's whole *career* was at stake!" And when, after Marilyn's death, Huston was asked whether he believed the star system had killed her, there was an explosion which expressed an idea which must have occurred to many but which nobody else had had the nerve to express: "The star system had nothing to do with it whatsoever. The goddam doctors killed her. They knew the girl was a pill addict. It's a hell of a tragedy." There are times, I think we may believe, when profanity may please God as the expression of an honest and generous warmth of feeling, though, as we shall see, Hollywood cannot be acquitted of all responsibility.

It was a committee of "goddam doctors" who elaborately "investigated" Marilyn's "case" and then labeled her a "probable suicide." Nine people out of ten omit the "probable" and think and speak of her as having killed herself, quite as if she had left a note in which her intentions were made clear. Perhaps they prefer to think of her in this way. Perhaps it even gives them a sense of superiority to think that she is dead while they are alive, though God knows that in any proper sense of the term, most of them are not nor ever will be. In many cases too—I make no doubt—their minds are so small that they have no room in them for any open questions. But except with that small group of people who are capable of analyzing evidence, Marilyn will certainly be set down with the suicides of cinema history, and with no further questions asked.

In her last interview with Richard Meryman, Marilyn said:

> It might be a kind of relief to be finished. It's sort of like I don't know what kind of a yard dash you're running, but then you're at the finish line and you sort of sigh—you've made it.

After her death these words were quoted out of context in an Associated Press dispatch as supporting the theory that she had killed herself. Later a fan magazine made a poster-like display of them. But John Livingston Lowes, whose great book, *The Road to Xanadu,* was one of the great critical and scholarly masterpieces of the last generation, used to warn his graduate students never to use a quotation until they had *looked it up in context and read what had been left out,* and there never was a case where this counsel might better be applied than here. For this is what was left out:

> But you never have—you have to start all over again. But I believe you're always as good as your potential.
>
> I now live in my work and in a few relationships with the few people I can really count on. Fame will go by and, so long, I've had you, fame. If it goes by, I've always known it was fickle. So at least it's something I experienced, but that's not where I live.

Even a moderately intelligent cat would know that this woman was not talking about being finished with her *life* but only with her *career.* She envisioned the passing of *fame,* and she expected to go on contentedly without it. It would be difficult to find any utterance by any actress which had less to do with suicide or which expressed a more normal attiude toward the vicissitudes of the dramatic career.

As I say, any moderately intelligent cat would understand this. It would take a journalist to misunderstand, and even he could do it only when misunderstanding gave him a chance to lie about a dead girl by twisting her perfectly innocent words so that they could be turned against her to make a more sensational story.

One fan magazine printed an agonized-looking picture of Marilyn on the cover[4] with a screaming headline: "THE MAN WHO KILLED MARILYN." You turn to the story, and what do you read? "If there was such a man he's unimportant. He's one in a long line. It doesn't matter. Marilyn was killed by everyone and no one." Another cover screamed: "MARILYN MONROE DIED OF A CONTA-

---

[4] To the best of my knowledge, Marilyn Monroe is the only star in film history whose death did not stop the use of her photograph on the covers of fan magazines.

GIOUS DISEASE." Open the filthy sheet (handling it carefully with a pair of tongs), and you will learn that the disease is "suicide," and that two other prominent stars (who are named) have been exposed to it.

A well-known news magazine began a brutal article about Marilyn with the statement that her death was long overdue. (On what basis has this been calculated, one wonders, and how long, then, can the writer be expected to live?) A serious periodical devoted to cinema art began a career article about her by declaring that it was "impossible not to feel sympathy for her," then proceeded to show none whatever.[5] The author of a high-priced, hard-cover book about movie stars[6] reports Miss Monroe's death a suicide, without any if's or and's about it, and upon this basis proceeds to work out one of his characteristic pseudo-psychological analyses on her.

If those who have gone away from this world are ever permitted to look back upon it, we may hope that they are spared the knowledge of such obscenities as these. But Marilyn would not have been surprised. She would not have expected to be treated fairly. She never had been. What would have surprised her would have been the recurrence of such words as "decency," "innocence," and "purity" in the tributes that have been paid to her.

Joshua Logan called her "one of the most unappreciated people in the world," and Richard Watts, Jr. has found the essence of her trag-

[5] Robert C. Roman, "Marilyn Monroe," *Films in Review*, Vol. XIII (1962), 449–68; cf. the letters about it, pages 565–67. Ridiculous as the judgments expressed in this article are, it is valuable for the bibliography of Miss Monroe's films contained in it. In the same issue of *Films in Review* as Mr. Roman's article is a review of the Brigitte Bardot film, *A Very Private Affair*, by Jean Cambon, who begins by observing that the affair in question was "about as private as Marilyn Monroe's suicide," and goes on to advise Mlle Bardot, "in the brief future in which she will still have sex appeal [she was in her late twenties], to entrust herself to a director less self-centered than [Louis] Malle." In a later review of *The Stripper* Joanne Woodward was told that her role could not have been worse acted if Marilyn had played it. Yet when the film anthology *Marilyn* appeared in the summer of 1963 it received a very favorable review, and Miss Monroe's picture once more graced the cover.

[6] Richard Schickel, *The Stars* (Dial Press, 1962).

edy in the fact that she never knew "how much people everywhere loved her." It is an astonishing thing that one of the most admired women in the world should also have been one of the most abused women in the world. Of course it was all right to admit that you liked her, but you were always expected to snicker slightly when you said it. She was snubbed by Hollywood figures who were unworthy to wash her linen. "Anyone who has ever felt resentment against the good for being the good," says Ayn Rand, "and has given voice to it, is the murderer of Marilyn Monroe." All through her career, she was pursued with articles dilating on the wretched conditions of her early life, and explaining how impossible it was, under the given conditions, to expect a happy ending. Even when Maurice Zolotow published his on-the-whole excellent biography of her, the jacket was decorated with a candid-camera shot of her grief-stricken face looking back upon the house she had shared with Di Maggio on the morning she drove away from it for the last time. The questions which reporters asked her were outrageous (was she wearing a garter-belt?) when they were not insane (how long did she think a whale could stay under water?); I cannot think of any other person of her distinction to whom they would have dared to address such questions. It is a great pity that it seems never to have occurred to Marilyn to answer such interlocutors with a slap in the face. That would have been good for a front-page story any time, and she might have had the additional satisfaction of knowing that she had pleased God.

Unfortunately she was not the face-slapping variety; she could be deeply hurt, but she achieved a freedom from resentment that almost matched that of her great idol Lincoln. She played the game, and she paid the price. What it costs to swing such a career as she had can never be known except by the person who experiences it, but surely the editors of *Vogue* did not exaggerate when they said, "That she withstood the incredible, unknowable pressures of her public legend so long as she did is evidence of the stamina of the human spirit." "Marilyn identifies powerfully with all living things," said Arthur Miller, "but her extraordinary embrace of life is intermingled with great sadness." She was an abnormally sensitive person; she would not, for example, walk out on a show, no matter how bad it might be, for fear of hurting the performers' feelings, and she is reported once to have tried to drag a cow into her house to get her in out of the rain and to have denied herself a Christmas tree because she could not bear the thought of the tree's being cut down. "You've got to wrestle this dame," said Clark Gable during the filming of *The Misfits,* "to keep her face toward the camera." When she could think of something smart to say in response to an impudent question, she would generally say it, and sometimes she scored, but such victories cost her more than they were worth. To the extent that she co-operated in building up the legendary Marilyn Monroe who was so different from the reality, she did, in the insanely confused attitude toward sex which prevails in America, help create the monster she had to live with for the rest of her days. But her responsibility was less than that of the studios and the publicity men, for she had never been through the mill before and did not know what was involved. They had, and they had seen it destroy others before her.

I cannot honestly say that I think Marilyn never posed for a picture that was in bad taste or never made a wisecrack that it would have been better not to have made. On the whole, however, I believe that her attitude toward her body was sane and wholesome and that we are all better off for her example than we would otherwise have been. I can see nothing vulgar in the famous calendar pictures for which she posed early in her career, and the nude swimming scene in "Something's Got to Give," as it was finally shown in the film anthology *Marilyn* (1963), was one of the gayest and most beautiful things ever put on the screen; I should really feel sorry for anybody who was capable of being shocked by it. As for the pictures taken at the very end of her life and published after her death in *Eros,*[7] these are not, despite the

[7] Vol. I, No. 3 (Autumn, 1962). Some of these photographs appeared again in *U. S. Camera Annual, 1964* (Duell, Sloan & Pearce, 1963). See also, the pictures and article, "MM Remembered: A Retrospective Tribute to a Hollywood Legend," in *Playboy* (January, 1964).

sensational preannouncement, properly speaking, nudes at all. Most of them are heads. Some are clothed. A few show her breasts through a veil. All are cut off at the waist. Nobody is going to be shocked by them except people who have not seen them. Incidentally we have another beautiful illustration of journalistic ethics in connection with these pictures and another example of the consideration habitually accorded Marilyn. After the pictures had been taken, Marilyn went over them with the photographer, approved the ones she was willing to have published, and made a big cross over the face of the others. But after she was dead, *Eros* printed the disapproved pictures, crosses and all, because they were "so interesting." I hasten to explain that these pictures were not rejected because they were too revealing but simply because, for one reason or another, Marilyn did not like them.

II

Let us try, for once, to get this sex business straight in its relation to Marilyn Monroe. Nakedness is obviously a thing into which we can read as many meanings as Melville read into the color white in *Moby-Dick*. If it means lust, it also means innocence and vulnerability, especially vulnerability, and this was a very important element in the appeal Marilyn made. Important as sex was in her public image, nobody who knew her ever considered her oversexed in her private life. She may indeed have been quite the opposite, as people who make sex an important element in their art often seem to be. Dame Sybil Thorndike has been quoted as saying that during the period when she was playing particularly gruesome roles on the stage, she enjoyed exceptionally sound and refreshing sleep. "I got it off my chest" was the explanation she gave. Marilyn was engaged in a business which characteristically puts a pretty crass commercial value upon sex. She never did. She did not "arrive" on the screen until she was twenty-six, which is not young for a film star, and she arrived then only by insistent public demand. Producers in general do not seem to have liked her even as an artist, and they never did anything for her until her tremendous popularity had made her such a valuable box-office property that they had to accept her on any terms—her own terms. She might have had stardom much earlier if she had not made up her mind from the beginning that she was going to win it legitimately; she would not sell herself for a place on the screen, as others have done.

She passed yet another test. Early in her career she enjoyed one of the richest friendships of her life with a man much older than herself who loved her devotedly and wished to marry her. For him she felt respect and affection, but because she could not convince herself that she loved him, she refused him, though they both knew that he had not long to live and that as his wife she would inherit a large fortune. This is not the behavior of a frivolous or ignoble woman. But people of Marilyn's (or Huck Finn's) temperament get no satisfaction even from doing right, and after he was dead, she reproached herself bitterly for not having given him what he wanted. Carl Sandburg, who knew her well, always found Marilyn "a sensible woman," and indeed her common sense failed her only when she passed judgment on herself. There is a deep earthy wisdom even in some of her broadest quips, and sometimes there is even more than this. Some of the shock that was awakened by her sexuality was mere prudishness, but some of it came, too, from those who are afraid of women—and of life—and Marilyn may well have cut deeper than she knew when she replied to critics of some of her more revealing photographs that "maybe they think girls should look like boys." In her own funny little way she once remarked, "I don't care for money. I just want to be wonderful," and who can deny that she was? All in all, few women can ever have paid a higher price for decency than this girl who became the Number One Sex Symbol of her time.

When Marilyn and Billy Wilder filmed on Lexington Avenue in the middle of the night the famous scene in *The Seven Year Itch* in which a gust of air from under the sidewalk blew her skirt about her shoulders, she was savagely attacked by a generally sensible religious journal and told that if the picture were released with this scene in it, she would become responsible for a fresh outbreak of sex crimes! If this is true, it is difficult to see why every girl who appears in shorts or puts on a bathing suit is not equally responsible, and life seems to grow quite too complicated to endure. This editorial is an excellent example of the harm that can be done by a hysterical approach to undress in the theater, for if you are going to read sinister intentions into so playful and harmless a scene as this, what indignation are you going to keep in reserve to deal with the real scavengers? And indeed Marilyn was attacked a dozen times for every attack that has been made upon the really vicious films, products of corrupt and depraved minds, which are exhibited all around us, and which go scot-free, especially when they are of European origin, make grandiose "artistic" pretensions, and take care to be very solemn and dull.

One of the most interesting passages in Zolotow's biography of Marilyn is his account of his conversation with her about Joyce's *Ulysses*. Had she read it? She had read it "here and there." Had she read Molly Bloom's soliloquy in the last chapter? "Oh," she replied, "the one with the words." Zolotow told her that Arnold Bennett had called it a superlatively fine study of a woman's psychology. Who, she wanted to know, was Arnold Bennett? Arnold Bennett was a novelist. But, she objected, he was a man. How would he know, anyway? Zolotow thought Bennett might have asked his wife, though he wasn't sure he was married. "I think he's crazy," replied Marilyn. "Both of them. Women don't have sex on their mind *that* much." "Do you?" he asked her. "Of course not," she replied.

I have no doubt that Marilyn meant the "Let's make love" which she whispered breathlessly several times during the unreeling of the credits in the film of that title to be very seductive, but to me it sounded much more like a little girl who was trying very hard to be a big girl. "How do I know about man's need for a sex symbol?" she once asked. "I'm a girl." The worst woman she was ever called upon to portray on the screen was the evil young wife in *Niagara*, and it was her least effective performance, for there was nothing in it for her to take hold of. She had had many contacts with evil, but she did not understand it, and she did not understand sex as a destructive power either, even from the woman's point of view, for she never destroyed anything. Milton has his Moloch tell us of the angels that

> *descent and fall*
> *To us is adverse.*

This was Marilyn's experience also. Hollywood gave her the cheapest and tawdriest materials to work with and the cheapest colloquial English to speak, but these things made no difference whatever. "I washed the adjective," wrote Emily Dickinson, signing a letter "Your Rascal" to a friend who had called her "damned rascal." Marilyn could have spoken the adjective and washed it too, for even common words lost their commonness in her mouth. Taken seriously, was there ever a more cynical, thoroughly immoral song than "Diamonds Are a Girl's Best Friend"? Marilyn, who was about as far from Lorelei Lee temperamentally as a female can be, made it as innocent as one of John McCormack's ballads. So, one fancies, though with a thoroughly different quality of personality, must Yvette Guilbert have cleansed her café songs in her Touluose-Lautrec period. In *The Seven Year Itch* Tom Ewell grabs Marilyn and kisses her violently, and they fall off the piano bench. When they have picked themselves up, he apologizes profusely. He cannot understand how it happened. "Nothing like this," he says, "ever happened to me before." "Really?" asks Marilyn in amazement, pulling her dress down from the middle of her thighs. "It happens to me all the time." Think of the implications of that, and then listen to the way she speaks the line; you will find it difficult to do both these things at the same time. But perhaps the best illustration of all this is her Cherie in *Bus Stop*. On the stage, William Inge's play deals with a tough saloon-hall girl who becomes a new woman through her love for a naïve and innocent cowboy. The scenario was retained in the film, and for all I know Marilyn may have thought she was playing the part in the same way, but simply because she was Marilyn Monroe, Cherie became as innocent as the boy himself, the whole realistic aspect evaporated, and *Bus Stop* turned into what it had never been before—a very beautiful, very touching, almost spiritual picture of young love, a lovely fairy story which had not quite cut the cord which anchored the balloon to the earth.

Personally I have never come across any evidence to indicate that Marilyn Monroe was a corrupting influence so far as sex is concerned; if I were going to attack her, I should have to take another line altogether. I am very sorry to say that I believe she inspired vandalism and theft, and I am sure that anybody who, like me, has had occasion to look up material about her in bound magazines in library files will know what I mean. If the article was illustrated—and who would be silly enough to publish an article about Marilyn without illustrations? —the chances are very good that it will not be there!

I don't like to go psychological on her at this point, but I must say that I think there was, to the end of her days, a conflict in her between her natural tendency to negotiate her most obvious asset and her increasingly consuming desire to be taken seriously as an actress. Perhaps this was not a real conflict, but if it was not, then the confused public attitude on the subject tended to make it seem one. Marilyn herself tried to resolve it in one of her most amusing utterances: "No matter how much a person learns about being a better actress, a person isn't going to change and wear high-necked, long-sleeved dresses and dye her hair black." Yet she did, from time to time, clear to the end, exploit her beautiful body in a way that she must have known might well work against the serious recognition she was trying to win, and I think I can understand why she did this. Life had rejected this girl in so many ways. This was the one thing that had always worked. When she took off her clothes, she was in full command of the situation, and nobody else could compare with her. I believe, therefore, that this mild form of sexuality had considerable survival value for Marilyn, and it was very fortunate for her (as well as for us) that she possessed it.

III

But I must go back here to pick up one or two lost stitches. I have said that Marilyn could not play *Bus Stop* the way William Inge wrote it, that she had to make Cherie over into Marilyn Monroe. Can we claim, then, that she was what she most wanted to be—an actress? Or did she break her heart trying to achieve something she did not have it in her to encompass?

The Strasbergs believe that potentially Marilyn was not only an actress but a great one, and that if she had lived, she would have had an important career on the stage, and their opinion cannot be lightly brushed aside, for they saw a great deal of serious work by Marilyn at the Actors Studio that the rest of us have not seen. When she and Michael Chekhov did Lear's reunion with Cordelia, he pounded the table and cried, "They don't know what they're doing to you!" Lincoln Kirstein, of the American Shakespeare Theater, declared of Marilyn Monroe that

> as a classic comedienne of grace, delicacy and a happy wonder, she certainly has had no peer since Billie Burke or Ina Claire. The lightness, justness and rhythm of her clowning often held hints of something more penetrating. Her comic tone was sometimes disturbingly ironic; her personal style was more lyric than naturalistic.

Under the right conditions, he thought,

> she certainly could have played magnificently Doll Tearsheet, Katharine the Shrew, Mistress Page, Portia. And if she had been granted another chance, in another life, in another society or culture, she could have played Cleopatra.

But this is what might have been. What did she do? Speaking for myself, I never saw anything of Marilyn's that led me to believe her capable of creating a character who was essentially different from herself. If that is what you mean by an actress, then Marilyn was not an actress, in her actual achievement at any rate. On the other hand, she seems to me to have been virtually the only star of these latter days who transcended the realistic limitations which the screen foolishly imposed upon itself when it accepted sound, and created a great mythopoeic image comparable to those created by the great stars of the silent era. That may not be acting, exactly, in the stage sense, but it *is* creative work, and it involves the employment of a human being's own mind and soul and body in the projection of a personality which sums up much of what life means to the people of the time. It has too often been carelessly assumed that Chaplin was Charlot, William S. Hart Rio Jim, Douglas Fairbanks His Majesty the American, and so on. Actually the matter is much more complicated than that. Probably there is no more Chaplin in Charlot than there was Booth in Hamlet, though the relationship may well have existed in somewhat different terms. But nobody ever became celebrated on either stage or screen simply by being himself; the theater is much too artificial, too much a world of its own to make that possible. If you want to see what a person looks like on the stage when he behaves "naturally" and acts like himself, you will find plenty of examples in any amateur production, and nothing seems more thoroughly artificial. The vitality of the kind of image we are talking about here is born between actor, audience, and the spirit of the time. There are times when you may, if you like, sneer at it as art, but you cannot reject it without rejecting life itself. Yet I am not for a moment saying that I think this, great as it is, is the only thing Marilyn could ever have learned to do, and I certainly would not wish to suggest that she lacked a sense of character or artistic integrity. In 1958 she and Richard Avedon made a really amazing series of photographs of her, for the Christmas number of *Life*,[8] as Lillian Russell, Theda Bara, Clara Bow, Marlene Dietrich, and Jean Harlow. The most beautiful of these photographs, though not the best interpretation, is the picture of Lillian Russell in tights, high-heeled shoes, an enormous, lilac-trimmed picture hat, and with her bosom bare, posing beside a very fancy, gold-plated bicycle. It was suggested to Marilyn that she should put her foot up on one of the handlebars, but she shook her head. "Miss Russell," she said, "would never do that." In *Bus Stop* she insisted upon a sleazy, torn costume, and her song in the saloon was just the amateurish, pitiful kind of thing that might be sung by such a girl as Cherie in such a place.

[8] December 22, 1958.

Marilyn's presentation of it thus, at the same time infusing it with her own subtle and highly sophisticated charm, to hold a vast audience which had not assembled in a cheap frontier saloon—all this added up to a classical example of superb screen technique.

That "Who was Arnold Bennett?" a few pages back is the other stitch to pick up. By asking this question Marilyn quite innocently but very effectively gave the lie to those who believed that her interest in intellectual matters was all pose. If she had been a *poseuse*, she would of course have pretended that she knew. As a matter of fact, she was one of the most truthful persons who ever lived. As she herself once remarked, "I have a certain stupid sincerity." When we do not recognize an allusion, most of us say "Oh?" in the wisest tone we can manage and pray that our ignorance will be overlooked, which it never is. When Marilyn was ignorant, she blurted it right out, for she always wanted to learn. "I don't consider myself an intellectual," she told a Chicago reporter. "And this is not one of my aims. But I admire intellectual people." Her formal education was cut off early, and even then she seems never to have studied anything except the subjects that were of direct interest to her, so that she got good grades only in English. But she must be one of the few starlets in Hollywood history who ever spent her evenings in class at U.C.L.A., and she is the only woman I ever heard of in my life who, when she began to earn money, opened her first charge account not at a dress shop but at a bookstore. When Philippe Halsman went to her house to take a series of pictures of her for *Popular Photography* in 1953, he was shocked to find little or nothing in her wardrobe that he wanted her to wear. The girl had no clothes. She only had books and phonograph records.[9]

Yet even her hunger for knowledge was not simple: with Marilyn —and for Marilyn—nothing was simple. She was so extraordinarily innocent a person to have come out of her milieu that a great many people found themselves unable to accept her innocence as anything but the most skillfully played of her roles. I think they were wrong about this, but there may have been times when she did not know her-

[9] Philippe Halsman, "Shooting Marilyn," *Popular Photography* (June, 1953).

self. It amused her to dramatize herself as the "dumb" little girl, and there were times when the little girl used her "dumbness" with astonishing cleverness. When, shortly before her death, she was asked whether she had any foreign languages, she replied with a laugh that she could hardly manage English. Yet when she was asked whether she knew that she was born under the same sign as Rosalind Russell, Rosemary Clooney, and Judy Garland, she replied almost haughtily that she knew nothing about these people, but that she shared her sign with Emerson, Whitman, Bernard Shaw, and Queen Victoria. And she was not merely clowning, for there was a sense in which she was quite right in feeling that such as these were her people. And if it is amusing (with one eye on *The Prince and the Showgirl*) to conjecture what Victoria might have made of her—or even Emerson— we can certainly feel that Whitman and Shaw at least would have understood.

But here again, the complication. For precisely because she lacked background, Marilyn was at the mercy of the people she happened to meet and consequently, I should guess, more or less limited to the writers, composers, artists, etc., who happened to be currently in vogue. This is always a terrible handicap to any honest person, and it was more than usually so to a person who was less typical of her time than she ever found out. I must say frankly that I think it was a sad day for Marilyn when she first heard of Freud, and I should like to have that statement taken without reference to what either you or I may believe about the value of Freudianism per se. Whatever her temperament or inclinations, it must be very difficult for an important film star to avoid becoming the center of her own world, the unique object of her own attention, and in a sense her own god, and Marilyn's terribly introspective nature plus the isolation forced upon her by the circumstances of her youth must have made the temptations which exist along this line unusually strong for her. I do not mean that I think her quite undiscriminating in her attitude toward psychiatrists (she is said to have told the doctors at the Payne-Whitney Clinic that they ought to have *their* heads examined), but I do believe that the Freudian technique as she understood it kept her attention focused upon the conditioning which flowed from what Conrad would have called her "brutally murdered childhood" to an unwholesome and perhaps ultimately disastrous degree, and I cannot help suspecting that either a good priest or a good Christian Science practitioner might have done more for her than any psychiatrist ever achieved. According to the newspaper reports, her own psychiatrist was not able to suggest anything better to her on the last night of her life than that she go out for an automobile ride, and some of the rest of us might have achieved that much without psychiatric training. It is interesting that Marilyn was exposed to Christian Science in her youth, through a woman whom she loved and honored almost beyond anyone else she ever met, and that she tried working at it, but it would not have been reasonable to expect a girl with her agonizing menstrual problem to meet with much success. Here, again, I must explain that I am expressing no opinion as to whether or not Christian Science could have solved that problem; I simply mean that it would not have been reasonable to expect her, as she was then, to have been enough of an adept to achieve it.

When Marilyn's marriage to Arthur Miller was announced, a lady who greatly admired the playwright put everybody who knew her in stitches by requesting to be informed of all and sundry what Mr. Miller could possibly "see" in "that girl"! Amusing as this is, it becomes tragic when you realize how close Marilyn came to agreeing with the obtuse lady. When she married Miller she was undoubtedly the most desired woman in the world, yet she is reported to have written on the back of her wedding pictures the words "Hope, Hope, Hope."

IV

The story of Marilyn's tragic childhood has often been told, and the narrative need not be repeated here. She was clear-sighted enough to know that "most of the people who are born in India and China or someplace lead lives that are much, much worse. The thing is I've taken it too hard." Nevertheless it was bad enough so that if she had turned out a veritable "tramp," nobody who ever knew her conditioning could have blamed her. She was about as far from being a "tramp" as any girl who ever lived. The invincible and irrefragable innocence of her spirit was triumphant to the end. Yet she was never able to heal the psychic wound that she had suffered or rebuild her shattered self-confidence. She ought to have known that her ability to rise above her environment as she did was the highest attestation to her worth that she could have asked for, but she never developed the arrogance that would have enabled her to perceive this. To the end of her life there was something in her that took the side of those who sneered at her. She made herself a world figure, but she could never satisfy her own impossibly high standards. In life and in art she tried so hard that she defeated herself.

So we find her telling an interviewer: "I haven't reached a dramatic crossroads yet. I've reached a comedy crossroads. I think I got it across in *Some Like It Hot*." And then came the characteristic qualification: "At least, let's say it got across at the box office." And after another pause, "Still, I don't know." When she began making records she declared, "I won't be satisfied until people want to hear me sing without looking at me." And then she added, "Of course, that doesn't mean I want them to stop looking." Others could no doubt match the perfectionism of the first statement. Still others could match the almost brutal candor of the second. It was the combination of perfectionism and candor that marked the utterance as coming from Marilyn Monroe and nobody else on earth. She even thought (poor child!) that she was getting old and losing her looks, yet when the scenes from "Something's Got to Give" were released at last they showed her in assured possession of a fragile, exquisite loveliness which even she had never possessed before and which surely none of us had ever seen surpassed. Yes, she had changed since she had made *The Love Nest,* and even since she had made *Bus Stop,* but with the change had come the promise that she would still be lovely if she lived to be ninety. What a pity it was that she could not have known!

Of the man who is probably the greatest singer of our time we are told that when he records he will do two or three "takes" of a song and then refuse to do any more. "That," he will say, "is as good as I can sing it." This is the way to be a great artist and survive. Marilyn wanted thirty or forty or fifty "takes," playing her scenes over and over, beyond what any other star had ever dreamed of doing, and until every actor in her company was exhausted, and even then she was never satisfied with what she had done. Look at the production shots of *Let's Make Love*[10] if you want a glimpse of her agony. It is reported that the "My Heart Belongs to Daddy" sequence in that film, which runs six minutes on the screen and gives an impression of complete gaiety and spontaneity, took her eleven grueling days to film. She never did complete her touching scene with Hope Lange in the bus in *Bus Stop*; Joshua Logan finally pieced it together from various shots, and Marilyn thought it was terrible. When she "doodled" while waiting for her call in the studio, she would scribble reassuring little notes to herself, exhorting herself not to be afraid; I do not know where you can match the pathos of this. As Billy Wilder well understood, it was this fear, not arrogance and not a desire to throw her weight about, that made it impossible for her to reach the studio on time. She probably made more agony of acting than any other actress who ever lived. No film can ever possibly be good enough to justify the suffering which it cost Marilyn to produce it.

In Henry James's great novel *The Tragic Muse,* Peter Sherringham accuses Miriam Rooth of only wanting a husband "to stand in the wing and hold your shawl and your smelling-bottle—!" But she replies unanswerably:

> "Holding my shawl and my smelling-bottle is a mere detail, representing a very small part of the whole precious service, the protection and encouragement, for which a woman in my position might be indebted to a man interested in her work and as accomplished and determined as you very justly describe yourself."
>
> "And would it be your idea that such a man should live on the money

[10] *Life* (August 15, 1960).

earned by an exhibition of the person of his still more accomplished and still more determined wife?"

"Why not if they work together—if there's something of his spirit and his support in everything she does?" Miriam demanded. *"Je vous at-tendais* with the famous 'person'; of course that's the great stick they beat us with. Yes, we show it for money, those of us who have anything decent to show, and some no doubt who haven't, which is the real scandal. What will you have? It's only the envelope of the idea, it's only our machinery, which ought to be conceded to us; and in proportion as the idea takes hold of us do we become unconscious of the clumsy body. Poor old 'person'—if you knew what *we* think of it! If you don't forget it that's your own affair: it shows that you're dense before the idea."

There can be no doubt that James has truly perceived and felici-tously stated what the actress needs, but those who find it are few. The great American contralto Louise Homer was one of the lucky ones. Her husband Sidney Homer—himself a great musician—used to say that it took the both of them to give a great performance— Louise on the stage and himself in the audience.

But here again, as with Freudianism, I must record my suspicion that the doctors did not help Marilyn much. I do not doubt that the "Method" which the Strasbergs taught her can produce fine acting; that much has been demonstrated often enough. But even at its best it seems to me unnecessarily wasteful of the actor's psychic energy, and I doubt that its devotees are ever in complete control of the effects which they create. "The less you feel a thing," said Flaubert, "the fitter you are to express it as it is." As her previous coach Natasha Lytess had realized, Marilyn had no psychic energy to waste; she needed des-perately to be released from the prison of self, not locked into it, and I cannot think of anybody more likely to be injured by making her own emotions, her own frustrations, her own sorrows her dramatic stock-in-trade.

In addition to Christian Science, Marilyn was abundantly exposed in her youth to the Southern California type of Protestant Evangelical Fundamentalism, and she tells us that she used to offer fervent inter-

rs for one pair of adopted parents, who, kind as they were
by all accounts to have needed them. Yet though they
ipty whiskey bottles and cigarette cartons to play with,
..... : may well have hurt her less than the religious fanatics
who would not let her go to the movies on Saturday afternoon because
Jesus might come again while she was there and find her among the
wicked people, and who warned her, when they put her to bed at
night, that she might die before morning and wake up in hell. I am
sure that Marilyn would be astonished if she could read my statement
that at heart she was a very religious person; she was under the impression that religion did not "work" for her. By the same token, I
am sure she would raise her eyebrows over all the writers who, since
her death, have described her as an exceptionally good and pure woman (this is one of the many reasons why we can be sure she deserves
these tributes), and for that matter we may be confident that nothing
could surprise her more than to find herself in such a book as this at
all. Though she was no materialist, she would never discuss religion
after she became a star; it is clear that there was a sore spot there and
the consciousness of an unsolved problem. When she married Arthur
Miller, she tried to embrace Judaism, but this can hardly have been
anything more than another of her pathetic attempts to "belong" at
last, to become part of a family, with no barriers left standing between
herself and the others. In art and in love, she sought what only God
can give, and it says much for her that though the marriage foun-
dered her relationship with her father-in-law survived, so that when
she died he felt as though he had lost a daughter; whatever else
Marilyn Monroe may have failed to achieve, she succeeded in her
lifelong quest for a father.

Family life was romance to this unconquerable idealist; it was wonderful to her because she never had it; if she had been brought up
in the normal way, she would have known that human beings can
be as devilish in family relationships as anywhere else, and frequently
are. She had always been cautious about personal entanglements, and
she was getting more so as she grew older, yet I am not sure that, if

she had lived, she might not well have attempted marriage again, nor that this time she would not have succeeded. She had pretty much all the domestic gifts and virtues. She stood by Miller loyally when he was in trouble for contempt of Congress, and perceived and denounced and repudiated the immorality of those who sought through her to bring pressure upon him; she sat upon her possessions lightly, yet was not, by movie-star standards, extravagant; she adored children and won the hearts of Di Maggio's son and Miller's sons without reserve. And though it is undeniable that she was in some aspects a dreamy girl, she did not, as some persons seem to imagine, drift through the world like a zombie. Who looked after Marilyn through most of her thirty-six years except Marilyn? and how many of those of us who think we are managing our personal affairs in a very satisfactory manner have demonstrated our survival value by proving our capacity to deal with anything like the difficulties which confronted her? Hitherto her attempts to have a child of her own had been foiled by a physical disability, but surgery was now supposed to have corrected that, and the future she saw beckoning her beyond her years of fame, in her final interviews, might conceivably have given her everything she had hoped for. It was once the fashion to blame her for Miller's lack of productiveness during his marriage to her; being married to Marilyn, we were told, was a full-time job. Both Miller and Marilyn deserve credit for the dignified fashion in which they kept their troubles, whatever they were, to themselves and out of the newspapers;[11] so far as I

[11] This statement was true when I wrote it; after the production, on January 23, 1964, of Miller's play, *After the Fall,* the most outrageous violation of privacy in the history of the drama, and its subsequent publication in *The Saturday Evening Post* (February 1, 1964), and in book form by the Viking Press, it remained true only for Marilyn, for Miller has now made the stage an analyst's couch and the world his psychiatrist. I am not, of course, saying that Maggie in this play *is* Marilyn or that Miller has said she is. Bue he *has* used enough material obviously derived from Marilyn to make the equation all but inescapable for all except the most critical and intelligent auditors. To draw such a portrait of a person you have been married to (especially when she is no longer in a position to call you to account for it) would be unpardonable in my book even if everything stated were true and set forth in a straightforward factual account, but Mr. Miller has done something inconceivably worse than this by

know, the only critical thing she ever said about him for publication was her remark that she thought him a better writer than husband: "I'm sure writing comes first in his life." But it is not reasonable to suppose that a wife as much interested in her husband's work as Marilyn was in Miller's, and as proud of it, would stand in the way of his doing it. We have Miller's own testimony that she was a "demon about my work" and drove him to his desk even when he did not wish to go there; it is also clear that she did for him all the practical things which any wife does for any husband—a great many more such things than many wives do.[12] Marilyn created glamour, but she was not herself greatly seduced by it. Handsome actors left her cold, and nothing

---

mixing his facts with obvious and demonstrable fictions and thus leaving his readers and his audiences without the necessary data to decide what, if anything, he wishes to affirm or to stand by. A work of art is not required to be faithful to the life situations which suggested it, but it should not be used merely to evade responsibility. These are materials whose employment puts an artist into the company of those who write anonymous letters.

Mr. Miller's failure to understand these things suggests a degree of insensibility comparable in its way to that of the Duke in Browning's "My Last Duchess," and it is comforting to note that the reception accorded *After the Fall* should have been nothing short of savage; no author in my time has been so "clobbered." At this point I myself should like to recall what Miller himself wrote of his wife in 1961: "To understand Marilyn best, you have to see her around children. They love her; her whole approach to life has their kind of simplicity and directness. I have not really helped her as an actress; Marilyn has perfected herself. . . . The thing is, Marilyn has become a sort of fiction for writers: each one sees her through his own set of pleasures and prejudices." With this we may compare Marilyn's own touching comments on her happiness in her life with Miller, in an interview with Lester David, June, 1957, published in *This Week Magazine* (April 12, 1964) under the title "Which Was the True Marilyn?" ("There's a feeling of being together—a warmth and tenderness. I don't mean a display of affection or anything like that. I mean just being together.") This article hit my desk as I was reading the galley proofs for this book.

Aside from the fact that she divorced Miller, what mysterious alteration did Miss Monroe undergo between the time Miller wrote his eulogy of her and the time he wrote his play? Perhaps it might not be out of order to recall James Russell Lowell's acute observation on Pope's remarks concerning Lady Mary Wortley Montagu, that "it is not in human nature for a woman to have had two such utterly irreconcilable characters as those of Lady Mary before and after her quarrel with the poet."

[12] *Look* (October 1, 1957).

could be more absurd than the notion that her public was made up of wild kids; it was not her pin-up pictures that attracted the admiration of such persons as Carl Sandburg, Isak Dinesen, Dame Edith Sitwell, and Lillian and Dorothy Gish. As she loved children on the one hand, so she also had great respect and affection for people who were much older than she was, and she was proud of the fact that she could count many such among her fans.

Marilyn Monroe wanted men, she wanted all human beings, to be good and kind and worthy of trust; she needed to have those she could believe in around her; what she valued most in love was not sensation but tenderness and understanding.[13] How touching is the scene in *The Misfits* in which she holds Montgomery Clift's head in her lap and lets him pour out his heart to her, her famous bare legs stretched out clear across the Cinemascope screen, and how much of herself she put into it. The need to worship is the hallmark of the religious spirit, and the little girl who worships a movie star may be as pure in her devotion as she who pays homage to a saint, provided she is doing the best that she knows. Marilyn, as everybody knows, found her ideal in Lincoln, and it was Arthur Miller's first appeal to her that he reminded her of Lincoln. If she had been merely a woman this might have served, but she was cursed and blessed by being an artist too, and whatever one thinks of the value of what she created, the devotion with which she gave herself to it was absolute. It was all she had, and it consumed her.

There are many different ways of classifying human beings, and I suppose one way would be to say that there are people who love actresses and people who hate them. To a modified degree, the same reactions may be observed in connection with other public figures, but

[13] Harriet Beecher Stowe would not seem greatly to have resembled Marilyn Monroe, yet Catherine Gilbertson (*Harriet Beecher Stowe,* Appleton-Century, 1937) might almost be speaking of the actress when she writes of Harriet: "Perhaps she sensed the menace in applause, a mob demonstration, likely at any moment to turn into hissing. It came upon her that she had no interest in fame, did not want it, had never wanted it. What she yearned for was what almost all women—almost all people—yearn for, an absorbing, sustaining, sheltering affection."

they are stronger in the theater, for only the actor gives *himself* to his audience, only he dramatizes his own personality, uses his own body as the instrument upon which he plays. Of course this is true of men as well as women, but it is true of women to an intenser degree, for not only are women incomparably the most personal creatures in the world—for a woman everything comes down to personal relationships in the last analysis—but in the theater a woman is allowed a much freer exploitation of her individuality than would be permitted a man. As long as there is a theater, consequently, people are going to feel very personally about actresses, and I quote once more from *Vogue*'s perspicacious tribute to Marilyn: "She has given a warm delight to millions of people, made them smile affectionately, laugh uproariously, love her to the point of caring deeply—often aggressively—about her personal unhappiness."

Now of course there is—or there may easily be—an element of mawkishness in all this, but there is also something which is valuable and precious. The actress embodies womankind. She dramatizes what other women have but cannot set forth in so glamourous an aspect. Mary Garden used to tell her admirers that other women were quite as interesting as she was if they would only learn how to look at them. I have known many foolish people who loved actresses. But I have known no man who hated actresses—and feared and mistrusted and slandered them—who was not also mean and narrow and hard and vindictive and envious and spiritually more than half dead.

Poe's statement that the death of a beautiful woman is the most poetic subject in the world has often been attacked. Surely, it has been argued, we ought to be more greatly moved by the death of a great man. Yes, our minds would seem to tell us so. But we are more than our minds, and I cannot but feel that a man—a young man especially —who should spontaneously *feel* it so in his inner abiding place must be something of a freak.

For what is the great sin of our time? Is it not the sin of treating human beings as means rather than as ends? Hawthorne thought that the unpardonable sin. So did Marilyn. Toward the end of her life she developed something of a mania on the subject of being "used." She was not a thing, and she was tired of being treated like a thing. Everybody who comes near me, she said, wants a chunk out of me. One of the most attractive pieces ever written about her is Hollis Alpert's in *The Dreams and the Dreamers*.[14] When he told her that she did not seem much like the articles he had read about her, she replied, "Maybe I shouldn't say this, but I've always felt those articles somehow reveal more about the writers than they do about me." Of course it would be absurd to pretend that we cannot maintain the sanctity and integrity of human personality without supporting the cult of the actress. But if we still believe that human personality is of value in this increasingly collectivist world, if we recognize the importance of dramatizing it, and making it vivid, and placing it where it can exert an appeal to men's imagination, if, in short, we wish to continue to be people and not turn into numbers, then we ought to think twice before we begin to take up too dim a view of the cult of the star.

What would have happened in this world if something else had not happened is always a fascinating subject for speculation, but one can never be definite about it. It is possible, as I have already said, that if Marilyn had lived, all her hopes and dreams might at last have been realized. On the other hand, her background and her heritage being what they were, it may even be that fate was kind. Her kingdom was not of this world, and she never felt quite at home here; few except the exploiters ever do, and there was nothing of the exploiter in her. She had her faults and her limitations; she was no design for a stained-glass window. But say the worst that can be said about her, and there was still something vastly admirable about this girl, a mingled quality of light and warmth that made her an instrument for the gods to play on. One of her famous flip remarks was that she didn't sun-bathe because she liked to be blonde all over. She was blonde all over in another sense too, for she was one of those rare women who both rouse passion and stimultaneously purge it, so that instead of turning in upon itself and generating poison, it broadens out to brighten and hearten

14 Macmillan, 1962.

all of life. Many stars have been admired. Marilyn was loved. Was? Is!
Love knows but one tense. As Ellen Terry wrote Bernard Shaw, "We
'can't lose' the few we love." She was like the girl in the Brahms folk
song:

> *Mein Mädel hat einen Rosenmund,*
> *Und wer ihn kusst, der wird gesund.*

But, as all movie fans know, kisses are not always physical, and now
that she is gone they must often be tempted to think of her in terms of
the lovely poem by Friedrich Rückert which was set to music by
Schubert:

> *O du Entrissne mir und meinem Kusse,*
> *Sei mir gegrüsst, sei mir geküsst!*
> *Erreichbar nur meinem Sehnsuchtsgrusse,*
> *Sei mir gegrüsst, sei mir geküsst!*

For that matter, the German Lieder are full of Marilyn and incomparable expressions of her lovers' feelings toward her, perhaps nowhere
more impressively than in the first stanza of Hermann von Gilm's
"Zueignung," which inspired one of Richard Strauss's greatest songs:

> *Ja, du weisst es, teure Seele,*
> *Dass ich fern von dir mich qüale,*
> *Liebe macht die Herzen krank,*
> *Habe Dank.*

Her own short life was crammed with physical suffering and mental
anguish, and it ended on a note of ambiguity, but only a fool could
call it a failure.[15] As the dying Dencombe says in Henry James's won-

---

[15] There have, of course, been no lack of such fools; this seems to be one article
that is always kept abundantly in stock. One of them is beautifully annihilated in what
I consider the finest article yet written about Marilyn—Lincoln Kirstein's "Marilyn
Monroe: 1926–1962," *Nation*, Vol. CXC (1962), 70–72 (I have already quoted from it
in another connection): "A Hollywood gossip columnist, who should know if anyone does, said that Marilyn Monroe's life was an absolute waste; one wonders what
he, in the brief watches of the night, thinks of what he does with his time." I do not
like to criticize Diana Trilling's article, in *Redbook* (February, 1963) (the publishers

derful story, "The Middle Years," "It *is* glory—to have been tested, to have had our little quality and cast our little spell. The thing is to have made somebody care." Marilyn made somebody care if anybody ever did, and untold thousands of men and women, thankful for what they saw of her, will always find life sweeter because she lived and sadder because she died. She never had a chance to play James's Daisy Miller, which is a pity, for she would have been incomparable in the role, yet many must think of her in the terms which Giovanelli at last applies to Daisy: " 'She was the most beautiful young lady I ever saw, and the most amiable.' And then he added in a moment, 'And she was the most innocent.' "

All judgments of human character are in the last analysis intuitive: you cannot really *prove* anything that matters to you. Pascal said that people must be known in order to be loved but that God must be loved in order to be known. There is also the gambler's definition of religion: betting your life on the existence (and, he might have added, on the goodness) of God. The gambler was right, but Pascal was wrong. Human beings too must be loved, and understood—for only in love is there understanding, and perfect understanding comes only with perfect love—on faith; sooner or later, even here, you reach the place where you must commit yourself to that leap into the dark which religion demands or else you must turn away. When Laura Benét asked Walter de la Mare whether he believed in immortality, he replied in the affirmative, then caviled at the word "believed." After all, he said, he could not say he "believed" in butterflies.

took a full-page advertisement to announce it to the readers of the *Saturday Review,* and the article itself was later reprinted in *The Paris Review* and in Mrs. Trilling's *Claremont Essays,* Harcourt, 1964), for its feeling is beautifully right, but Mrs. Trilling does have a few factual errors. Thus, the official finding was not suicide but "probable suicide"; Richard Meryman's interview in *Life* came out before Marilyn's death, not after, though the issue containing it was still on the stands when she died; Marilyn was alone the last Saturday night of her life because she chose to be, not because she had not been invited out. Mrs. Trilling also seems to me to assert (1) that Marilyn committed suicide: (2) that we don't know whether she did or didn't; (3) that she probably didn't, and that (1) she was and (2) wasn't more highly sexed than other people.

I am sure I shall be accused, in some quarters, of attempting to canonize Marilyn Monroe. This is not important, for what insensitive and uncomprehending people may say about me is of no more significance than what they have always thought and said about her. Actually, of course, I have done nothing of the kind, for I have admitted all her faults and limitations freely. There were many elements in her complicated character, but at heart she belonged to that variety of human being called pilgrim. "I'm trying to find myself as a person. Sometimes that's not easy to do. Millions of people live their entire lives without finding themselves. But it is something I must do." In this respect she often reminds me of Katherine Mansfield. "My work," she said again, "is the only ground I've ever had to stand on. To put it bluntly, I seem to have a whole superstructure with no foundation. But I'm working on the foundation." I am not sure that if she had lived she would have become a great artist. I think it entirely possible that art might have represented only one stage in her development. What I *am* sure of is that she *would* have been a great human being.

Who failed her, and why, is not, at this point, very important. If she failed herself, it was because there are limits to human resources and the capacity of human beings to endure suffering. She was pure of heart. She was free of guile. She never understood either the adoration or the antagonism which she awakened. Because she was herself incapable of malice, she met it, when it was directed toward her, with a kind of dazed incomprehension, and because she never knew how different she was from other people, she did not grasp what her admirers saw in her much more clearly. There is not the slightest evidence that she ever experienced envy or jealousy; cruelty would have been completely outside her range even if she could have brought herself to desire it. When you happen to be made like that, what real comprehension can you have of the meanness of other people, and how can you possibly be qualified to cope with them? In a sense, perhaps, we may even say that a person who is incapable of cruelty deserves no credit for being kind, but this surely need not prevent us from loving her. The difficulty, however, is that unless we love her, we fall into grave danger of hating her, for the simple reason that her life and her nature constitute a judgment upon ours. But I have surely written of Marilyn to little purpose if I need to explain here that I trust her and believe in her, and that I am as sure as I can ever be of anything that her soul inhabits that world of light where the excellent becomes the permanent.

In paradisum deducant te Angeli: in tuo adventu suscipiant te Martyres, et perducant te in civitatem sanctam Jerusalem. Chorus Angelorum te suscipiat, et cum Lazaro quondam paupere aeternam habeas requiem.

BIBLIOGRAPHY

I. Jenny Lind

The present writer's *Jenny Lind* (Houghton Mifflin, 1931), of which the present study is a revision and condensation, contains an extensive bibliography of books and articles about, or containing references to, Jenny Lind. Of the items therein listed I will here repeat only two: (1) the authorized biography of Jenny Lind—Henry Scott Holland and W. S. Rockstro, *Memoir of Madame Jenny Lind-Goldschmidt: Her Early Art-Life and Dramatic Career, 1820–1851* (2 vols., London, John Murray, 1891); (2) the book written by Jenny Lind's daughter —Mrs. Raymond Maude, *The Life of Jenny Lind* (London, Cassell, 1926).

Since my book appeared, three books about Jenny Lind have been published in English—all written by women and all, I think, excellent: Laura Benét, *Enchanting Jenny Lind* (Dodd, Mead, 1939); Joan Bulman, *Jenny Lind, A Biography* (London, James Barrie, 1956); Gladys Denny Shultz, *Jenny Lind, The Swedish Nightingale* (Lippincott, 1962). Miss Bulman's seems to me the most important of these books; it also contains a bibliography. Laura Benét's book was intended primarily for young readers.

II. Sarah Bernhardt

There are many books about Sarah Bernhardt in a number of languages, and they cannot all be listed here. Neither do I intend to cite any articles except those which have been mentioned in my notes.

Much the fullest bibliography of books and articles about Sarah Bernhardt is in Ernest Pronier, *Une Vie au Théâtre: Sarah Bernhardt* (Geneva, Editions Alex. Jullien, n.d.). The most recent substantial study of her at the date of this writing is André Castelot, *Sarah Bernhardt* (Paris, Le Livre Contemporain, 1961).

The American edition of her autobiography, *Memories of My Life,* was published by Appleton in 1907. Lysiane Bernhardt's *Sarah Bernhardt, My Grandmother,* translated by Vyvyan Holland (London, Hurst & Blackett, Ltd., n.d.), was, in a way, designed as a sequel to the autobiography, for Bernhardt asked Lysiane to write it and furnished her with material for it. See also Bernhardt's technical book, *The Art of the Theatre,* edited by Marcel Berger (Dial Press, 1925).

The following books were written from personal knowledge: May Agate, *Madame Sarah* (Home & Van Thal, 1946); Sir George Arthur, *Sarah Bernhardt* (Doubleday, 1923); Mme Pierre Berton, *The Real Sarah Bernhardt* (Boni and Liveright, 1924); Reynaldo Hahn, *Sarah Bernhardt: Impressions* (London, Elkin Mathews & Marrot, Ltd., 1932); Arthur William Row, *Sarah the Divine* (Comet Press Books, 1957); Suze Rueff, *I Knew Sarah Bernhardt* (London, Frederick Muller, 1951); and Louis Verneuil, *The Fabulous Life of Sarah Bernhardt* (Harper, 1942). Verneuil's book is virtually a full-scale biography and an excellent book in every way.

See, further, Maurice Baring, *Sarah Bernhardt* (Appleton-Century, 1934), a brilliant little study; G. G. Geller, *Sarah Bernhardt* (London, Duckworth, 1933); Jules Huret, *Sarah Bernhardt* (Lippincott, 1899). The best independent study, in English at any rate, is certainly Joanna Richardson's *Sarah Bernhardt* (London, Max Reinhardt, 1959).

III. Ellen Terry

Ellen Terry's autobiography is *The Story of My Life: Recollections and Reflections* (Doubleday, Page, 1909). The later edition of this work—*Ellen Terry's Memoirs,* with a Preface, Notes and Additional Biographical Chapters by Edith Craig and Christopher St. John (Putnam, 1932)—is valuable for the added material, but there are differences from the earlier text which are not explained by the editors' prefatory statement. See, further, Ellen Terry, *The Russian Ballet* (Bobbs-Merrill, 1913) and *Four Lectures on Shakespeare* (Martin Hopkinson, 1932). Her famous letters to Bernard Shaw are in *Ellen Terry and Bernard Shaw: A Correspondence* (Putnam, 1931), and a much smaller collection to an unnamed friend may be read in *The*

Heart of Ellen Terry (London, Mills & Boon, Limited, 1928). With all her published writings except her letters Ellen Terry had the help of Christopher St. John.

There are books about Ellen Terry by Charles Hiatt, *Ellen Terry and Her Impersonations: An Appreciation* (George Bell and Sons, 1898); Clement Scott, *Ellen Terry* (Stokes, 1900); T. Edgar Pemberton, *Ellen Terry and Her Sisters* (Dodd, Mead, 1902); Christopher St. John, *Ellen Terry* (John Lane, 1907); and Edward Gordon Craig, *Ellen Terry and Her Secret Self* (Dutton, 1932). Marguerite Steen's *A Pride of Terrys: Family Saga* (Longmans, 1962) covers the whole Terry clan. In Christopher St. John's anonymously published novel, *Hungerheart* (Methuen, 1915), Louise is Ellen Terry and Sally her daughter, Edith Craig, but I have never seen this book. There are many references to Ellen Terry in Bram Stoker's *Personal Recollections of Henry Irving* (Macmillan, 1960)—see also his article, "The Art of Ellen Terry," *Cosmopolitan,* Vol. XXXI (1901), 241–50—in W. Graham Robertson's *Time Was* (Hamish Hamilton, 1931), and in Laurence Irving's *Henry Irving* (Macmillan, 1952).

Valuable articles containing personal reminiscences of Ellen Terry are Alice Comyns Carr, "Ellen Terry: Recollections of a Long Friendship," *Fortnightly,* Vol. CXVIII (1922), 230–43; Sir Johnston Forbes-Robertson, "Ellen Terry," *London Mercury*, Vol. XVIII (1928), 492–96; Gwenillian F. Palgrave, "Ellen Terry: A Tribute," *Cornhill,* Vol. CLII (1935), 1–10; Harcourt Williams, "Ellen Terry," in *Sixteen Portraits of People Whose Houses Have Been Preserved by the National Trust,* edited by L. A. G. Strong (London, Naldreth Press, 1951). See, too, Frederick A. King, "A Rose Cottage in Kent," *Craftsman,* Vol. XXIV (1913), 293–99.

The phrase used as the title of this portrait is Christopher St. John's.

IV. Julia Marlowe

The authorized biography is Charles Edward Russell, *Julia Marlowe, Her Life and Art* (Appleton, 1926). A much shorter, earlier memoir, copiously illustrated with photographs by B. J. Falk, is John D. Barry,

Julia Marlowe (Boston, E. H. Bacon and Company, 1907). E. H. Sothern wrote *Julia Marlowe's Story* in the first person, as if his wife were speaking. Edited by Fairfax Downey, it was published after her death by Rinehart, in 1954. See also Sothern's charming autobiography, *The Melancholy Tale of "Me," My Remembrances* (Scribners, 1916).

The following articles appeared over Julia Marlowe's by-line: "The Future of the Historical Romance for the Stage," *Independent,* Vol. LIV (1902), 1531–35; "Stage Work and the Stage Aspirant," *Good Housekeeping,* Vol. LIV (1912), 325–32; "Why I Am Leaving the Stage," *Ladies' Home Journal* (January, 1916). Two valuable articles by Elizabeth McCracken are "Julia Marlowe," *Century,* Vol. LXXXIII (1906), 46-55, and "When the Public Does Not See the Actress—Behind the Scenes with Julia Marlowe," *Ladies' Home Journal* (April, 1913). See also Gustav Kobbé, "The Actress We Know as Julia Marlowe," *Ladies' Home Journal* (February, 1903); Karl von Herrmann, "How Julia Marlowe Climbed Vesuvius," *Ladies' Home Journal* (November, 1905); Clara E. Laughlin, "Back of the Footlights with 'Juliet,'" *Ladies' Home Journal* (May, 1907).

William Winter's most elaborate commentaries on Julia Marlowe are in *The Wallet of Time,* II (Moffat, Yard, 1913), and *Vagrant Memories* (Doran, 1915); see also John Ranken Towse, *Sixty Years of the Theater* (Funk and Wagnalls, 1916); Augustus Thomas, *The Print of My Remembrance* (Scribners, 1922); and S. Morgan-Powell, *Memories That Live* (Toronto, Macmillan, 1929).

About 1921 Sothern and Marlowe recorded for the Victor Company a series of scenes from *Romeo and Juliet, The Merchant of Venice, The Taming of the Shrew, Twelfth Night,* and *Julius Caesar.* Though Sothern's voice recorded more successfully than Miss Marlowe's, the result was still a valuable series of souvenirs.

V. Isadora Duncan

The items listed in this bibliographical note should be supplemented by reference to my footnotes and the bibliography in Paul Magriel's anthology, *Isadora Duncan* (Holt, 1947); see also *Bulletin of Bibliog-*

raphy, Vol. XVI (1936–39), 173–75. Doris Hering, "To Dionysius— With Love," *Dance Magazine* (December, 1957), gives an account of the Irma Duncan Collection, now in the Dance Collection of the New York Public Library, with quotations from unpublished material.

Two books were published over Isadora Duncan's by-line: *My Life* (Boni and Liveright, 1927) and *The Art of the Dance,* edited by Sheldon Cheney (Theatre Arts, Inc., 1928).

My Life was importantly supplemented by three other early books: Irma Duncan and Allan Ross Macdougall, *Isadora Duncan's Russian Days and Her Last Years in France* (Covici-Fride, 1929); Mary Desti, *The Untold Story: The Life of Isadora Duncan, 1921–1927* (Liveright, 1929); Maurice Dumesnil, *An Amazing Journey: Isadora Duncan in South America* (Ives Washburn, 1932). Barring its amazing errors in proper names, Macdougall's *Isadora: A Revolutionary in Art and Love* (Nelson, 1960) is the best general account of the whole life. David Weiss, *The Spirit and the Flesh* (Doubleday, 1959), is "A Novel Inspired by the Life of Isadora Duncan"; cf. his article, "Isadora Duncan—Actress," *Dance Magazine* (February, 1960). See, too, the photographs in Arnold Genthe, *Isadora Duncan: Twenty-Four Studies* (Mitchel Kennerley, 1929), and cf. his *As I Remember* (Reynal and Hitchcock, 1936).

Walter Terry's *Isadora Duncan: Her Life, Her Art, Her Legacy* (Dodd, Mead, 1964) did not appear until after my manuscript had been completed. I have read it with interest, for it contains valuable material not elsewhere available, but I have taken nothing from it. I did, however, make use of Mr. Terry's article, "The Legacy of Isadora Duncan and Ruth St. Denis," *Dance Perspectives 5* (1960).

The following deal with Isadora Duncan as a dancer: Carl Van Vechten, *The Merry-Go-Round* (Knopf, 1918); Ernest Newman, "The Dances of Isadora Duncan," *Living Age,* Vol. CCCIX (1921), 606–607; Blanche Evan, "Road to the Dance," *Theatre Arts*, Vol. XIX (1935), 27–34; Irma Duncan, *The Technique of Isadora Duncan* (Kamin Publishers, 1937); Lillian Moore, *Artists of the Dance* (Crowell, 1938); Richard Guggenheimer, *Sight and Insight* (Harper, 1945);

Winthrop Palmer, *Theatrical Dancing in America* (Bernard Ackerman, 1945); Walter Sorell, ed., *The Dance Has Many Faces* (World, 1951)—cf. his "Isadora Duncan: An American Memento," *University of Kansas City Review,* Vol. XXI (1954), 95–102; Agnes de Mille, "The Revolution of Isadora," *New York Times Magazine* (September 14, 1952).

In the following the emphasis is on life rather than art: Sisley Huddleston, *Paris Salons, Cafés, Studios* (Lippincott, 1928); George Seldes, "What Love Meant to Isadora Duncan," *Mentor* (February, 1930); Princess Der Ling, *Lotos Petals* (Dodd, Mead, 1930); Robert Edmond Jones, "The Gloves of Isadora," *Theatre Arts* (October, 1947). There are biographical portraits in William Bolitho, *Twelve Against the Gods* (Simon and Schuster, 1929), and Louis Untermeyer, *Makers of the Modern World* (Simon and Schuster, 1955).

See, further, Floyd Dell, *Women as World Builders* (Forbes & Company, 1913); H. T. Parker, *Eighth Notes* (Dodd, Mead, 1922); Anon., "Burnt Offering," *Harper's Magazine,* Vol. CLVIII (1929), 246–49; Marie-Louise De Meeus, "A Star Danced," *Cornhill Magazine,* N.S., Vol. LXXII (1932), 544–51; Janet Flanner, *An American in Paris* (Simon and Schuster, 1940); Mercedes de Acosta, *Here Lies the Heart* (Reynal, 1960).

VI. Mary Garden

The most important single source of information is *Mary Garden's Story,* written in collaboration with Louis Biancolli (Simon and Schuster, 1951). But the many magazine articles published over Miss Garden's by-line are quite as interesting and sometimes more so. I list them here in chronological order:

"The Debasement of Music in America," *Everybody's,* Vol. XVIII (1908), 232–36; "Opera and the People," *Everybody's,* Vol. XX (1909), 249–58; "The Girl Who Sings," *Harper's Bazaar,* Vol. XLIV (1910), 176; "Acting in the Lyric Drama," *Century,* Vol. LXXXI (1911), 585–88; "My Working Theory of Beauty," *Delineator,* Vol. LXXVII (1911), 230; "The American Girl and Music," *Good House-*

keeping, Vol. LVI (1913), 168–74; "The Opera Singer and the Public," *American Magazine* (August, 1914); "A Mary Garden Mood— Some Adventures of My Destiny," *Forum,* Vol. LXI (1919), 469–77; "The 'Know How' in the Art of Singing," *Etude*, Vol. XXXVIII (1920), 439–40; "Your Career in Opera," *Ladies' Home Journal* (September, October, November, 1921); "My Life," *Hearst's International* (December, 1923; January, February, March, April, May, 1924); "The Secret of Lasting Youth," *Good Housekeeping* (August, 1924); "Love and Let Love," *Collier's* (January 8, 1927); "Why I Bobbed My Hair," *Pictorial Review* (April, 1927); "I, Mary Garden," *Ladies' Home Journal* (September, 1928); "We Are What We Are," *Ladies' Home Journal* (January, 1930); "The Climb," *Ladies' Home Journal* (March, 1930); "These Couriers," *Ladies' Home Journal* (April, 1930); "The Heights," *Ladies' Home Journal* (June, 1930); "Monte Carlo for a Night," *Ladies' Home Journal* (July, 1930); "Love and Marriage," *Ladies' Home Journal* (September, 1930); "Of Me I Sing," *Collier's* (March 4, 1933).

Among books and articles by other hands, the following will be found of interest: William Armstrong, "A Wonderful New Singer," *Cosmopolitan,* Vol. XLIV (1908), 295–301, and "The Girlhood of Mary Garden," *Woman's Home Companion* (August, 1911); Karleton Hackett, "How Mary Garden Made Her Debut in Opera," *Theatre,* Vol. XIV (1911), 214–18, vii; Jane Heap, "A Decadent Art" and "Mary Garden," in Margaret Anderson, ed., *The Little Review Anthology* (Hermitage House, 1953); James Huneker, *Bedouins* (Scribners, 1911); Edward C. Moore, *Forty Years of Opera in Chicago* (Liveright, 1930); Katharine Metcalfe Roof, "The Return of Mélisande," *Touchstone,* Vol. II (1918), 582–84, 619; Oscar Thompson, *The American Singer* (Dial, 1937); Carl Van Vechten, *The Merry-Go Round* (Knopf, 1918) and *Interpreters* (Knopf, 1920).

VII. Marilyn Monroe

Much the fullest account of the life of Marilyn Monroe is in Maurice Zolotow, *Marilyn Monroe* (Harcourt, Brace, 1960). Pete Martin, *Will*

Acting Spoil Marilyn Monroe? (Doubleday, 1956), contains an abundance of good talk and even more fascinating pictures. John Pascal, *Marilyn Monroe,* published in magazine format by Popular Library, Inc., 1962, is surprisingly good for this kind of book, and George Miller, *Marilyn: Her Tragic Story* (Escape Magazines, 1962), is certainly worth reading. Both these items are abundantly illustrated. Except for a few good pictures, Joe Franklin and Laurie Palmer, *The Marilyn Monroe Story* (Greenberg, 1953), is worthless. The chapter on Marilyn in Ezra Goodman, *The Fifty-Year Decline and Fall of Hollywood* (Simon and Schuster, 1961), though unsympathetic, contains a few items worth noting. James Goode's *The Story of* The Misfits (Bobbs-Merrill, 1963) gives a detailed account of the making of Marilyn's last film.

A number of very important articles relating to Marilyn are mentioned in my footnotes. Of prime importance are the interviews with Richard Meryman and Alan Levy. To the Meryman interview should be added his article, "A Last Long Talk with a Lonely Girl," *Life* (August 17, 1962). Flora Rheta Schreiber, "Remembrance of Marilyn," *Good Housekeeping* (January, 1963), contains the moving recollections of one of the few people who really loved and understood Marilyn—her father-in-law, Isadore Miller. Carl Sandburg's recollections are in *Look* (September 11, 1962). See, also, Cecil Beaton, *The Face of the World* (John Day, 1957).

For my purposes, the most valuable of the other articles not listed elsewhere are Robert J. Levin, "Marilyn Monroe's Marriage," *Redbook* (February, 1958); Jon Whitcomb, "On Location: Marilyn Monroe," *Cosmopolitan* (December, 1960); "Mosaic of Marilyn," *Coronet* (February, 1961); Alice T. McIntyre, "Making the Misfits or Waiting for Monroe or Notes from Olympus," *Esquire* (March, 1961). I do not care much for James T. Farrell's "Waif to Woman," *Coronet* (January, 1957), but it is certainly a historic piece of Monroviana. A run through the *Reader's Guide* will uncover a good many other items, especially those of a pictorial character: *Life, Look,* and *Collier's* were always very generous to Marilyn in every way.

INDEX

In the main entry for each, the seven women considered in this book are entered under their full names; elsewhere in the index, initials are employed.

Books by Edward Wagenknecht

BIOGRAPHY: *The Man Charles Dickens* (1929); *Mark Twain: The Man and His Work* (1935, 1961); *Longfellow, A Full-Length Portrait* (1955); *Mrs. Longfellow: Selected Letters and Journals* (1956); *The Seven Worlds of Theodore Roosevelt* (1958); *Nathaniel Hawthorne, Man and Writer* (1961); *Washington Irving: Moderation Displayed* (1962); *Edgar Allan Poe, The Man Behind the Legend* (1963).

HISTORY: *Cavalcade of the English Novel* (1943); *Cavalcade of the American Novel* (1952); *Chicago* (1963).

CRITICISM: *Values in Literature* (1928); *A Guide to Bernard Shaw* (1929); *Utopia Americana* (1929); *A Preface to Literature* (1954).

ABOUT THE THEATER: *Lillian Gish, An Interpretation* (1927); *Geraldine Farrar, An Authorized Record of Her Career* (1929); *Jenny Lind* (1931); *The Movies in the Age of Innocence* (1962); *Seven Daughters of the Theater* (1964).

ANTHOLOGIES: *The College Survey of English Literature*, with others (1942); *Six Novels of the Supernatural* (1944); *The Fireside Book of Christmas Stories* (1945); *The Story of Jesus in the World's Literature* (1946); *When I Was a Child* (1946); *The Fireside Book of Ghost Stories* (1947); *Abraham Lincoln: His Life, Work, and Character* (1947); *The Fireside Book of Romance* (1948); *Joan of Arc, An Anthology of History and Literature* (1948); *A Fireside Book of Yuletide Tales* (1948); *Murder by Gaslight* (1949); *The Collected Tales of Walter de la Mare* (1950); *An Introduction to Dickens* (1952); *Chaucer: Modern Essays in Criticism* (1959); *Stories of Christ and Christmas* (1963).

INTRODUCTIONS: *The Chimes,* by Charles Dickens (Limited Editions Club, 1931); *Life on the Mississippi,* by Mark Twain (Limited Editions Club, 1944); *A Tale of Two Cities,* by Charles Dickens (Modern Library, 1950); *Great Expectations,* by Charles Dickens (Washington Square Press, 1956); *The Wizard of Oz,* by L. Frank Baum (Reilly & Lee edition, 1956); *The Art, Humor, and Humanity of Mark Twain,* edited by Minnie M. Brashear and Robert M. Rodney (1959); *The Innocents Abroad,* by Mark Twain (Limited Editions Club, 1962); *Great Expectations,* by Charles Dickens (Harcourt, 1963); *The Prince and the Pauper,* by Mark Twain (Limited Editions Club, 1964).